A Dog for the Kids

Also by Mordecai Siegal

Good Dog, Bad Dog (with Matthew Margolis)
Underdog: Training the Mutt, Mongrel & Mix-Breed
    (with Matthew Margolis)
The Good Dog Book
The Mordecai Siegal Happy Pet/Happy Owner Book
The Good Cat Book
The Simon & Schuster Guide to Cats
Happy Dog/Happy Owner Book

A Dog for the Kids

Mordecai Siegal

Little, Brown & Company
Boston   Toronto

FIRST EDITION

LIBRARY OF CONGRESS CATALOGING IN PUBLICATION DATA
Siegal, Mordecai.
  A dog for the kids.
  1. Dogs.   2. Children and animals.   I. Title.
SF427.S57   1984   636.7   84-21824
ISBN 0-316-79007-9

*Unless otherwise noted, all photographs
are by Mordecai Siegal.*

MV

Designed by Patricia Girvin Dunbar

*Published simultaneously in Canada
by Little, Brown & Company (Canada) Limited*

PRINTED IN THE UNITED STATES OF AMERICA

For my only daughter, Ida Justine
— a very dear and special person

Contents

Acknowledgments

Words cannot express my deep feelings of gratitude and admiration for my partner, my sometime collaborator, my confidante, my best friend, my mentor, and my inspiration . . . my wife, Victoria.

The magnificent breed portraits were photographed by Creszentia Allen, perhaps the finest photographer of dogs and cats in the world. She claims she was taught all she knows by her husband and collaborator, Ted Allen. They have been working together for many, many years and have produced great animal photos gracing more than twenty books, hundreds of magazine articles and the walls of many fortunate people. Among the leading magazines their work has appeared in are *Town and Country* and *House Beautiful*. Their exquisite photographs have appeared on the covers of *American Kennel Gazette*, *Dog Fancy*, *Cat Fancy* and *National Geographic* magazine's children's edition, *World*. Grosset & Dunlap published two books of their photographs, *Dogs* and *Cats*. Their color photographs have the distinction of hanging on the walls of the Cat Fanciers' Association offices and are no strangers to the American Kennel Club, either. This author wishes to express his pleasure and gratification in having breed photos by Creszentia Allen in his book.

A great debt is owed to dog trainer Nancy Strouss of People Training For Dogs for her many kindnesses, her loyalty and her invaluable advice and assistance. The same for her colleague, Debra Feliziani.

The youngsters and their dogs who so graciously appeared in the dog-training photographs are Ben Terk, his mother Judy Terk, their young friend Edward Randall and their Siberian husky, Glaze; Matthew and Amy Steigbigel and their English springer spaniel, Tiffany; Mark and Amelia Sadowsky and their mixed breed, Angel. Baby Katherine Aaby, her mother Donett and their wonderful golden retriever, Madame General, CDX (but you can call her Jenny if you know her). Thank you.

Many thanks to Steve Willett, director of Gaines Professional Service, and to Tom O'Shea of Gaines Dog Care Center for allowing the use of some of their terrific photographs.

Appreciation to Bart Campbell of Alpo Dog Food for use of some material from the booklet, "Puppies, Parents and Kids," and to Don Hyman, too.

Some of the nutritional research material was supplied by Dr. Jim Corbin, professor of Animal Science, University of Illinois at Urbana-Champaign and to Mark Morris, Jr., D.V.M., Ph.D., of Mark Morris Associates in Topeka, Kansas. With deep gratitude.

It's nice to know that the Pets Are Wonderful Council is out there in Chicago doing all the great things they do for everyone in the pet world. The photographs they allowed us to use in this book are great and I do thank them.

To two of America's great dog trainers, Capt. Arthur Haggerty and Matthew Margolis, thank you so much for sharing with me your wealth of knowledge, advice, aid and comfort. I am proud to call you my friends.

Thanks to Carol Benjamin, noted author and dog expert, for her friendship and encouragement.

A note of gratitude to a brilliant photographer, Shelley Seccombe; Dr. Susan D. Siegal of the West Village Veterinary Hospital (no relation); Aida B. Ferrer, one of the very knowledgeable librarians of the American Kennel Club Library; Tina Carroll, director of the Pet Information Bureau; Rose Mary Bergmann of the 4-H Club of Morristown, New Jersey, who taught me that the four H's stand for Head, Heart, Hands and Health; Pedigrees Catalog of Spencerport, New York, for the use of their photos; Winthrop M. Hodges, Mary Tondorf-Dick, Caroline E. Patterson and Stephanie Holmes of Little, Brown and Company; and to Mel Berger of the William Morris Agency, to whom I owe much more than ten percent.

*   *   *

Finally, I would like to express my admiration and gratitude to Dr. Boris M. Levinson, Ph.D., who pioneered the field of animals in the service of mental health. His two books, *Pet-Oriented Child Psychotherapy* and *Pets and Human Development,* not only made this work possible but paved the way for the entire subject of the human/companion animal bond in psychology, prisoner rehabilitation, pets for the elderly, pets for the infirm of every stripe. It is a privilege to take this opportunity to afford Dr. Levinson the recognition he so richly deserves. Those of us involved in the world of dogs owe him a great deal. He started it all.

A Dog for the Kids

One

What Dogs Mean

to Children

Childhood begins with a wet slap while hanging upside down. A half-forgotten dream, it is the gradual process of becoming a human being. Children are delicate saplings, vulnerable but overflowing with joyful promise. They are beautiful. They are also valuable. The worth of the world can be found in the innocent vision of children. They are the gift of renewal and our only hope. Somewhere between the first breath of infancy and the last complaint of adolescence, adoring parents must step back and let them go. But before that uncertain step is taken one should assess the quality of a childhood inevitably spent in delight, wonder, agony and human fruition. Success and failure are relative terms, one not necessarily canceling the other. Keeping score is without value but acceptance of our young as they are while continuing support and encouragement is priceless. Holding two little arms as two little legs wobble their first step in significant. Wiping tears and tickling bellies and explaining the rain are also significant. Childhood is a measurement of time during which one grows to full height and humanity. It is not complete without the reflection of ourselves in nature. Children and dogs complete the equation. Children are important and so are the dogs who share their lives.

Most dogs are initially purchased for the benefit of children. Parents aren't really sure why they do this, other than it seems to be a good idea. Puppies are sweet looking and adorable and give unsuspecting parents the notion that they make wonderful toys. The truth is they are

3

nothing at all like toys. Puppies quickly become grown dogs, certainly a lot sooner than children become adults. A grown dog bears little resemblance in appearance or behavior to the puppy it once was.

There is a new dog in the house. It's cheaper than a season in Europe, a house on the beach or even summer camp. The kids would rather have a doggie than any of those things.

"A dog of my own. Oh, boy."

It's baby powder, *Sesame Street* and training wheels all rolled into one delicious pie. The magic moment of arrival is a giggly, near-hysterical time for kids, canines and innocent bystanders. The dog somehow knows he has ended his perplexing journey and found a home. His new family looks way down at him on the floor, scoops him up and cuddles him like a newborn. The froth, however, begins to settle with the first yelp of the dog and cry of the child. A tail was pulled and a finger nipped. The dog poops on the carpet and the little mistress and master step in it. There is a howl and a holler as parents, pup and pupils run for the hills. How do you handle a hungry dog with *nasty* coming from both ends?

A turning point has been reached in the relationship between family and pooch and it's only the first hour of arrival. Unless the parents know what they are doing, things are going to get worse. There is probably nothing quite as miserable as the first seven nights with a newly adopted puppy or young dog. If you don't know what to do, you are probably ready to forgo the animal's innocence and quietly strangle it. But, alas, the children are watching. The new member of the family must be treated with kid gloves. Getting dogs and kids to hit it off on a permanent basis, much less learning to live with dog behavior, requires some understanding of dogs, of kids, and of dogs and kids together.

In view of all this, one must ask, why get a dog at all? The answer is easy. Because the canine connection could easily become the most valuable experience your child will ever have short of school and four years with an orthodontist. There are two uniquely valuable aspects to giving your child a dog. First, there is the value to the parents, and second, what it means to the child.

If you ask any child why she or he wants a dog, the answer will have something to do with fun. For kids, dogs are stimulating and great playmates. They do play well together and if you visit a good nursery school or kindergarten you will quickly discover that play is the principal activity. However, if you look closely you will also discover that the play is carefully orchestrated. Although there are many periods of "free play" most of the time is spent in *playlike* activities. The reason for this is that professional teachers and child experts understand that play is a learning experience. It is a reenactment of what is learned through the process of repetition, emulation and, of course, instruction. Dogs are great teachers.

But this new member of the family means more than play to a child. Every child needs a friend who will remain constant and loyal without qualifying the relationship. This kind of friend will not exact a price in exchange for solace and comfort. In the day-to-day living of any child there are many troubled times, often because of transitional periods of growth and development. There is a period of disequilibrium for every child prior to the achievement of new accomplishments, from learning to walk or speak to accepting a maturing body. Each new phase brings with it fear of the new way of being and a refusal to give up the old way. Trading off the security of dependency for the unknown factors of independence creates stormy emotions and a deeply felt ambivalence. This is true for every child. When an infant crawls into a room, leaving the family behind in another, it is a significant first step to separating from mother and father and going off into the frightening world of adulthood. Do you remember how many times your child came crawling back from the empty room to the safety and comfort of your presence?

· A normal dog responds sympathetically and most lovingly to the somber moods of children with quiet companionship or lively enticements to play or at least relate. It is a lucky child who has a pet during those times when life is difficult and the world does not seem to be a pleasant place. When a child is confused and troubled, her four-legged friend will always be there to offer a bit of warmth and friendship, consistency and unquestioned loyalty, and an unflagging desire to catch her eyes. Dogs are better than chicken soup. The love of a dog will ease the pains of growth. It gives a child a very real sense of security and identity, enabling the youngster to take some large risks and enter the next phase of growth and development. The dog is always there for the sad, happy, eager or anxious kid.

From the parents' view, dogs provide the opportunity for emotional and psychological growth. To use an old-fashioned term but one that is too long forgotten, dogs help children develop *character*. The way a child learns to handle and care for an animal helps in developing a

healthy self-image. When children like themselves they believe they are worthwhile people. When children do *not* have a sound and healthy self-image, if they do *not* like themselves or if they believe others do not like them, they tend to show it by being aggressive or withdrawn. They may hurt others in order to ease their own inner pain. They may also withdraw into a shell, a personal private world, to protect themselves from what they believe is rejection. Obviously, the primary source of self-esteem in the very young comes from parents and then peers. But do not discount the influence of living with a dog.

Of all that children derive from their pets, including understanding birth, death, growth and relationships, one of the most worthwhile lessons is *leadership.* I don't mean leadership in the sense of high-school graduation speeches or militaristic virtues, but rather in the vital areas of independence, self-sufficiency and competent self-management. If leadership is understood as the willingness to assume responsibility, to make decisions, to risk failure, then a child living with a pet is, indeed,

involved with leadership. Dogs are capable of bringing out the best in a child or helping parents create values that are more learned than inherited. Parents become partners with the family dog and influence the development of self-control and inner focus in their children. It is not accomplished with mirrors or by regarding the dog as an assistant teacher. One does nothing unusual with the dog other than giving it normal care and attention. But parents must teach the children to regard the pet as a playmate, friend, and *dependent* member of the family. This will promote a sense of responsibility for the dog's care, with the motivating factor being the reward of play and companionship.

By helping a child set realistic goals in regard to caring for the family dog, he or she is more apt to experience the elated feelings of achievement and success. This in turn allows for feelings of competence in dealing with life problems as they are encountered. All children can help in some degree with feeding, walking, grooming, training and loving the dog. Even some medical problems can be handled by kids.

Allow your kids to shop for the dog's needs, participate in the decision-making process (e.g., food selection, toys, bedding, training). It is quite reassuring for the child to discover that she has an important role in her family because they care about how she feels and what she thinks, says and does. It is rewarding to encourage the kids to express their thoughts, feelings and ideas concerning the dog. Discussions about the dog's welfare are not only useful but give the *entire* family an opportunity to relate to each other about something meaningful.

The initial decision to acquire a dog for the kids may have been based on an impulse, a desire to give your children yet one more plaything, or because of other parents' influence. Although these are not really the best of reasons, still, the initial decision was a good one, with the parental heart in the right place. For whatever reason you decided to get a dog, it was a fortunate, valid idea. Parents are the unsung heroes of dog ownership. They deserve awards and medals for leading the way to happy pet relationships. When a child begs for a puppy, and most do, it is Mom and Dad who really accept the brunt of the work and do so because they know it brings pleasure and happiness. They recognize the special place dogs have in American family life.

THE FAMILY WAY

What Dogs Can Mean to Different Children

The typical family.   It is probably not possible to define the typical family, but for the purpose of exploring various situations in which dogs live I will try. Here I refer to a group where one or more children live with both parents. There are no unusual situations demanding more of the dog or the kids than the typical, day-to-day activities and problems. To the kids in this situation a dog is a sort of brother or sister without all the bickering and competition for attention.

The dog becomes a pal and a teacher at the same time. It's no secret that children are intensely interested in animals and all things pertaining to animals. This offers parents the unique opportunity to stimulate learning in their children and, at the same time, wield significant influence in developing character traits based on important moral codes of behavior. Learning to relate to a dog automatically involves a child's ability and desire to be fair minded and humane. Studies have revealed that in families across America the most popular member of the household is the pet. Most people regard their dogs as full-fledged members of the family. The reasons given are that dogs and other pets are responsive to the family's feelings and anxieties. Many stated that their pets are sensitive to family illness, depression, anger, tension, turmoil, happiness and excitement. New friendships and social contact resulted because of the animal's presence in the house. There is even evidence of greater family harmony along with more hours spent together. Many of these surveyed pet owners like to think of their furry friends as being near "human" because of their feelings and contributions to the quality of family life.

In a typical family situation the dog can mean a great deal to the kids, but primarily as a dog. Which is to say that a pet is a superb companion and playmate demanding of the children kindness and some sense of responsibility. In this most typical of all family life-styles the dog is highly valued but at the same time related to without intensity or unusual need.

The divorced family.   There is no possibility for a dog, new or otherwise, to play the role of a missing parent. We have all been exposed to those who foolishly, or sensibly, use an animal as a substitute human. But in the case of children trying to cope with a broken family it is not only foolhardy but risks psychological damage. People cannot be replaced. Children should not be asked to feel better about something when they do not. When adult responses are asked (or demanded) of a child, it tends to retard emotional growth. Trying to fill a void with a dog when that void is caused by the loss of a person is to court emotional retreat and a feeling of failure. It is heaped upon all the other bad feelings brought about by family change.

One's mother or father or one's dog, for that matter, can never be replaced if you believe that we are all one-of-a-kind. Mothers and fathers are the primary relationships in the lives of children. They are the role models for kids, the source of safety, security and what's real and what isn't. A dog can never fill that bill. However, dogs can be quite important to children in other ways during the crisis of family change.

The most common negative feelings in children during and after a divorce have to do with guilt, a sense of loss, and most destructive of all, the loss of self-esteem. Children tend to believe that they, somehow, have caused their parents to separate. This feeling, plus the sense of failure by comparison to families that have not split up, helps to create a very poor self-image. A dog can help a child improve his self-image.

Feeling good about oneself is the primary benefit to a child who lives with a dog. Learning to handle and care for a dog competently helps in developing a positive self-image. That sense of self also comes from the

feeling of being loved and needed by the animal. The consistency of a dog's affection, his needs, his unqualified acceptance of human care-takers will break through all emotional barriers in children and with one slurp across the face make a child feel better. After all, if a kid is certain of being loved and needed, how can he feel bad about himself? How can he have doubts about his worth? A dog can make him happy and happiness is an ongoing feeling that can grow within and stay for a lifetime.

Single-parent family. The problems connected with one parent leaving home because of divorce or the death of a parent are compli-cated and difficult. Here the role of the dog is to help the child feel competent and worthwhile. But in the case of the single-parent home where the mother (most often) has chosen a life-style of single parent-hood from the very beginning, the dog's place is unique. While not ac-tually a substitute parent, the dog becomes an integral part of the family, almost to the extent of equal status and importance. The family dog is more like a brother or sister, with greater standing and privilege than the average pet. It is pointless to place a value judgment on this arrangement because the adult involved has, one assumes, given the matter much thought and is committed to the life-style.

11

The decision to have a child without living with a spouse is a private matter, although most child experts do not approve on the grounds that the welfare of the child is not served. I can think of no family situation where the dog is more valuable than in the single-parent arrangement. As previously stated, the dog is a member of the scant family and probably adds much to the child's feeling of having what other children have. The parent must make every effort to make a success of having a dog and that can be pretty difficult what with hours devoted to a job, daycare or babysitter service and the exhaustion felt at the end of a completely used day. It will be difficult, indeed, caring for the dog's needs, especially a young dog in need of housebreaking and obedience training.

The reward will be in the comfort and security provided to the child by the dog. The family pet becomes an important factor in the child's life. It represents a fleshing out of the family structure plus a constant, reliable source of added love and comfort. A devoted dog, one who has been trained to behave himself, takes up a great deal of the emotional slack for the child whose needs can drain one human being. Single parents do much for their children and for themselves when taking on the chore of living with a dog. It is worth all the bother connected with the first months with a puppy. The canine family addition is as essential as burgers, shakes and fries and a Snoopy glass, too.

12

Handicapped kids.   A child with a physical or mental defect that prevents him or her from enjoying the activities of so-called normal children is considered handicapped. The need for parental love and guidance notwithstanding, the greatest gifts given to such children are self-esteem, pride and as much independence as possible. A dog can do that for the handicapped child, at least in part. Family and community support are the most important elements in succeeding, but having a dog has its place and good effect.

The most useful role the dog plays for a handicapped child is that of faithful and loyal friend. Dogs have no prejudice toward other dogs or people. Race, religion, sexual orientation or physical and mental capacities play no role in the giving or withholding of affection or approval. Once a person makes the effort to relate and take charge of a dog, the two creatures connect for life. It is one of nature's gifts. Even the most handicapped of children can do something involving a dog's needs. The giving of affection or approval is not taken lightly by the dog and is received with more than a little gratitude. The stroke of a brush or filling of a food bowl are not difficult tasks but mean a great deal to the dog, who will regard the handicapped provider as a benevolent master or mistress. When a pet comes to a handicapped child in need of something and that child is able to fulfill the need, the dog has done his job well.

Rich kids, poor kids, kids from large families, and the only child.   The benefits of having a dog are the common denominator of kids living these diversified life-styles. Both rich and poor kids learn the same lesson from living with and caring for a dog. A coyote-looking mutt or Cavalier King Charles spaniel both must take to the street to obey the demands of digestion. The kids in charge of humble or grand dogs must still clean the doggie-do from the streets to obey the laws of most cities. Caring for dogs requires work, effort and intelligence. These are the same requirements for managing money or learning to acquire it.

To an *only child* a dog is both friend and relative offering companionship while demanding the same sort of sharing as would a brother or sister. This child will learn to respect the needs and feelings of others by satisfying the demands made on him or her by a dog. If he or she doesn't, the dog will not relate to his or her satisfaction. If you don't play ball, your dog won't roll over.

Conversely, a dog living in a family with many children offers an op-

portunity for some exclusive attention to the child that works for it. A dog cannot relate to the entire clan at once, at least not all the time. For the caring, giving child in a large family the dog will extend itself with something extra, almost with gratitude. Here, the pet is really the *family* dog in the fullest sense of the word and offers the parents a unique opportunity for shared responsibility. This will require a serious discussion and working out of who does what for the dog. Schedules and work charts are useful and a spirit of cooperation is absolutely necessary. Taking care of the dog should be a family project that draws everyone together. Each member of the family will benefit in some way from the experience.

It is quite clear that children and dogs have an undeniable need for each other. Those who spend the better part of childhood together will have something more valuable than money in the bank or straight A report cards. The free expression of emotion, the desire to live with others and the ability to accept responsibilities are part of entering the adult world. Children learn much of this from dogs they have known and loved. What a bunch of lucky dogs!

Two

Which Dog?

I f you ask a child to pick a dog, he may point and say, "I want the big orange one," and you and the family get stuck with a furry cow that's bigger than your kitchen. Don't do it. Be brave and tell the kids to do their homework when the subject comes up. I advise you to leave this decision to the grown-ups. If you aren't happy with the new family dog, then sooner than you can say *scoop law* everyone is going to be miserable. Trust me.

Acquiring a dog is as easy as having a baby. If you stay in one spot long enough something will happen. Try to make a decision out of the event. Stay away from pet shop windows full of huggable puppies with their noses smack up against the glass, begging for you, just you alone. Watch out for sad stray dogs, neighbors bearing gifts, rescued dogs, abandoned dogs, and dogs that follow your children home. For those who feel the pressure rising from the family ranks with subtle hints around the breakfast table like, "Please pass the dogberries," or "My cereal says snap, crackle and pup," look them in the eye and respond with something official like, "Thank you for your suggestions. They are being considered by the management!" The best thing is to do nothing until you have given the matter some intelligent thought.

Unfortunately, most people enter the world of pet ownership through a series of chance circumstances and uncontrolled impulses. More puppies are purchased each year as a last-minute Christmas gift than at any other time. Dogs that are gifts are like in-laws who come to

15

live with you shortly after being introduced. It is to be trapped at a pot-luck supper. Do not obey those very human responses to the chance dog. Acquisitions of this sort can be correctly classified as accidents. Obviously, many happy pet situations can come out of the aforementioned possibilities, but the risk of disenchantment is quite high.

When human beings are dissatisfied with a pet dog, it means the animal doesn't fit in with their life-style. The apartment or house was too small, the animal was too big, too wild, too grumpy, too untrained, too expensive, too little, too exuberant, too friendly or not friendly enough. In any case the animal's future, indeed its very life, is in jeopardy. When getting divorced from a pet the choices are limited and not very pleasant for the dog. One may find it another home (not too easy to accomplish); place the dog in a shelter (where it will probably be put to death); abandon it (immoral for the human and deadly for the dog). It is very hard on children to face giving up a dog, even if it bit someone or destroyed fifteen thousand dollars' worth of furniture. It can be an emotional wrench, one you'll not forget so easily. The best way to avoid such a situation is to be certain you get the right dog for the conditions in your house.

The most common reason for people acquiring dogs is companionship and that's about the best reason there is. Of course there are always dogs who work for a living but very rarely are they in a pet situation. There are many, many who maintain show dogs and campaign them for the pleasure and sport of it. This is a legitimate activity enjoyed by the most humane and knowledgeable dog lovers in the country. There is also a place for children in the world of show dogs. The American Kennel Club sanctions "Junior Showmanship" competition at AKC all-breed or specialty shows. Here, kids between ten and seventeen years of age are judged in the ring on their ability and skill as show dog handlers. Ribbons, prizes and awards are given to the winners. For more information contact the American Kennel Club, 51 Madison Avenue, New York, New York 10010.

Of late, some people have acquired dogs for protection but have exchanged one danger for another. Without consummate professionalism watch dogs and attack dogs can be lethal, especially to children, who innocently come in contact with them. It is essential before acquiring a dog that you ask yourself why you want it, how will it function in your life, and if that reason is conducive to fifteen years of pet ownership. Nothing less will do.

WHERE TO GET A DOG

Adoption agencies. For economy or humane considerations there is no better place to obtain a dog or puppy than your local animal shelter. Most cities and towns maintain a dog pound, SPCA-type organization or animal adoption agency and they can be found by looking in the Yellow Pages under "Animal Shelters." Adopting a dog from an agency is a good deal for the animal as well as the human. Its life will in all likelihood be saved from euthanasia. The pet will cost far less than in any commercial situation. It is possibly the least expensive way to purchase a dog.

Most agencies today require that the animal be neutered so that it will not be able to add to the enormous population of homeless pets, though not all have this requirement. Some shelters perform the service for reduced rates or no fee at all. Do not be surprised if you are asked to sign a contract agreeing to have the animal spayed (for a female) or castrated (for the male) within a set period of time. There are many good reasons to comply. It is not only humane but also healthy for the dog and *very* convenient for the dog's new family.

Breeders. Noncommercial and serious amateur breeders are the ideal sources for the best of the purebred dogs. This is especially important if you are at all interested in the show ring and the high price of the dog is not too serious a problem. The noncommercial breeder is in the process of developing a line of dogs that will enhance his or her reputation and sense of fulfillment. He or she strives for breed perfection with the help of an understanding of genetics and socializing techniques. Such breeders are, as a group, knowledgeable about selecting good dogs for mating and are in constant touch with other serious breeders. This type of breeder is usually interested in "breaking even" financially with not much thought of profit, or at least large profit. Noncommercial breeders enjoy the demands of breeding and developing winning dogs that eventually become Champions of Record with the American Kennel Club. With few exceptions they are ethical and quite selective about to whom they will sell one of their pups.

Many commercial breeders are just as knowledgeable and ethical as those amateurs. Although they are involved with breeding as a business, high standards are often the case. However, it is difficult for those who are not acquainted with the world of dog breeding to sort out who is producing sound, healthy dogs on a selective basis and who is not. I am a bit more than cautious when a storefront operation selling puppies and young dogs sports blue ribbons and mounted plaques indicating champion dogs. It is a style of exploitation that is obviously being used as a sales tool and not necessarily indicative of high-quality dogs. Many breeds have been overpopularized and subsequently ruined by mass-breeding while the breeder utilizes a few winning dogs for display and sales purposes. Before you buy a dog, find out about the seller and his stock. Ask around. Do not be afraid of blunt questions about any dog's parents and progenitors and get the answers in writing if you can.

Pet shops.   Some pet shops breed their own dogs while others obtain their animals from decent, local commercial breeders. These often produce sound dogs of "pet quality," which simply means the dogs are not absolutely perfect representations of their breed. However, because of the laws of supply and demand, many pet shops must obtain their "merchandise" from sources that can supply the quantity needed for a large business. This is where the trouble starts for the typical dog owner.

A large number of puppies sold in many pet shops come from so-called puppy mill operations that are scattered throughout the midwestern part of the United States. Arkansas, Kentucky, Iowa, Nebraska, Kansas, Missouri and Illinois are the main sources of puppies bred under the most dreadful, inhumane and unhealthy conditions imaginable. A puppy mill is usually a small farm that maintains a cramped, dirty kennel area jammed with male and female dogs that are constantly mating, gestating and whelping puppies in large quantities. There is no genetic consideration, no culling out those that are either unhealthy or from unhealthy parents. Certainly, dogs that are hyperactive, vicious, nervous, overly shy are not taken out of the breeding program. The same is true of dogs possessed of one illness or another. Eye disease, hip disorders and all manner of ailments are ignored in such operations. Everything that breathes is mated as if on an assembly line. Time is money. Indiscriminate breeding is money.

Interestingly, many a good dog was purchased from a pet shop and there are always enough exceptions to the rule to give one doubt. But there is no way for a novice dog owner to know for sure what he or she is getting into. Many dog diseases such as hip dysplasia, progressive retinal atrophy and congenital heart defects do not show up until the

dog has grown somewhat. There are many, many illnesses and defects that are simply passed from one generation to another of puppy mill dogs. However, in all fairness and accuracy the same could be true of a reputable breeder's stock. The principal difference is that the breeder is more likely to make good on a defective dog and in most instances will make efforts to eradicate the defect from his or her line of dogs. The facts are, however, that the large majority of dogs in the United States are purchased from pet shops.

HOW TO SELECT A DOG

There is no such thing as an ugly puppy. They are all appealing and lovable, and many of us want to take them all home on first sight. With their large, pleading eyes and impish stances they creep right into your heart and make it very difficult to choose one from the many available. But you must maintain your cool so you do not purchase the first furball that licks your finger and yelps for your attention, because he may have ringworm, be a potential fear-biter and suffer from deafness all in one package. How would you know if the seller didn't tell you? You must make some effort to discriminate between puppies that are physically and mentally sound and those that are not.

It is impossible to predict how an eight- to twelve-week-old puppy is going to turn out, but the dog's pedigree will tell you something. If there are several champions in the dog's genealogy, you are on the right track. If possible, examine the pup's dam or sire. One or the other (sometimes both) should be available for inspection if you are dealing with a breeder. Assuming you have done your homework and familiarized yourself with the standards of the breed, you can tell to some degree if the dog in question is half good. Because most breeders take great pride in their bloodlines, they will try to steer you to a good specimen. Most of you will be purchasing a dog as a pet rather than for the show ring and will be shown a "pet quality" dog. Do not be put off by the term or upset because the breeder will not sell you a show dog. They are only interested in having the best examples of their breed "campaigned" for a champion title in the show ring. Pet quality dogs are almost always perfectly healthy dogs with sound temperaments. Quite often it is one slight flaw that makes the difference. Perhaps one hind leg turns out just a bit or the nose color is slightly off or some other "flaw" that would disqualify the dog for the ring is present. "Pet quality" dogs are, for the most part, the best pet dogs in the world.

Beware of overly shy, timid or aggressive puppies. What is heartwarming or cute at twelve weeks can be quite destructive at six or eight months of age. *Do not buy the puppy but the dog he will grow into.* Look for an outgoing, friendly dog who comes right up to you and does not hide in the corner or run in terror.

A healthy puppy has clear, bright eyes. The teeth should be almost white and the gums pink. Sometimes there is a natural black-spotted pigmentation on the gums. This is normal. There should be no liquid or crusty discharge from the animal's eyes, ears or nose. Its coat must be loose, supple, low-lustered with no bare patches. If there is one puppy that is obviously in bad health either in the pet shop or in a breeder's kennel do not pick any dog from that group. Pass them by.

Look for unnatural markings or discoloration in the eyes. A puppy with a distended belly may have internal parasites or some other ailment. If the dog has just been fed, the belly will be distended from that, too. View the pups two hours after feeding time. Do not pick a dog that is fat, thin or unusually different from the rest of the litter. Watch for continual rubbing of the eyes, ears or nose. This could be a sign of skin disease, external parasites (mites) or infection. Some puppies are born deaf. Test for deafness by gently clapping your hands behind the dog and watch for a response. Do not purchase a puppy that is suffering from diarrhea or bloody stools.

With the breeder's permission, hold the puppy in your arms with the belly facing up. If the dog submits with ease and pleasure, his temperament is just fine. If he squirms desperately to get away, he is either aggressive or nervous. If he whines and whimpers, he may be shy or timid. This is important for you to know. Most children are best matched up with a dog of sound, even temperament. Do not pass up a dog with a passive or retiring temperament if you happen to have a quiet, shy child. That could work out perfectly. The point is that there is probably the right child for almost every dog. It's up to each parent to decide how to match a dog of a given temperament with a child of a specific personality type. Some quiet, gentle children do best with an outgoing dog. The dog may draw the child out of his shell. These are highly personal decisions to be made by parents for one-of-a-kind kids and dogs.

Having selected a puppy, get a written record of the dog's inoculations indicating the dates, amounts and types. Find out if the animal has just been wormed and any other medical history. This will help your veterinarian. Seek a written guarantee that the puppy can be returned if, after a veterinary examination, he is found to be in poor health. Do not leave without official papers from the American Kennel Club if the dog is represented as AKC registered. In most cases the litter has been registered and you will be given a form to mail to the AKC with the registration fee. This is a proper procedure.

Before making a final decision about selecting a breed of dog, you would be well advised to attend as many local dog shows as possible. As a matter of fact, attending local dog shows is a good idea even if you know what you want. A *benched show* is the best kind for this purpose because the dogs must remain in portable kennels (dog crates) until the judging is completed. At a benched show you will have the opportunity to tour the benching area and closely examine the dogs and talk to their owners who are either noncommercial or amateur breeders. More than likely you will make contact with a quality source for the dog of your dreams. If not, you can look for breeders' classified advertisements in *Dog World Magazine, Dog Fancy Magazine,* or *Pure Bred Dogs —* *American Kennel Gazette* (AKC) or the classified ads in your local newspaper. If all else fails write to the American Kennel Club for a list of breeders handling the breed that you are interested in (American Kennel Club, 51 Madison Avenue, New York, New York 10010). One last word about selecting a dog. There is probably no one who deals with all the breeds in every conceivable living situation other than the professional dog trainer. It is only from the trainer that you can get a truly objective opinion about any breed of dog as a pet or worker. Seek out an experienced, reputable dog trainer and go to him or her for top-flight advice.

WHICH BREED FOR YOUR KIDS?

Of all the questions of dog ownership, I can think of none more important than which breed to choose. That initial decision is without a doubt the most important one. The second most important decision is selecting a dog with a good temperament. Temperament is more important than looks, intelligence or cost. It is better to have a good-natured mutt with a scruffy multicolored coat than a manicured toy poodle who will open your veins when you go near his food bowl. If you are in the process of selecting a dog for your children, you owe it to yourself and your family, and to the dog as well, to go about the process with some degree of knowledgeability. Common sense will not necessarily help you.

Apart from aesthetics, selecting a specific breed of dog has more to do with how it fits in with your living conditions and your family situation. Some dogs have a hard time in a cramped apartment because they are quite active. There are breeds that are large, vigorous hunters with an incredible ability to run and yet become quite inactive indoors. That would describe some surprisingly large breeds. It is an interesting set of qualities and ideal for some home situations.

What seems more logical than getting a toy breed of dog for a young child? Unfortunately, it is not the best thing to do. Many of the toy breeds are not suitable for children. Despite the fact that toy breeds are among the finest of all dogs, the very qualities that make them so desirable to adults are exactly what make them unsuitable for children. These demanding little creatures like to think of themselves as the blessed event of the family and become quite competitive with, if not downright intolerant of, children. Several of the toy breeds are openly hostile toward children while others are just too fragile for rough-and-tumble play. Pomeranians, as a rule, do not like children. A Yorkshire terrier can break a bone just by falling off the bed. This is not to say that, in some instances, children and various toy breeds do not hit it off. Older, gentler children or those who are more introspective will develop lifetime relationships with small dogs.

The American Kennel Club recognizes 137 breeds and breed varieties. These are separated into seven groups plus one *class* designated as *Miscellaneous* for breeds close to AKC recognition. Officially, most (but not all) of the very small breeds are part of the Toy Group. There are 17 breeds within that category. All these small dogs range in height between six and twelve inches from the shoulder and between one and fourteen pounds, depending on the breed and selectivity of the breeder. The smallest of these dogs are referred to as "teacups." An older, considerate child can live with and care for any one of them. But the more typical child should not be saddled with a dog he can accidentally harm or with a dog who might not want to share the spotlight of childhood.

The same is true for many of the terriers, especially the smaller ones. West Highland white terriers are adorable, loving family dogs but do not necessarily want to be the exclusive companion of a child. Airedales are larger, more protective but somewhat stubborn animals with lovable and unlovable traits. Pugs are among the toy breeds that love and adore children. They are also quite rugged and make excellent playmates, except in the summer heat. Poodles are extremely intelligent, come in three varieties (toy, miniature and standard) and shed least of all breeds. The miniature and standard poodle are the most suitable of the three for children. English springer spaniels are among the best dogs for kids because of their ability to relate to them and their easygoing temperament. Fox terriers are superstars. They are probably the most charming of all. These outgoing dogs do tricks and try anything to get your attention. However, they are highly sensitive and excitable and unbelievably active indoors. They are capable of driving your family quite mad with their energy, barking and demand for attention. They are also quite scrappy with other dogs. Each dog breed has a little something different to offer the first-time dog owner.

When you select a dog breed, try to find out what exactly that breed was used for in its traditional role. For example, most people are not aware that the poodle is essentially a retriever and one of the finest swimmers in the canine kingdom. The name poodle comes from the German, *pudeln,* meaning to splash in the water. In France it is called *caniche,* from the French word *canard,* meaning duck. Obviously, the poodle was a vigorous water dog assisting the duck hunter. This tells you that a poodle has all the marvelous qualities of a retriever and needs exercise and mental stimulation as well. An occasional swim is a blessing for these dogs. If you read about the qualities of retrievers, you will be in a position to judge whether this breed suits your family needs.

It would be a mistake to believe that one breed or mixture is smarter, cleaner, or more lovable than another. An animal from well-bred stock with proper care and training is more likely to be the ideal pet than any other. The correct approach for choosing a dog is not which dog is best, but which dog best suits you. Do you like a huggy-kissy pet or one with an aloof sense of self? Large or small animal? Long-coated or short, and do you have the desire to fuss with a coat requiring daily grooming? Do not begin to shop for a dog until you've answered these basic questions. How much time, for instance, can you devote to grooming, exercise or play? Various breeds require more or less attention to these matters. Are your kids very young or around ten years of age? Do you want a male or female dog? There are many aspects to each sex that must be taken into account so that a sound choice can be made. Stud fees for males and valuable litters from females are not realistic considerations for the average pet owner with no knowledge or facilities for animal husbandry. There is no profit to be gained from dog breeding if you are an inexperienced amateur; therefore, it should not be a factor in selecting male or female.

Male dogs are larger animals and normally eat more food than females of the same breed. They are somewhat more independent and consequently more difficult to obedience train, or at least require more handling. The male of the species is more likely to wander away (sometimes permanently) than the female and certainly gets into more fights with other dogs. Many people admire these qualities and would be more attracted to male dogs. The machismo of a large male dog can be quite appealing for some.

Female dogs go into *heat* twice a year. This is called *estrus* and each period lasts approximately three weeks. During this time the animal secretes an odorous fluid intended to attract male dogs for the purpose of mating. When no puppies are desired the female dog must be kept away from all possible exposures to male dogs, and that means being locked indoors. Many dog owners consider this a nuisance while others consider it a small inconvenience in exchange for a gentle, easy-to-manage animal that tends to stay home.

The stereotypical attributes of males and females can be missing or distorted in an individual dog by poor breeding or early environmental influences such as gun shots, car backfires or physical abuse. A viable option for solving some of the less desirable male or female traits is to spay the female (*ovario-hysterectomy*) or castrate the male, assuming you have no intention of showing or mating the animal. These are very common procedures and highly recommended to enhance the animals' adaptibility to family life while eliminating the possibilities of unwanted puppies.

45 BREEDS THAT LOVE CHILDREN

To help parents select a dog for their kids, a gallery of forty-five breeds is offered on the following pages. These breeds are accepted by many dog experts to be good with children. That means they actually like kids and enjoy their company. It does not account for individual dogs within these breeds that may not hold true to their predictable breed traits. As mentioned before, mass-breeding operations have managed to produce millions of puppies that do not maintain the original breed characteristics. Most of these show up in pet shops. However, both commercial and noncommercial breeders have managed to make their negative contributions. Your only protection is to buy from a reputable source, get some form of guarantee, examine the puppy's parents where possible, look for a pedigree *and read as much as you can about the breed of your choice.* Go to the public library for reference sources on dogs, buy one of the many good books available, go to dog shows and talk to the experts.

Most of these forty-five breeds are from the existing dog groups as established by the American Kennel Club. The groups are known as *Sporting, Hound, Working, Terrier, Toy, Non-Sporting,* and *Herding.* Among those breeds mentioned are dogs of every conceivable size, shape, temperament and tendency. The idea is that every household is different in matters of taste, desire and need. You are certain to find at least one or two breeds that match up with your requirements. The one thing all these breeds have in common is a fondness for children. Beyond that they are as different as night and day. Read *all* the information about the breed you are most interested in, but especially where it discusses the dog's personality.

A brief word about the cost of a dog. Because prices change so quickly with the cost-of-living and all other economic considerations, any price mentioned would become invalid before this book went to press. In each breed article we do give you some indication of the cost of the breed. The code used is: *Moderate* — under $300; *Expen-*

sive — $300 to $500; *Very expensive* — over $500. Please bear in mind that these prices are relevant for a short time. By the time you read this the prices will certainly have risen.

If the breed you are most interested in does not appear on these pages, that does not necessarily mean you should forget it. There are many responsible breeders of those not mentioned producing lovable, adaptive dogs representing their original characteristics. Many breeds are not mentioned simply because of the limitation of space. But the sad truth is that many dogs of several breeds have been more radically changed by poor breeding practices and/or mass-breeding than others. There are no absolutes, however. Dog trainer/author Carol Benjamin purchased one of the best golden retrievers I ever met from a pet shop many years ago. Her late dog, Oliver, was loved and respected by many people in the Dog Fancy, *including staff members of the American Kennel Club itself. There are no rules to this game. You are at the mercy of pure luck and your own diligent research efforts. To quote the grave marker of James Thurber's Airedale, Muggs, "Caveat Canem."*

SPORTING DOGS

German Shorthaired Pointer

Origin: The history of hunting dogs goes back long before written records were kept. In nineteenth-century Germany, hunters and breeders wanted to combine the separate abilities of the different hunting breeds — pointing, trailing, retrieving on land and water, keen scenting, hardy endurance — into one beautifully formed dog. After years and generations of work they achieved the German shorthaired pointer. This breed is popular among nonhunters as well because German shorthairs are particularly intelligent, loyal and loving.

Height at shoulder: Males — 23 to 25 inches
　　　　　　　　　　Females — 21 to 23 inches

Weight: 　　　　　Males — 55 to 70 pounds
　　　　　　　　　　Females — 45 to 60 pounds

Grooming: There is some shedding but the coat is very short. A brushing now and then is good for the coat.

Cost: Moderate

Creszentia Allen

*German
shorthaired
pointer*

Capabilities: German shorthairs make wonderful watchdogs because they will bark at any strange sound. The German shorthair is too gentle by nature for guard work. (A good guard dog must attack if needed.)

Training tip: Start early. As loving and loyal as this breed is, remember this is a hunting dog. German shorthairs need a very firm, strong, consistent hand from a very early age. They can be very strong willed and stubborn without it.

Housebreaking: A breed so used to the outdoor life is more difficult to housebreak. Begin early, be firm, stick to a very rigid schedule, and don't be surprised over the years when mistakes happen. Get right back to the strict schedule and firm attitude.

Aesthetic quality: Brown and white athlete

Personality: Older children can appreciate the German shorthair's friendship and faithfulness. They can also go on the long, long daily walks and runs necessary to keep this breed in even temper and good physical shape. Younger children would be overwhelmed. German shorthairs need a lot of companionship. They hate to be left alone. Without enough exercise and company they can become destructive, chewing everything in reach and barking and howling till relief comes. City living is usually too confined for such an active hunting breed. Even with outdoor exercise the German shorthair remains very active indoors. Many teenagers feel exactly the same way and enjoy playing chase and race with this handsome canine.

Creszentia Allen

Golden Retriever

Origin: Goldens were bred like the other retrievers in the nineteenth century. But the golden was bred by Lord Tweedmouth's gamekeepers on his Scottish estate called Guisachan. A male yellow retriever named Nous was mated to a Tweed water spaniel named Belle in 1867 or 1868. From that romantic setting comes our present day golden retriever.

Height at shoulder: Males — 23 to 24 inches
Females — 21½ to 22½ inches

Weight: Males — 65 to 75 pounds
Females — 60 to 70 pounds

Grooming: This beautiful, slightly wavy fur does shed. Regular brushing will help.

Cost: Expensive.

Capabilities: The golden is so easygoing and gentle that guarding is simply not in its nature. On the other hand a golden can be a totally trustworthy companion for a child. They often serve as dog guides for the blind.

28

Training tip: This is an extremely responsive breed. Training seems very easy because they are so willing to please. But these are hunting dogs whose minds can wander. Give the commands and the praise in a calm voice and be sure each command is obeyed properly.

Housebreaking: Retrievers are comparatively easy to housebreak.

Aesthetic quality: Honey-colored, graceful dogs with lovable faces

Personality: Goldens love everyone, understand everything. They are intelligent, dignified, considerate and perfect for young children, toddlers, babies or of course older children. That is not to say that they are boring. If the child wants to play ball or run or just be silly, the golden can do that too. They can adjust to almost any life-style in the city or the country, but they deserve to get some daily exercise and a swim now and then.

Labrador Retriever

Origin: Like the other retrievers, the Labrador comes from Newfoundland. However, it was not crossed as often to the hunting dogs of England. In the mid nineteenth century the earl of Malmesbury and the duke of Buccleuch each sponsored the breeding of pure Labradors in England. The real mystery is how Labrador retrievers came to Newfoundland. They must have arrived by ship, since there were apparently no native dogs on the American continent. But such records were never kept. If not for the English we would not have these magnificent dogs. They all but disappeared in Newfoundland when a dog tax was imposed.

Height at shoulder: Males — 22½ to 24½ inches
Females — 21½ to 23½ inches

Weight: Males — 60 to 75 pounds
Females — 55 to 70 pounds

Grooming: This shiny, short, close-lying, black or yellow coat sheds a little but not excessively. Brushing is helpful. Retrievers love water, so baths can be fun.

Cost: Moderate

Capabilities: Labradors are amazingly versatile dogs. Of course they hunt and retrieve but they also make good guard dogs and watchdogs

Creszentia Allen

Labrador retriever

while remaining gentle and trustworthy with children. Many Labs have been trained as dog guides for the blind.

Training tip: Training such an intelligent animal is easy providing the trainer stays in charge. The Labrador's intelligence can make him mischievous if he is not controlled. Demand a lot from a breed with so much potential, and begin early. Give them generous praise.

Housebreaking: Begin early and stick to the schedule. Some Labradors make a mistake now and then and some don't.

Aesthetic quality: Staunch, powerful dignity

Personality: Labs are as intelligent, devoted, reliable and even-tempered as a dog can be. They are active indoors and need to run outdoors and yet they can adjust to city life well. They are large, assertive dogs that relate very well to toddlers and young children as well as older children. They love to "retrieve" balls and sticks and are expert swimmers. After all, they worked for the fishermen in their Newfoundland days.

Creszentia Allen

English Setter

Origin: Bird dogs have been very important to the English hunter throughout their history. Four hundred years ago the English setter was bred from various spaniels, including the Spanish pointer. In addition to its superb skill in the field, the English setter has an extraordinary beauty. Though it is seen in solid colors or a solid color and white, it is most recognizable in its "belton" coat (white with flecks or freckles of the darker color).

Height at shoulder: Males — 25 inches
Females — 24 inches

Weight: Males — 60 to 70 pounds
Females — 50 to 60 pounds

Grooming: The setter's flat, straight coat needs expert trimming now and then. Frequent brushing keeps them in good condition. There is some shedding.

Cost: Moderate

Capabilities: The English setter's greatest trait is patience. They have an easygoing, laid-back quality not suited to guard work, though they can sometimes function as watchdog.

Training tip: In training, the English setter's patience can become stubborn resistance. Try coaxing, insistence and ecstatic praise. Never get tough with an English setter. It doesn't work. Begin early and always be firm and consistent.

Housebreaking: Setters are not easy to housebreak. Begin early, stick closely to the schedule, and always praise the successes. Admonish the failures but don't use physical punishment. Begin immediately with housebreaking and skip paper training. The transition from one to the other adds to the confusion.

Aesthetic quality: Magnificent form and grace on point or in motion — coat color, pattern and texture glorious

Personality: Affectionate, loving, gentle English setters are quiet and relaxed inside but require long vigorous runs outside every day. They also require undying love and devotion from every member of the family. They can be remarkably patient with toddlers and young children or they can give big kids a run for their money. Adjustment to apartment life is quite good.

Gordon Setter

Origin: In the late eighteenth century, the duke of Gordon gave his name to the already existing black and mahogany setter. The duke developed the breed to locate birds in the field at his castle in Scotland. In the middle of the nineteenth century, the Gordon setter brought its expertise to America.

Height at shoulder: Males — 24 to 27 inches
Females — 23 to 26 inches

Weight: Males — 55 to 80 pounds
Females — 45 to 70 pounds

Grooming: The setter's flat, slightly wavy coat sometimes needs expert trimming. There is some shedding. Regular brushing helps.

Cost: Moderate

Creszentia Allen

*Gordon
setter*

Capabilities: Unlike the other setters, the Gordon can be trained to guard. They have a more protective nature than the English or the Irish but they retain the setters' love of children.

Training tip: Begin early and be very firm. The Gordon is stubborn. Habits once established are difficult to break.

Housebreaking: Try not to paper train a Gordon. The transition to housebreaking is confusing for them. They have the typical setter difficulty with housebreaking. Stick to rigid schedules and begin early.

Aesthetic quality: Strength and great dignity in a black and tan coat

Personality: Gordons are hunting dogs and usually do best in the country. With long outdoor runs they can settle down when they come inside. Like the other setters, the Gordon likes a lot of attention from its family and in return takes excellent care of all the children from infancy to adulthood.

Creszentia Allen

Irish Setter

Origin: This easily recognized Irishman was created at the beginning of the eighteenth century in Ireland, of course. It was red and white then and still is in Ireland. It is bred strictly for that solid, mahogany-red color in America only.

Height at shoulder: Males — 27 inches
                         Females — 25 inches

Weight: Males — 70 pounds
                         Females — 60 pounds

Grooming: The flat, straight setter coat needs expert trimming now and then. There is some shedding. Regular brushing keeps the dog in good condition.

Cost: Expensive

Capabilities: In addition to their hunting talents Irish setters are good entertainers. They are very playful and like to clown around. Guard work is out of the question, but some Irish setters are good watchdogs.

Training tip: Begin early and be very firm. The Irish setter shows that typical setter stubbornness.

Housebreaking: The Irish setter, like his fellow setters, requires strict housebreaking schedules. Begin with housebreaking as early as possible. Skip paper training. It causes confusion. Be firm, consistent and diligent.

Aesthetic quality: Shining, breathtaking, chestnut red coat

Personality: Without training the Irish setter can be much too playful for very young children. They are big dogs who like to romp and play with big kids. This is not a sedate dog. Irish setters love and need miles of outdoor exercise every day and then come inside to be very active for the rest of the day. A country setting is best for them.

Brittany Spaniel

Origin: The "French" spaniel is very popular at field trials. Brittanies resemble setters as much as spaniels, but their tails are always short, like those of their fellow spaniels. Unlike the other spaniels, the Brittany is often born with a short tail. They were used to hunt woodcock in western France long before records were kept.

Height at shoulder: Males and females — 17½ to 20½ inches

Weight: Males and females — 30 to 40 pounds

Grooming: These spaniels shed a little. They need brushing regularly and trimming now and then.

Cost: Moderate

Capabilities: These hunters are warm, friendly companion dogs that can serve as watchdogs because they will bark at outside sounds and intruders. Although more assertive than the other spaniels, they are not suitable for guard work.

Training tip: Brittanies respond to obedience training a little more readily than some of the other hunting breeds, but they still need an early beginning, a firm hand, a consistent routine and a strong-willed trainer.

Creszentia Allen

*Brittany
spaniel*

Housebreaking: Housebreaking goes pretty well considering this is a hunting dog, but begin early and be consistent.

Aesthetic quality: Tall orange or brown and white spaniel

Personality: If given enough outdoor exercise, Brittanies do well in the city. They love children and play well with them, but they are large dogs and quite active even inside so they would probably overwhelm most toddlers. All Brittanies are affectionate, gentle and outgoing. Occasionally one will become attached to one person in a family. So make sure everyone is involved with the dog's daily routine to avoid singular attachments.

Clumber Spaniel

Origin: The dukes of Newcastle lived in Clumber Park, Nottingham. As far back as the nineteenth century they bred an uncharacteristic spaniel from various dogs imported from France. These dogs are shaped like spaniel cousins of the basset hound and have an excellent nose for finding game. They made their appearance in America in 1883.

Height at shoulder: Males and females — 16 to 19 inches

Creszentia Allen

Clumber spaniel

Weight: Males — 55 to 65 pounds
                       Females — 35 to 50 pounds

Grooming: These spaniels shed a little. They need regular brushing and trimming now and then.

Cost: Expensive

Capabilities: They're good hunters but don't look for a guard dog or a watchdog here.

Training tip: Clumbers give leisurely responses. Just begin early, be patient and consistent and don't give up.

Housebreaking: This chore goes pretty well. Stick to the schedule.

Aesthetic quality: Heavyset, cartoonlike face

Personality: There is no need to hurry for a Clumber. Outdoor exercise is important but they would just as soon wait till tomorrow. Small apartments are fine despite their size because of their sedate temperament. A Clumber is affectionate and gentle and a tower of patience with toddlers and small children. He can become attached to one person, so encourage everyone in the family to relate to him every day. His style of play is very subtle. Clumbers need to be coaxed.

Creszentia Allen

Cocker Spaniel

Origin: The always popular and easily recognizable cocker (often called the American cocker) is one of the smaller breeds of the ancient spaniels. It takes its name from the woodcock which it can find, flush and retrieve so well. The breed was introduced in America in the 1880s. By the middle of the twentieth century, the cocker spaniel had become one of the most popular and prolific breeds in the country. After suffering some breeding problems as the result of indiscriminate mass production, the cocker spaniel is now regaining its deserved position as an ideal American dog.

Height at shoulder: Males — 14½ to 15½ inches
Females — 13½ to 14½ inches

Weight: Males — 25 to 28 pounds
Females — 23 to 26 pounds

Grooming: Cocker spaniels shed. They need regular brushing, and trimming by an expert.

Cost: Moderate

Capabilities: Cockers are not meant to be guard dogs, but they can make good watchdogs.

Training tip: These are bright, responsive animals. Because they are essentially hunting dogs, it is a good idea to begin early. Resist their irresistible expressions and demand obedience to all your commands. Cockers respond very poorly to physical abuse. Always avoid hitting, but especially with a cocker.

Housebreaking: A good reason for sticking to the obedience training is because it helps the housebreaking. Hunting breeds, and the cocker is a hunting breed, have lived outdoors in kennels for so many generations that controlling bodily functions for the indoor life can be a difficult task. Begin housebreaking early and stick to a schedule. Praise success. Admonish failure but without physical abuse, including rolled-up newspapers.

Aesthetic quality: Sweet, small dog with big hanging ears and big gentle eyes.

Personality: A well-bred cocker can live happily in a city apartment, getting a fair amount of outdoor exercise and remaining even tempered and moderately active indoors. Cockers are gentle, cheerful and easy to get along with. They are wonderful companions for children of all ages. Just be sure to get a well-bred puppy. A large family would do well with a cocker because the dog can give personal attention, love and play to each member.

English Cocker Spaniel

Origin: The English cocker is slightly larger than the American cocker and is closely related to the English springer spaniel. The English began to breed spaniels separately by size in the late nineteenth century, but they all retain that splendid, engaging spaniel personality.

Height at shoulder: Males — 16 to 17 inches
Females — 15 to 16 inches

Weight: Males — 28 to 34 pounds
Females — 26 to 32 pounds

Creszentia Allen

English cocker spaniel

Grooming: English cockers shed. They need regular brushing and expert trimming.

Cost: Moderate

Capabilities: Anyone should be able to get along with an English cocker, including an intruder. However, they will bark at strange noises or when someone comes to the door, making them effective watchdogs.

Training tip: This breed trains rather easily, especially for a hunting breed. They are responsive and willing to please if the trainer is consistent and firm.

Housebreaking: Patience may be required. Stick to rigid schedules, begin early, praise successes, scold but never hit for failures.

Aesthetic quality: Long, hanging ears and graceful sporting lines

Personality: Marvelous, adaptive English cockers can do well in the country and the city with some outdoor exercise. They are moderately active indoors, certainly active enough to show a house full of children a good time. English cockers are well suited to all ages. They are so adaptive and loving that any child flourishes in their presence.

Creszentia Allen

English Springer Spaniel

Origin: These spaniels are named for their ability to "spring" the birds from cover, forcing them to fly up. The smaller cockers flush woodcock, a low-flying bird. Springers and cockers are considered land spaniels, though they can retrieve from water if needed.

Height at shoulder: Males — 20 inches
Females — 19 inches

Weight: Males — 49 to 55 pounds
Females — 46 to 50 pounds

Grooming: They need regular brushing and expert trimming. English springers shed.

Cost: Moderate

Capabilities: Springers can serve as watchdogs but not guard dogs. They are expert hunters and companions.

Training tip: English springers respond well for a hunting breed. They are eager to please and responsive. Take advantage and give them a good, consistent, early obedience course.

Housebreaking: Typical hunting dog difficulties with housebreaking occur in this breed, too. A conscientious obedience course can help. Begin the housebreaking early and stick to a schedule.

Aesthetic quality: Long, hanging ears and graceful sporting lines

Personality: These are good city or country dogs. They are active and need exercise, the kind a group of children can give them. Though they are larger than other spaniels, easygoing springers are usually gentle with toddlers and playful with older children. Like all spaniels they love retrieving games with balls and sticks.

Weimaraner

Origin: This is another magnificent German hunting dog created by dedicated breeders in the nineteenth century. The weimaraner, named for the court at Weimar, was bred to hunt large game such as wolf, bear, deer and wildcat. There is no large game to hunt in Germany now, and little elsewhere for that matter, so the weimaraner has been adapted to bird hunting, which suits the breed equally well.

Height at shoulder: Males — 25 to 27 inches
Females — 23 to 25

Weight: Males — 70 to 85 pounds
Females — 55 to 70 pounds

Grooming: There is some shedding, but the coat is short. Periodic brushing is good for the dog's coat.

Cost: Moderate

Capabilities: Weimaraners make wonderful watchdogs. They will sound the alarm at any unfamiliar noise. Many of them can be trained to guard and attack, but such training requires an expert. These dogs do not guard naturally, and if trained to do so need constant supervision.

Training tip: Begin early, very early; be firm; be consistent; never waver. These are hunting dogs who have been bred to follow their own

Creszentia Allen

Weimaraner

instincts, not those of their owners. Unless the owner wants the dog to track a mountain lion or bring a wild pheasant home for dinner, there may be a conflict of interests. Teach this breed, from the beginning, that the owner makes all the decisions and must be obeyed every time.

Housebreaking: Hunting breeds accustomed to outdoor living are much more difficult to housebreak. Weimaraners must begin early, be given rigid schedules, and be corrected firmly.

Aesthetic quality: Sleek, iridescent gray hunter

Personality: These dogs are bright and develop very personal relationships with each member of the family. They are wonderful for active older children who have the time and energy to give them long, daily runs and lots of active personal attention. Weimaraners are very active indoors as well, so they are not well suited to a sedentary household or to city living. Small children usually find the weimaraner too large and active to play with comfortably.

HOUNDS

Creszentia Allen

Basset Hound

Origin: Bas in French means a "low thing" or "dwarf." A dog referred to as a basset was mentioned in 1585 in a French treatise on badger hunting. But the basset hound appears to have been used most often for hunting rabbits, hares and deer in France and Belgium. It looks like a bloodhound on short legs and shares that dog's ability to follow a scent.

Height at shoulder: Males and females — 14 inches

Weight: Males and females — 45 pounds

Grooming: This breed sheds, but at least the coat is short. Otherwise they just need an occasional brushing.

Cost: Moderate

Capabilities: Creating a quiet, relaxed atmosphere is one of the basset's most noticeable qualities, but it will act as watchdog if no one else will do it. Guarding is out. They are much too easygoing for guard work.

Training tip: Bassets are very responsive. Just don't expect quick responses. Give them more praise than correction. Flattery will get you everywhere.

Housebreaking: Early obedience training along with early housebreaking are the best insurance. Some basset hounds do have trouble with this chore.

Aesthetic quality: Long, low, heavy and calm, with a deadpan expression

Personality: Cooperative, gentle, cheerful bassets need their family's attention and love. They are not very active indoors but deserve a good walk outdoors, which makes them ideal for the city. Toddlers are handled with the patience of Job and quiet older children will value the loyalty and friendship offered by a basset. Only a very active teenager might be disappointed when the dog preferred a game of Scrabble to a game of catch.

Beagle

Origin: The Romans found beagle packs in England when they arrived. The English used them for hunting rabbit. *Beagle* means small, for they are the smallest of the hounds. Although they have been bred for centuries in packs, they adapt well to living individually in families. The beagle as we see it today in America was developed in the 1880s. They are bred in two varieties, different only in size. The 13-inch variety and the 15-inch variety both resemble the English foxhound in miniature and both participate in AKC beagle field trials.

Variety 1

Height at shoulder:	Males and females — to 13 inches
Weight:	Males and females — 15 to 20 pounds

Variety 2

Height at shoulder:	Males and females — 13 to 15 inches
Weight:	Males and females — 18 to 23 pounds

Creszentia Allen

Beagle

Grooming: Beagles have some shedding, but the coat is short. Occasional brushing is good.

Cost: Moderate

Capabilities: Announcing the approach of strangers is well within the beagle's talents, but not guarding.

Training tip: Circumvent an inborn stubbornness by beginning the training early. Give a lot of praise and demand a lot. Be firm but never punish. Beagles respond very poorly to punishment.

Housebreaking: Housebreaking is difficult if begun late. Get an early start and there is no problem. Rigid schedules always help.

Aesthetic quality: The Snoopy look

Personality: There is a reason why beagles are so popular. They are sweet-natured dogs that seem to be genuinely happy. However, popularity breeds indiscriminate breeding, so be sure to get a well-bred puppy. Beagles hate to be left alone. They need a lot of outdoor exercise and are fairly active indoors, but many have made the adjustment to apartment living well. They are gentle enough for toddlers and playful enough for older children.

46

Black and Tan Coonhound

Origin: Black and tans are scent hounds; they live by their noses. They have been bred from English Talbot hounds, bloodhounds and foxhounds for their ability to hunt by scent and for their beautiful black and tan coats. Obviously these hounds specialize in raccoons, but they also excel in trailing deer, mountain lion and bear.

Height at shoulder: Males — 25 to 27 inches
                          Females — 23 to 25 inches

Weight: Males — 65 to 85 pounds
                          Females — 60 to 80 pounds

Grooming: There is some shedding of the short coat. The dog needs a brushing now and then.

Cost: Moderate

47

Capabilities: Black and tans can function as watchdogs and even now and then as guard dogs, although it is not their primary talent. Primarily they are scenting hounds.

Training tip: These are responsive dogs. Do not be too exuberant when praising them. They need to concentrate.

Housebreaking: They have surprisingly few problems in this area, but don't take a hound for granted.

Aesthetic quality: Sleek, black, athletic hunting dog

Personality: This is a large, energetic animal that needs extensive, daily, outdoor exercise, which usually means a country setting is best. However, he is calm indoors. Such a large, active dog would seem to be too much for a toddler, but if the child doesn't mind, the black and tan doesn't. They are very patient, easygoing members of the family. What they don't like is being left alone.

Irish Wolfhound

Origin: This medieval giant hunted the Irish elk (six feet at the shoulder) and the wolf for kings. There is even mention of this enormous dog in Roman history. But by the nineteenth century the Irish wolfhound was almost extinct. The breed was saved by a Scottish officer in the British army, Captain George A. Graham.

Height at shoulder: Males — 32 to 34 inches
Females — 30 to 32 inches

Weight: Males — minimum 120 pounds
Females — minimum 105 pounds

Grooming: This wiry, rough coat needs regular brushing, trimming and stripping (plucking out loose fur with one's fingers). There is also some shedding.

Cost: Very expensive to acquire and to feed

Capabilities: They are beautiful to look at and easy to live with but they are not suitable as watchdogs or guard dogs.

Creszentia Allen

*Irish
wolfhound*

Training tip: Be firm. These dogs must be controlled because of their size. A consistent early beginning is the best way. Irish wolfhounds will respond quite well when they know you mean it.

Housebreaking: Irish wolfhounds have no problem with housebreaking, but begin early.

Aesthetic quality: Lovable, smiling giant

Personality: They do not like to rush. Wolfhounds are easygoing cooperative dogs who *must* be pushed to take their long daily gallops. Being inactive indoors allows them to adapt to city life well. Older children are better suited to the wolfhound. Small children might be overcome by their size. They are especially good at rough play with big kids. But these very large dogs have shorter life spans.

Creszentia Allen

Otter Hound

Origin: From the early thirteenth century in England there was a need to hunt otter. Man and otter were in competition for fish. In the nineteenth century it became a sport, and otter hounds were kept in packs. But most of the otters are gone now in England, as are most of the otter hounds. The dog's happy-go-lucky quality is beginning to appeal to Americans.

Height at shoulder: Males — 24 to 27 inches
                        Females — 22 to 26 inches

Weight: Males — 75 to 115 pounds
                     Females — 65 to 100 pounds

Grooming: This rough, shaggy coat needs some care and brushing to keep that tousled look. There is shedding.

Cost: Moderate

Capabilities: These are happy, friendly dogs who do a little watching but no guarding.

Training tip: Otter hounds are difficult to train. Be firm and consistent. Begin early and stay with it. Training is important for such a large dog.

Housebreaking: Keep rigid schedules and be very firm. Housebreaking is a difficult chore for the otter hound. Begin early.

Aesthetic quality: Playful, shaggy giant

Personality: The ancient but rare otter hound is best suited to country living. They are happy, easygoing dogs who love everyone, but they should never be off leash or out of the owner's control. They will take off after a wild animal and wonder where they are miles later. Big children have a great time with these big dogs, but small children need a different breed.

WORKING DOGS

Bernese Mountain Dog

Origin: Named for the canton of Berne in Switzerland, this canine serves the Swiss farmer herding, pulling loads, and guarding the farmhouse and stock. The Bernese has been closely identified with the basketweavers for centuries, helping transport their shipments to market. Progenitors of the breed were brought to Switzerland by the Romans. Selective breeding was not begun until the end of the eighteenth century. These are large, stately animals with heavy medium-length fur. They can be comfortable outdoors through an entire winter but they need the closeness of their families.

Height at shoulder: Males — 23 to 27½ inches
Females — 21 to 26 inches

Weight: Males — 80 to 105 pounds
Females — 75 to 90 pounds

Grooming: The Bernese does shed, though not excessively. A good brushing once or twice a week will keep its coat in good shape.

Creszentia Allen

Bernese
mountain dog

Cost: Expensive

Capabilities: An owner can ask his Bernese to guard the house and children, to warn of approaching strangers, to haul loads on a cart, or to sit back and play with the kids and have a good time.

Training tip: These dogs are very intelligent and sensitive. They do not need harsh or loud corrections. A gentle voice and a patient manner will work wonders for the Bernese. Praise them as soon as they have obeyed a command and be generous with the praise. Training need not begin at a terribly early age, but socializing should. The puppies are adorable and should get a lot of human companionship as early as possible.

Housebreaking: No problem

Aesthetic quality: Big, sturdy black dog with a white face and chest

Personality: Children of any age will be ecstatically happy with a Bernese mountain dog. They tend to lean on someone they love. If that someone is a small child, some supervision might be necessary. They are gentle, even-tempered and patient. People outside the dog's immediate family are usually ignored. This breed deserves a decent amount of outdoor exercise but remains reasonably relaxed and quiet indoors, so it does well in the city.

Creszentia Allen

Boxer

Origin: They are called boxers because they tend to begin a fight by swinging their front paws. Fighting is what they were bred to do hundreds of years ago. The breed as we know it was developed long ago in Germany by crossing bulldogs, terriers, probably Great Danes and mastiffs. After bull-baiting and dog fights were outlawed in the middle of the nineteenth century, the boxer was used in police and guard work. It still makes a fine guard dog, but the viciousness has been bred out in the twentieth century to make the boxer an excellent, affectionate pet.

Height at shoulder: Males — 22½ to 25 inches
Females — 21 to 23½ inches

Weight: Males — 60 to 70 pounds
Females — 50 to 60 pounds

Grooming: Care of the boxer is easy. There is some shedding, but the coat is short. An occasional brushing is good.

Cost: Moderate

Capabilities: Clearly the boxer is an excellent guard dog and a companion. He is also a good watchdog.

Training tip: Boxers can be stubborn if training begins too late. Begin early, at about three months old.

Housebreaking: These dogs housebreak well when taught early in life.

Aesthetic quality: Majestic stance and wise expression

Personality: Boxers have intelligent, dominant personalities but surprisingly enough get along well with children. They love to play and romp with older kids. Most little children would have a hard time holding their own. The city suits this breed as well as the country. They are moderately active indoors and out. Boxers are very popular, so look for a well-bred puppy.

Great Dane

Origin: This giant breed was mentioned in eighteenth-century European animal studies and most likely existed before that. It was used to hunt the ferocious wild boar. At that time the French called it the Great Dane, although the dog does not have any connection with Denmark. Concentrated breed development of the Great Dane took place in Germany in the nineteenth century where it is called *Deutsche Dogge* (German mastiff).

Height at shoulder: Males — no less than 30 inches
Females — no less than 28 inches

Weight: Males — 135 to 150 pounds
Females — 120 to 135 pounds

Grooming: Occasional brushing is all a Dane needs. There is some shedding but the coat is short.

Cost: Expensive to acquire and to feed

Capabilities: Danes make good watchdogs but not guard dogs.

Creszentia Allen

Great Dane

Training tip: Sometimes sensitive, sometimes stubborn, these dogs need a lot of praise. Be gentle and coaxing, not harsh.

Housebreaking: They housebreak well if taught early.

Aesthetic quality: Majestic, graceful and dignified

Personality: Danes must be exercised outdoors every day whether they feel like it or not. Most living situations will do because Danes are so easy and agreeable. They do well in the city and can adapt to even small apartments, but more space is desirable. Children could have trouble with the dog's desire to lean on those he likes: A child cannot support a 150-pound dog. But if the dog is taught not to lean from the very beginning, the problem can be avoided. These are not very active dogs, so they are good with small children. Very large dogs have shorter life spans.

Creszentia Allen

Newfoundland

Origin: This breed was developed on the northeastern Canadian island of Newfoundland to help the fishermen with their nets, save shipwrecked men, haul heavy loads, and protect the children. The "Neuf" performs all of these tasks to perfection. There is no record of what dogs went into the breeding of the Newfoundland several hundred years ago, but they must have been imported, because there were no dogs native to the American continent.

Height at shoulder: Males — 28 inches
                        Females — 26 inches

Weight: Males — 150 pounds
                        Females — 120 pounds

Grooming: This breed has a medium-long outer coat and a heavy undercoat, both of which shed year round. In the late spring and early fall they shed heavily to prepare for the new season. A lot of brushing is necessary.

Cost: Expensive to acquire and to feed

Capabilities: Technically Newfoundlands are not guard dogs because they won't naturally protect buildings or boundaries, but they will usually come to the protection of their children. Neufs are truly canine nannies. They will also function as watchdogs.

Training tip: The Newfoundland is very responsive and willing to please, so the training should not be difficult. Be gentle and patient. This breed is very sensitive to harsh treatment; it makes them shy. They respond best to generous praise.

Housebreaking: No problem.

Aesthetic quality: A massive black bear

Personality: Although they are quite large, they are splendid with toddlers as well as older kids. Neufs are always affectionate. They love water almost as much as they love their families. If possible, swimming is the best exercise for these big, happy, reliable dogs. Such a large animal needs a large home, but it can be in the city or the country. They are inactive indoors like most large breeds and like most large breeds they have a short life expectancy.

Samoyed

Origin: The Samoyed people live in northwest Russia, near Finland, with their happy, laughing, white dogs. The people and the dogs have lived there longer than recorded history. These dogs have herded reindeer, pulled heavy loads on sleds, and protected their families while maintaining their phenomenal good spirit. They are much admired for their sumptuous white fur.

Height at shoulder: Males — 21 to 23½ inches
Females — 19 to 21 inches

Weight: Males — 50 to 75 pounds
Females — 40 to 55 pounds

Grooming: The medium-length outer coat and the heavy undercoat shed all year round. In late spring and early fall they shed heavily to prepare for the change of season. This heavy shedding is a form of natural dry cleaning for these white dogs. Northern dogs have strong weather-resistant coats that tend to stay cleaner than other breeds. If they have romped through mud, just clean the dirty area and keep the

Creszentia Allen

Samoyed

regular baths to a minimum. Regular brushing to remove the loose fur is most important.

Cost: Moderate

Capabilities: The Samoyed is a good watchdog but not a guard dog. They do like to pull sleds.

Training tip: They like to pull people, too. Training must begin early. These are strong, stubborn dogs that need convincing. They ignore punishment, so firm, consistent obedience training is very important.

Housebreaking: Begin early and stick to the schedule rigidly. Be patient. Reward success every time; admonish failures, but don't bother punishing. Samoyeds have trouble with housebreaking, but eventually they succeed.

Aesthetic quality: Luxurious, thick, white fur coat

Personality: The Samoyed is a very happy, playful, active animal. He is slightly calmer than the Siberian husky, so he is better for younger children, but with supervision. Samoyeds are happiest in large apartments or houses. This dog needs a lot of exercise inside and out, but he does seem to do well in the city.

Creszentia Allen

Siberian Husky

Origin: The Chukchi natives bred the Siberian husky to pull sleds over the long expanses of snow and ice in the Russian northeast. These dogs work in teams to pull light loads over incredible distances. They are very popular at sled dog races in the United States and Canada.

Height at shoulder: Males — 21 to 23½ inches
Females — 20 to 22 inches

Weight: Males — 45 to 60 pounds
Females — 35 to 50 pounds

Grooming: The harsh outer coat and the heavy undercoat shed all year long. In the late spring and early fall they shed heavily to prepare for the new season. The heavy shedding and the dog's natural habit of cleaning himself somewhat like a cat make frequent baths unnecessary.

Cost: Moderate

Capabilities: Pulling sleds and playing are the Siberian's talents. Guarding or watching are out of the question. They don't even bark, they howl.

Training tip: Siberians are very stubborn and playful. Be firm, authoritative and consistent. Begin early and give firm corrections. This is a very strong breed.

Housebreaking: This chore is sometimes difficult. Siberians need frequent walks, strict schedules and an early beginning. They are impervious to punishment, but strict adherence to the obedience course will create the self-discipline necessary for successful housebreaking.

Aesthetic quality: Mischievous wolf

Personality: These happy, happy dogs need to run, play and see people and lots of children. They are energetic, medium-sized dogs that seldom calm down. Small children would be overwhelmed. Huskies hate to be left alone. Huskies do best in large apartments or houses where there is room for all that energy, but many huskies have adjusted to city life.

TERRIERS

Airedale

Origin: The old English terriers were bred to hunt fox, rats, weasels and other nuisance rodents in the English countryside. In the early nineteenth century these old terriers were bred with the popular otter hound to combine the superior eyesight and hearing of the terrier and the superior scenting ability of the otter hound all in one hardy, courageous dog. The cross was so successful that the resulting Airedale (named for the Aire River Valley) was shown in its own competition in 1879 at the Airedale Agricultural Society Show. The breed has flourished ever since because Airedales can adjust to so many various life-styles. They are the largest of the terriers and perhaps more restrained than some of their cousins.

Height at shoulder: Males — 23 inches
Females — 22 inches

Weight: Males — 50 to 60 pounds
Females — 45 to 55 pounds

Grooming: The rough, wiry quality of the terrier coat needs very little care. The softer undercoat will periodically loosen to make way for new growth. Those with the time and patience should hand pluck out the loose, dead undercoat by pulling the tufts between the thumb and forefinger. However, those with a busier schedule can take the dog to a professional groomer to be trimmed and clipped. Except for the loosened undercoat, which stays on the body till plucked, there is very little shedding. Regular brushing is good.

Airedale

Cost: Moderate

Capabilities: The tenacious quality needed to hunt rats and the loyal hound spirit have made the Airedale an excellent guard dog. These dogs have been used by the military and the police because they will execute their commands even when wounded. Of course Airedales are courageous, indefatigable hunters and trusted companions.

Training tip: When Airedales are trained as young puppies they learn quickly, easily and willingly. They accept human dominance at this early age, which is important. If allowed to go untrained, an Airedale can become stubborn and difficult to control. This strong, independent spirit always needs a firm, decisive trainer.

Housebreaking: Well-taught puppies become well-housebroken dogs.

Aesthetic quality: Dominant, alert dignity

Personality: Older children have a great time with Airedales. They can run and jump and wrestle endlessly. But fifty pounds of boundless joy is too much for younger children. Airedales like to run and play a lot inside and outside until a stranger comes along, then they become aloof and distant. Airedales are territorial and may fight with strange dogs and therefore require early obedience training. They are usually polite to outsiders, both people and dogs, unless attacked. If they or their families are attacked, they are fearless. Despite the high energy level, this breed adapts to the city life-style well.

Creszentia Allen

Border Terrier

Origin: Where Scotland borders northern England the farmers have been plagued by the hill fox for hundreds of years. Their defense is the border terrier. They are tough little dogs who can hunt and kill a fox, no small feat. This breed may be difficult to obtain but not impossible. The American Kennel Club can be of help in locating a breeder. They are more commonly found in England and Scotland.

Height at shoulder: Males — 13 to 14 inches
Females — 11 to 12 inches

Weight: Males — 13 to 15½ pounds
Females — 11½ to 14 pounds

Grooming: The wiry top coat and soft undercoat shed a little, but regular brushing is all that is needed.

Cost: Moderate

Capabilities: Borders make good little watchdogs. They are too small for guarding but they make excellent ratters.

Training tip: These are responsive dogs, especially for a terrier. They do not respond well to harsh treatment: it could make them timid. Give them praise and encouragement and be consistent.

Housebreaking: Like most terriers, this one should not have housebreaking problems.

Aesthetic quality: Scrappy, scruffy little tough guy

Personality: Borders are the most calm of the terriers while still maintaining the terrier personality, which makes them ideal for children, young and old. Borders do not like to sit around, though. They are very active dogs inside as well as outside. City life is fine if they get enough exercise and if they are introduced to the noise and hubbub as puppies.

Cairn Terrier

Origin: The cairn stems from the Isle of Skye and the West Highlands of Scotland, as does the West Highland white terrier. These little terriers are all wonderful, feisty hunters of rodents and small game. There are very specific descriptions for the cairn by the middle of the nineteenth century. Dorothy's Toto was a cairn who was typically devoted to his mistress as they searched for the mythical land of Oz. They are very partial to their own families and indifferent to "outsiders." The spirit of a two-and-a-half-year-old is retained for a lifetime in this breed. However, the cairn may not want to share that particular spotlight with a human two-and-a-half-year-old. Older children can get along with a cairn much better.

Height at shoulder: Males — 10 inches
Females — 9½ inches

Weight: Males — 14 pounds
Females — 13 pounds

Grooming: The care of a cairn is easy. They have the rough outer terrier coat and the soft undercoat. Now and then that undercoat needs to be plucked (the loose hair pulled out with the thumb and forefinger). Regular brushing is good.

Cost: Moderate

Capabilities: Just as they would threaten rodents and foxes hiding in the rocks, they will warn of strangers at the door. They are small and

Creszentia Allen

Cairn terrier

unsuited to actual guard work, contrary to what they may think. A cairn's self-image is quite sound.

Training tip: Cairns are terriers. They are stubborn and sometimes aggressive. So begin early and be patient. Be firm and be consistent; don't let them get away without obeying every command just because they are adorable.

Housebreaking: Some little dogs are difficult to housebreak, but not this one. A cairn is a neat, tidy little animal. Just show him what to do.

Aesthetic quality: Little tough guy

Personality: All cairns love their families and are very devoted to the members of their own household. Some cairns enjoy company, even a house full of strangers, but some do not. They can live in a city apartment happily or they can run all over a large estate. Adaptability is a trademark of this intelligent breed. Certainly with older children they are splendid. With younger children some cairns are too feisty, too scrappy. Then again, some young children are too feisty for a little dog. As tough as the cairn is, he is not a big-boned tower of patience. He can't take the indiscriminate pounding some very small children might mete out.

Creszentia Allen

Fox terrier
(wire)

Fox Terrier (Smooth and Wire)

Origin: Both varieties of fox terrier were bred from other terriers in nineteenth-century England. They were used with packs of foxhounds. When the larger dogs ran a fox to ground the fox terrier burrowed into the tunnel for the kill. As foxhunting waned, the fox terrier became more popular in the show ring and in high-fashion settings. Remember Asta in the *Thin Man* movies?

Height at shoulder: Males — to 15½ inches
Females — proportionately lower

Weight: Males — 17 to 19 pounds
Females — 15 to 17 pounds

Grooming: There is little shedding. But the wirehaired variety needs regular brushing plus visits to the professional groomer for clipping. The smooth variety needs a brushing only now and then.

Cost: Moderate

Capabilities: These are wonderful watchdogs. They will bark at any sound or unusual circumstance. But they are not guard dogs.

Training tip: Begin early. Be consistent and firm. This breed is bright and responsive if the training is very consistent. When a fox terrier is given his own way, his stubborn streak begins to show.

Housebreaking: Some fox terriers have more difficulty with house-breaking than others. Don't wait to find out. Begin training early and be firm.

Aesthetic quality: Alert, clever and playful

Personality: They need busy, active, older children who want to play. A fox terrier's outdoor exercise does not have to be jogging, but he needs a lot of time to chase balls and see what's going on. Such active dogs need a fair-sized home in the city or country. Be sure to explain to the child and the dog that the child must be in charge at all times. Fox terriers like to take over if given a chance. Small children are usually not dominant enough, or fast enough, or alert enough to handle this breed. These dogs require a gentle-but-firm hand plus one who can out-wit them. They are very clever, and quite stubborn. They can make you laugh at their tricks and frown at their scrappiness. They are wonderful for older kids and teenagers.

Soft-Coated Wheaten Terrier

Origin: This terrier with the unusual fluffy fur comes from Ireland. From all accounts it was a dependable farm dog, protecting livestock and hunting small vermin, for hundreds of years while other terriers were gaining fame in the show ring. In 1937 it was recognized by the Irish Kennel Club, on St. Patrick's Day to be exact. And on St. Patrick's Day, 1962, the Soft-Coated Wheaten Terrier Club of America was founded in Brooklyn.

Height at shoulder: Males and females — 18 to 19 inches

Weight: Males and females — 35 to 45 pounds

Grooming: The wheaten's coat is unusual for a terrier. It is fairly long, soft and wavy. There is very little shedding, but daily brushing is important to keep the fur from matting.

Cost: Expensive

Capabilities: This is apparently a terrier of all trades. Watchdog is at the top of the list, followed by hunting, herding and then guarding. They do guard but they are better watchdogs.

Training tip: Wheatens are somewhat easier to train than other terriers. They are willing to please and very bright. Don't let them go

Creszentia Allen

Soft-coated wheaten terrier

without obedience training, though. That terrier stubbornness will surface.

Housebreaking: No problem

Aesthetic quality: Alert beige terrier with long, fluffy fur on his face

Personality: The wheaten is an even-tempered animal. He remains gentle in spite of his fairly high activity level, indoors and out, so he is wonderful for younger children when many of the terriers are not. As long as he gets enough exercise he does well in the city.

West Highland White Terrier

Origin: Westies go back at least to the middle of the nineteenth century in Scotland. They come from the common terrier stock of Scotland that gave us the cairn, the Scottie and the Dandie Dinmont. These all white terriers were often known as Reseneath or Poltalloch terriers after the estates of their breeders. Colonel Malcolm of Poltalloch had

Creszentia Allen

*West Highland
white terrier*

the name officially changed to West Highland white terrier in the first decade of the twentieth century. The white coat was valued because the dog was much easier to see when hunting. The darker, earth-colored dogs could sometimes be mistaken for the vermin they were chasing, leading to tragic mistakes.

Height at shoulder: Males — 11 inches
                        Females — 10 inches

Weight: Males — 17 to 20 pounds
                        Females — 15 to 18 pounds

Grooming: Believe it or not that sparkling white coat is easy to keep. Too much bathing makes it more difficult. Dry shampoo and regular brushing keep the natural oils distributed throughout the coat and do more to keep the white color clean than soap does. Westies do not shed very much, but they have the terrier hard outer coat and the soft undercoat that needs plucking when it loosens. Just gently pull the clumps of loose undercoat with the thumb and forefinger. It may take a little practice.

Cost: Moderate

Capabilities: A Westie can serve as watchdog, hunter or entertainment director. They are not good guard dogs. Not only are they too small, the West Highland white basically likes company and visitors, and though assertive, he is not an aggressive dog.

Training tip: Unlike some other terriers, Westies are not stubborn, so training is a reasonably simple, straightforward affair. These are very bright dogs. Just follow the basic training course.

Housebreaking: This breed is easy to housebreak.

Aesthetic quality: Alert, perky and white

Personality: Happy, active, sociable Highlanders enjoy life as long as they are loved, and who could not love them? Some Westies could be too impatient for a toddler or very young child. Like most terriers, a Westie will only put up with so much. But older children and Westies are a perfect combination. This breed is very active indoors and needs to play a lot. They are very active outdoors as well. However, they make wonderful apartment dogs because they do not need an enormous amount of space for all that activity.

T O Y S

English Toy Spaniel

Origin: *Spaniel* means "from Spain" and the English toy spaniel does have Spanish origins. However, this spaniel has a deep break in the line of the nose, which means a pushed-up nose like the pug or the Pekingese. This feature was probably developed in China or Japan. There is evidence of English toy spaniels coming from Japan to England in 1613. These luxurious little dogs come in four coat colors: King Charles (black with mahogany-tan markings on the face, chest and legs), Prince Charles (white with black and tan patches), Ruby (solid chestnut red) and Blenheim (red and white).

Height at shoulder: Males and females — 9 to 10 inches

Weight: Males and females — 9 to 12 pounds

Grooming: There is some shedding with this breed, but not much. Regular brushing keeps the coat from matting.

*English
toy spaniel*

Cost: Moderate

Capabilities: Companionship

Training tip: Like other spaniels these toys are responsive and willing to please.

Housebreaking: Most members of this breed housebreak easily.

Aesthetic quality: Elegant, cheerful, pug-nosed

Personality: English toys are charming in every way. They make perfect apartment dogs because they require very little outdoor exercise and are calm indoors. This is the only really small breed recommended, and unfortunately it is very rare. Younger children would be too rough for this dog as would very energetic older ones.

Pug

Origin: The Chinese are usually given credit for developing animals with pushed-in noses. They probably developed the ancient pug. The breed has a long and varied history. There is evidence of the pug in ancient Tibetan monasteries, with William, prince of Orange, in sixteenth-century France and with Napoleon and Josephine in eighteenth-century France. They are called *pugs* because of their similarity to marmoset monkeys, which were also called pugs in the early eighteenth century.

Creszentia Allen

Pug

For all that long, illustrious history, the pug has served strictly as a love object. These are very affectionate little toy dogs.

Height at shoulder: Males and females — 10 to 12 inches

Weight: Males and females — 14 to 18 pounds

Grooming: There is some shedding, but the coat is short. Occasional brushing is good. The care of the pug is really easy.

Cost: Moderate

Capabilities: Companionship

Training tip: Pugs can be stubborn. Be gentle and patient and don't give too many corrections. Because of their wheezy breathing they can't take hard tugs and pulling on the leash.

Housebreaking: There should be no problems.

Aesthetic quality: Worried little tough guy

Personality: Bright, affectionate, easygoing pugs are ideal for small apartments. They are not very active and do not need much exercise. Considerate school-age children are perfect with pugs. Toddlers and rambunctious children of any age could be too rough for the dog. A pug is loving and gentle with a child of any age. He is one of the sturdiest of the toy breeds, but he should always be treated with respect. They are often seen in pairs (a brace).

NON-SPORTING DOGS

Creszentia Allen

Bichon Frise

Origin: Bichon-type dogs lived in the Dark Ages throughout the Mediterranean region. They thrived during the Renaissance in Spain, France, and Italy. For hundreds of years they were kept as pets. No hunting or herding for the Bichon. Their job is entertaining and giving unending love and devotion. They are experts. After such a long history in Europe they made the trip to the United States in the 1950s and were accepted by the American Kennel Club in the 1970s.

Height at shoulder: Males and females — 8 to 12 inches

Weight: Males — 14 to 20 pounds
              Females — 11 to 18 pounds

Grooming: This abundant, curly white coat almost never sheds! However, there is extensive brushing involved and regular visits to a professional groomer for trimming.

Cost: Expensive

Capabilities: Companionship is their principal talent, though they sometimes serve as watchdogs.

Training tip: Training should be easy. They are very responsive.

Housebreaking: Be patient and diligent about the schedule. After perfection seems to be reached there could be lapses, so never give up that rigid schedule.

Aesthetic quality: Fluffy little white ball

Personality: The Bichon is so happy and sweet natured, busy and active, that it is extremely easy to live with, especially in an apartment. Although very active indoors, it needs comparatively little outdoor exercise. They are really the size of a large toy dog, so they can't withstand rough treatment from young or active children.

Boston Terrier

Origin: Born and bred in Boston in the 1870s from the mating of an English bulldog and a white English terrier, Boston terriers serve the sole purpose of giving and receiving affection. They always seem to have a smile on their wide little faces.

Height at shoulder: Males and females — 15 to 16 inches

Weight: Males and females:
lightweight — under 15 pounds
middleweight — 15 to 20 pounds
heavyweight — 20 to 25 pounds

Grooming: There is some shedding, but the coat is short. Occasional brushing is good. The care of the Boston terrier is really easy.

Cost: Moderate

Capabilities: Companionship is their primary function, but they do make good watchdogs.

Creszentia Allen

Boston terrier

Training tip: There is the terrier stubborn streak here, so be patient. Expect a Boston to be responsive, particularly when the training is consistent and firm and the praise is exuberant.

Housebreaking: Include as many walks as possible in the housebreaking schedule and don't be surprised when mistakes happen. Bostons are sensitive to punishment, so simply admonish when necessary and praise lavishly when appropriate.

Aesthetic quality: Round eyed, round bodied and wise

Personality: Bostons are easy to love and live with. They make wonderful city dogs because they need minimal outdoor exercise even though they are somewhat active indoors. They are not much bigger than some of the toy breeds, so some caution should govern how the children play with them, but Bostons can have a great time with any age child.

Creszentia Allen

Bulldog

Origin: This affectionate homebody was originally bred to attack bulls for sport. When bull-baiting was abolished in England in 1835, the bulldog nearly vanished with it. The few people still interested in the breed for its own sake created the bulldog we know today. The courage remains but the fighting instinct has been deliberately bred out.

Height at shoulder: Males — 15 to 16 inches
Females — 14 to 15 inches

Weight: Males — 50 pounds
Females — 40 pounds

Grooming: There is some shedding, but the coat is short. Occasional brushing is good. Bulldogs do need their mouths wiped at times each day.

Cost: Expensive

Capabilities: This is a suberb guard dog. He is always gentle and does not become aggressive until absolutely necessary. He doesn't bark much, so as a watchdog he isn't very effective.

Training tip: When training is begun early, bulldogs are very responsive. If too much time goes by, a stubbornness could set in.

Housebreaking: No problem

Aesthetic quality: A wheezing, snoring, drooling, magnificent animal

Personality: These legendary tough guys need and give loyalty and affection. Bulldogs only live up to their ferocious looks after extreme provocation. Any space, any place is fine since they need minimal exercise. Bulldogs love everyone in the family, including the cat. They are particularly strong and patient, which is a good combination for toddlers. They are poor at jogging and romping, which could be a drawback for an active teenager.

Dalmatian

Origin: Dalmatians are obviously named for Dalmatia, a coastal province of Yugoslavia, where they have lived for at least two hundred years. But the people of many countries claim the Dalmatian as part of their history and culture. His service in fire houses is legendary, but then so is his service as a "coach dog," which he is sometimes called. The English have called him the "Spotted Dick" and the "Plum Pudding Dog." The Dalmatian also has a long history with the Gypsies. Clearly this is an adaptable, popular dog.

Height at shoulder: Males and females — 19 to 23 inches

Weight: Males and females — 50 to 65 pounds

Grooming: Dalmatians do shed, but the coat is very short and flat. Regular brushing helps.

Cost: Moderate

Capabilities: These dogs have served their many admirers in many ways. They can haul loads, herd flocks, or serve in the military as sentry dogs. They can hunt and retrieve fowl, follow a scent, or hunt large

Creszentia Allen

Dalmatian

game. They have performed in circus acts and been trained for guard work. They work well with horses and have tremendous endurance.

Training tip: Dalmatians require a calm, firm, patient trainer. Because the dog can be excitable, praise him quietly and gently. Dalmatians are intrinsically stubborn, but their desire to please their owners is so great that they overcome that innate resistance.

Housebreaking: This breed housebreaks with no problems.

Aesthetic quality: Black spots on a large white dog

Personality: These active, strong dogs need a lot of exercise inside and out. Active children with a love for running and romping would be good for a Dalmatian. This dog is probably too big and active for very young children. When buying a Dalmatian for children be sure to go to a reputable breeder who can show you good steady bloodlines. The city is all right if the dog is exercised faithfully.

Creszentia Allen

Keeshond

Origin: For several hundred years the pet dog in Holland has been the keeshond. It was named for Kees de Gyselaer of Dordrecht, the political opponent of the prince of Orange in the latter part of the eighteenth century. Before that it had simply been "the people's dog." The prince of Orange won the contest, causing the keeshond to decrease in numbers until 1920, when the baroness van Hardenbroek became his patroness. Keeshonds now enjoy international acceptance.

Height at shoulder: Males — 18 inches
                          Females — 17 inches

Weight: Males — 40 pounds
                          Females — 35 pounds

Grooming: The harsh outer coat and the heavy undercoat shed all year long. In late spring and early fall the shedding is heavier to prepare for the new season. Frequent brushing helps. Frequent baths don't.

Cost: Moderate

Capabilities: These are principally companion dogs, though they can perform as excellent watchdogs.

Training tip: Keeshonds are responsive and easily trained.

Housebreaking: No problem

Aesthetic quality: Foxlike face with heavy coat of northern dogs

Personality: These easy-to-live-with dogs can adapt to all life-styles. They get along well with children of all ages and they can handle city life well for an active dog. A reasonable amount of exercise is good for them.

Poodle (Miniature and Standard)

Origin: The name *poodle* comes from the German name *Pudel* or from *pudeln* (to splash in water) and the poodle itself evidently comes from Germany, though its history goes so far back that there are no conclusive records. The French poodle is a misnomer, although the French do indeed love the dog. They call it the *caniche* (duck dog). The breed began as a standard poodle, a water retriever of remarkable skill and intelligence. They are also famous as dancers and tricksters. The poodle is always clipped, whether in a natural, even, sporting clip or one of the fancy show clips, because his fur grows like human hair; it does not stop. Unclipped, the poodle's coat is very difficult to manage. Poodles come in three varieties — toy, miniature and standard. Only the miniature and standard varieties are recommended for children.

Miniature Poodle

Height at shoulder: Males and females — over 10 inches to 15 inches

Weight: Males — 15 to 20 pounds
Females — 12 to 18 pounds

Standard Poodle

Height at shoulder: Males and females — over 15 inches

Weight: Males — 45 to 60 pounds
Females — 40 to 50 pounds

Poodle (miniature)   *Poodle (standard)*

Grooming: There is almost no shedding, but the poodle needs regular brushing and regular trips to a professional groomer for clipping.

Cost: Moderate

Capabilities: Some standard poodles can be trained for guard work. All poodles are good watchdogs. Most of them love to swim. Standards can be trained to hunt fowl, and miniatures can be trained to do all kinds of tricks.

Training tip: Poodles are extremely bright and responsive. They can learn just about anything they are taught.

Housebreaking: No problem

Aesthetic quality: Sculpted, cosmopolitan sophisticate, or rugged sporting dog depending on coat clip and life-style

Personality: Poodles win all popularity contests because they are extremely intelligent, cooperative and sensitive to their owner's needs. Only a poorly bred poodle shows any negative qualities. Miniatures need as much living space as standards because they are more active. Both varieties need daily outdoor exercise. Standards are large, active dogs that could overwhelm a toddler. Now and then a miniature is too high-strung for a very small child. Both sizes are wonderful with older children.

HERDING DOGS

Creszentia Allen

Bearded Collie

Origin: These herding dogs from southern Scotland were painted by Gainsborough in 1771 in a portrait of the duke of Buccleuch. Their ancestry seems to hearken back to the Magyar Komondor of Central Europe. The bearded collie offers Americans an opportunity to own a very new old breed. The beardie was not bred in America until the 1960s.

Height at shoulder: Males — 21 to 22 inches
Females — 20 to 21 inches

Weight: Males — 45 to 55 pounds
Females — 40 to 50 pounds

Grooming: Considering this breed's double coat (hard outer coat and downy undercoat), there is not as much shedding as one might think. But regular, thorough brushing is required.

Cost: Expensive

Capabilities: Beardies will herd sheep, cattle and children. They are good watchdogs but not guard dogs.

Training tip: These are responsive, easily trained dogs.

Housebreaking: There are no particular problems.

Aesthetic quality: Fluffy, medium-sized sheepdog

Personality: Beardies are splendid with all children but they do tend to think they are in charge. A medium to large apartment makes city life a reasonable choice since exercise is important to this dog both indoors and outdoors.

Bouvier des Flandres

Origin: The Bouvier served as a cattle drover for the farmers and butchers of northern France in the late nineteenth century. Many were lost when northern France was captured in World War I, but some survived working in the French military.

Height at shoulder: Males — 24½ to 27½ inches
Females — 23½ to 26½ inches

Weight: Males — 85 to 100 pounds
Females — 75 to 90 pounds

Grooming: Like all these herding dogs, the Bouvier has a longer, harder outer coat over a shorter, downy undercoat. Shedding continues all year round but is heaviest in the late spring and early fall when the coat adjusts to the new season. The Bouvier will need regular, thorough brushing plus visits to a professional groomer for trimming.

Cost: Expensive to acquire and to feed

Capabilities: Bouviers are wonderful, effective guard dogs and watchdogs as well as drovers.

Creszentia Allen

Bouvier des Flandres

Training tip: Luckily this breed trains well, because they are large, powerful dogs that must not go untrained. They are very bright and willing to please, so all Bouviers should be well behaved.

Housebreaking: No problem.

Aesthetic quality: Large, woolly, dominant animal

Personality: This large, exuberant dog loves and needs to run. He is probably best for older children because he is so energetic; however, he settles down once he is inside. Apartment living is possible if the apartment is large enough and the outdoor exercise is daily. Bouviers are happiest when they are with their own families, especially the children.

Creszentia Allen

Collie
(rough)

Collie (Smooth and Rough)

Origin: *Collie* comes from the English word *colly,* meaning black. The original collies before the nineteenth century were either black or black and white. The famous sable and white coloring was developed around 1870, along with the tricolor and the blue merle (blue-gray and black marbled). Both the well-known rough-coated collie and the less famous smooth-coated come in sable and white, tricolor, blue merle or white (which also has some sable, tricolor or blue-merle markings). Because of Lassie everyone knows that collies are sheep herders from the Scottish Highlands.

Height at shoulder: Males — 24 to 26 inches
Females — 22 to 24 inches

Weight: Males — 60 to 75 pounds
Females — 40 to 65 pounds

Grooming: Both the smooth- and the rough-coated collies have double coats. The outer coat on the rough variety is long and stands out from the body to give that typical "Lassie" look. The outer coat on the smooth variety is short and lies flat to the body. Both varieties have a short, dense undercoat. Both varieties shed, especially in the late spring and early fall when the coat adjusts to the new season. Regular brushing is essential, but collies do not need much clipping or trimming so a professional groomer is not necessary unless the rough coat has been neglected for a period of time.

Cost: Expensive

Capabilities: Herding, protective instincts make the collie an excellent watchdog. In addition, many collies can be trained to guard.

Training tip: All collies should be very bright and responsive and easily trained. Begin early to avoid a stubbornness that can develop in an untrained dog. Avoid punishing a collie: they are sensitive and respond poorly to punishment. Hitting them can make them aggressive.

Housebreaking: There should be no problems.

Aesthetic quality: Graceful, warm, dignified beauty

Personality: These are affectionate, intelligent, loyal dogs who take their family responsibilities seriously. Young children and toddlers must seem like spring lambs to them, needing a lot of care. If given enough outdoor exercise they are not too active inside and adjust to apartment living well. Be sure to get a well-bred puppy for children.

German Shepherd Dog

Origin: At the end of the nineteenth century a number of different German herding dogs were bred together for their intelligence and herding ability. Conformation was considered only as it affected the dog's performance in work. The result was the German shepherd dog. It lives to serve its human master. The German shepherd can be taught any number of tasks and is famous for service to blind persons, the police and the military. Nearly forgotten is its talent as a herder.

Height at shoulder: Males — 24 to 26 inches
Females — 22 to 24 inches

Weight: Males — 75 to 85 pounds
Females — 60 to 70 pounds

Grooming: The shepherd has the herding dog's hard outer coat and downy undercoat that sheds all year round, but particularly in the late spring and early fall. They need a lot of brushing but no professional care.

Cost: Expensive

Creszentia Allen

German shepherd dog

Capabilities: This breed's abilities are its reason for being. They are superior guard dogs and watchdogs and wonderful, devoted companions. They even have good noses and are often trained to detect hidden bombs or narcotics.

Training tip: The German shepherd dog is eminently trainable. The dog is so intelligent that punishment is offensive. These are very bright, sensitive dogs. Abuse is counterproductive. Simply correct unwanted behavior with a dominant demeanor and consistently praise achievement.

Housebreaking: No special problems

Aesthetic quality: The classic image of the faithful and noble friend

Personality: Shepherds need the respect and love of their families above all else. The children are their self-determined responsibility. All ages and types of children will be well cared for. Exercise is important. Shepherds are powerful, active dogs and will be active indoors even with a daily outdoor exercise period, so a small apartment is not appropriate, but they will adjust to any environment if necessary. The reports of aggressive behavior from German shepherd dogs could refer only to a poorly bred or mistreated animal, so select a well-bred puppy from a responsible breeder.

Creszentia Allen

Shetland Sheepdog

Origin: The Sheltie descends from the same Scottish sheep herders as the modern collie. But the Sheltie is a much smaller version. The people of the Shetland islands, off the northern coast of Scotland, allowed the Sheltie to develop quietly and go unnoticed by the rest of the world until the beginning of the twentieth century.

Height at shoulder: Males and females — 13 to 16 inches

Weight: Males and females — 15 to 20 pounds

Grooming: The long outer coat and downy undercoat shed all year long, especially in the late spring and early fall when the coat adjusts to the change in temperature. Regular brushing is essential.

Cost: Moderate

Capabilities: Warning strangers and sounding the alarm to strange noises are well within the Sheltie's talents, but guarding is not.

Training tip: This is a sensitive breed and as such does very poorly when punished or treated harshly. They become shy if mistreated. Train them easily and gently to maintain their sweet temperaments.

Housebreaking: There should be no problems.

Aesthetic quality: Miniature version of Lassie

Personality: Shelties need older, more thoughtful children who will not roughhouse with them. Even though they are relatively small, they like outdoor exercise and remain moderately active indoors. This is a good choice for apartment dwellers if the dog is introduced to the environment early. An older dog seeing buses and hearing taxis for the first time may be frightened.

Pembroke Welsh Corgi

Origin: Henry I brought Flemish weavers to England in 1107. They made their home in southwestern Wales. With them came their dogs, who descended from northern Spitz-types. They are known today as Pembroke Welsh Corgis. The *Cardigan* Welsh corgi is descended from the dachshund, but because the two corgis were interbred in the nineteenth century they are very similar in appearance now. Pembrokes are the corgis with pointed ears and almost no tail. The Cardigans have more rounded ears and long tails. For hundreds of years the corgis served their masters by nipping the heels of neighbors' cattle to keep them off their master's share of grazing land.

Height at shoulder: Males and females — 10 to 12 inches

Weight: Males — 27 to 30 pounds
                   Females — 25 to 28 pounds

Grooming: The medium-length outer coat and downy undercoat shed all year long, especially in the late spring and early fall. Regular brushing is helpful.

Creszentia Allen

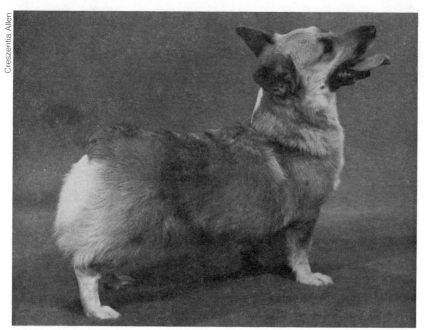

Pembroke Welsh corgi

Cost: Moderate

Capabilities: Corgis are natural guard dogs and watchdogs.

Training tip: They are very bright and learn easily.

Housebreaking: There should be no problems.

Aesthetic quality: Foxlike head on long, low, tailless body

Personality: The Pembroke is a bit more outgoing than the Cardigan and probably relates to children more easily, although they both like children. Older children usually get along with this breed better because their dominance is more acceptable to these decision-making cattle dogs. These dogs are very active indoors but because of their short legs do not require too much outdoor exercise. Apartments, houses or acres of countryside are all fine.

MISCELLANEOUS CLASS

Creszentia Allen

Cavalier King Charles Spaniel

Origin: European palaces and portraits of the sixteenth, seventeenth and eighteenth centuries were filled with toy spaniels. Many of them in those years looked just like the Cavalier of today. In the nineteenth century, the toy spaniel was bred for a more domed head and a pushed-up nose. This is the English toy spaniel. Interest returned to the original dog when an American, Roswell Eldridge, offered a prize at Crofts Show in England in 1926, 1927 and 1928 for the dog most like the old "nosey" type. The Cavalier King Charles spaniel was developed from those dogs and some larger spaniels. The Cavalier has the ability to scent and flush game in the field if trained or to serve as the perfect house pet, a rare combination in a small dog. The Cavalier comes in the same colors as the English toy. The breeders of the Cavalier in this country are very conservative about the expansion of the breed. It does not yet compete in a regular class in the American Kennel Club but rather remains in the nebulous Miscellaneous Class.

Height at shoulder: Males and females — 12 to 13 inches

Weight: Males and females — 12 to 18 pounds

Grooming: There is a little shedding. Regular brushing keeps the fur from matting.

Cost: Very expensive

Capabilities: Companionship or flushing fowl for the hunter.

Training tip: They are very responsive and eager to please.

Housebreaking: Frequent walks, consistent schedules and patience will help. The Cavalier sometimes has difficulty with housebreaking.

Aesthetic quality: Elegant, classic, cheerful

Personality: Cavaliers are loving and playful with all children. They have the spaniel talent of being able to relate to every member of a large family as though each person were the favorite. The Cavalier is not as delicate as the English toy spaniel but young children and toddlers should be supervised. This breed is a delight to live with and extremely easy to care for. They are reasonably active indoors but do not need extensive outdoor exercise, which makes them wonderful city dogs.

IDEAL MUTT

The earliest wolves to leave the prehistoric forests and join human campfires were the first mutts. It is with some justification that humans conjure romantic visions of mutts. Part wolf, part coyote, part fox, the first mutts were the forerunners of today's purebreds. More people live with mutts than any other dog.

The principal difference between purebreds and mutts is the predictability of look, type and, to a lesser degree, behavior of the purebred. Mutts should not be confused with mixed-breeds. A part-poodle, part-spaniel is fairly obvious. The so-called cock-a-poo is thought of by many pet owners as an actual breed. If the dog's parents are known but of different breeds, you can at least guess what the puppies will be like. Not so with a mutt. Mutt puppies are mystery dogs. This type of dog is an adventure in genetics.

Mutts, or mongrels, generally fall into one of several categories of physical appearance. The most basic mutt type is a small to medium *coyote-fox*-looking dog. The fur is most often red to brown with a white blaze on the chest. Next is the *police dog* look. These are medium to

Creszentia Allen

Ideal mutt

large dogs most often seen with a gray to black coat. They resemble German shepherd dogs. A fairly common mutt type is the medium-sized *spitz* look. They are most often white or white and black with a furry mane and curly tail. They derive from the *northern* or *sled-dog* types. There is a *spaniel*-looking mutt and a *setter*-looking mutt. Among the most popular are those that are obviously from terrier breeds. The breed most common in films, TV and commercials is a me-dium to large *shaggy terrier* type that resembles an old English sheep-dog, otter hound or bearded collie. Then there are the small to medium *wire-haired terrier* types. These are very popular. One often finds a small to medium, *smooth-coated terrier-hound*-looking dog with white fur and black patches. Nipper, the immortal RCA dog, is the prototype. A toy-size mutt is a rarity, but they are around. The most commonly admired mutt is the medium-sized dog that looks like a *yellow Labra-dor retriever.* It always has a wise, engaging look in its eyes.

Generally speaking, if the mongrel puppy is large for his age and has big paws he will grow into a large animal that could be too much dog for small children. Another clue to look for is how the puppy behaves in his litter or in his cage. Just as when choosing a purebred puppy, pick the one who comes to the front and wants you to take him home. He will probably enjoy the children more and be a little easier to train. A dog's temperament is far more important than its look. You would be sur-prised how quickly one comes to love a sweet-natured, intelligent dog that may at first seem something of an eyesore. It is a universal truth that a dog's beauty, like a child's, is from a source deep within and hid-den from the uncaring.

Three
Understanding
Your Dog

To the family trying to cope with a dog that eats furniture, dumps on the bed, barks at the landlord, and lifts its leg on shopping carts loaded with bags of food I offer my sympathy. More than that, I offer this chapter. Believe it or not, a great deal can be accomplished with a dog when you understand why he does what he does. Knowing the basics of dog behavior helps you decide how to solve the dog's living problems. You see, you only have three ways to proceed to make a dog more livable. One, you can have the dog obedience trained (either by a trainer or a member of the family). Two, you can manipulate the dog's living conditions to accommodate his particular difficulties as well as your sensibilities. Three, you can try some type of behavior modification as practiced by dog psychologists. Actually, all dog training can be regarded as a form of behavior modification.

After living with a dog for several months many will proclaim that he is neurotic. When they leave the house he pees on the carpet and leaves a mess someplace. This is always interpreted as spite work for having been left alone. But is a dog neurotic or spiteful if, when confronted with a set of circumstances that parallels a similar situation in the wild, he obeys every impulse that is true to his nature? It is not reasonable to expect a dog to behave differently just because the demands of domesticity clash with natural canine behavior.

Is your dog unable to develop and sustain a meaningful relationship? Does she scramble for cheap thrills in order to hide from reality? These

93

are human problems, as are other aspects of neurotic behavior. Dog owners who announce that their pets are neurotic seem to get an undeserved pleasure in the telling. Pet owners need to understand the difference between "normal" and "problem" behavior and forget the word "neurotic" when it comes to animals.

If your dog were to chain-smoke and pace all night, it would probably be neurotic. But if it did that, it would not be a dog. On the other hand, if it quakes with fear during a thunderstorm, it definitely has a dog problem. It is possible to take a specific fear, a phobia if you will, and generalize it to a point where the dog is irrationally frightened of all manner of things that are not really threatening, such as unknown people and moving cars.

The most common forms of canine problem behavior are housebreaking failures, aggressiveness (threatening, biting, attacking), failure to obey humans, nervousness (barking, digging, chewing, jumping, or running away), fear responses (cringing, hiding, shaking, nipping, wetting, chewing, barking), phobias (fear of confinement, isolation, thunder, strangers, outdoors, mechanical noises, etc.). I'm sure you can add more to this list.

In many cases, something in the living environment is disturbing the animal. This could range from the ringing of the telephone to something a child is doing. There are other aspects of childhood that could disturb or frighten a dog. As a child gets older it grows bigger and for some dogs it threatens their position of dominance in the family or pack structure. This is where a knowledge of basic dog behavior will help.

Obviously, abusive or inhumane treatment will alter a dog's behavior. A death in the family, a divorce, a child going off to school for the first time, and boarding the dog are events that can almost guarantee a response in the dog's nervous system. Boredom and loneliness, however, are the two greatest factors in creating problem behavior in dogs. Aggressive dogs may be expressing a medical problem or the result of early abuse. The same can be true of a shy or nervous dog. Moreover, a dog may inherit these qualities from its progenitors or follow its breed characteristics to the extreme due to poor breeding. The problem is often solved by firmly establishing a subordinate attitude in the dog and a dominant attitude in the human. Dog trainers are extremely helpful in effecting this change. It has been my experience that few behavior problems are unsolvable. I recommend a professional dog trainer or a do-it-yourself dog training book. If the problem persists, then see one of the new breed of animal psychologists and pass the Kleenex. Actually, the nature of many problems — and their solutions — becomes clear when you understand basic dog behavior.

BASIC DOG BEHAVIOR

Dogs will behave in certain predictable ways providing they have been influenced by outside factors such as the behavior of the dog's mother, littermates or human beings. What puppies and human babies have in common is the influence of early experiences and their profound effect on later behavior. *Dog behavior is determined by genetics and shaped by environmental influences.* This is all facilitated through the sensory mechanisms (eyes, ears, nose, etc.) acting upon the nervous system. There are known factors in basic dog behavior that are present at birth in all dogs. In other words, one could say that there is such a thing as *classic dog behavior* by which to measure the behavior of all dogs.

It must be understood that the dog, with all its variety of breeds, is a descendant of the wolf. From the Chihuahua to the Saint Bernard, all dogs are related to each other and share the wolf as their common ancestor and present-day cousin. Even wolves vary in size, color and characteristics. The great physical and behavioral differences among dog breeds are the result of twelve thousand years of domestication plus the genetic tinkering of those involved in breeding them. Still, it is a safe statement, if not altogether proven, that dog behavior is a *modified* form of wolf behavior. A great deal is known about wolf behavior and has been successfully applied to the study of dogs.

The most important aspects of classic dog (or wolf) behavior are: 1. They live in groups known as *packs*. 2. They form social attachments. 3. They require a leader. 4. They claim territory. 5. They survive by hunting prey animals for food. 6. They mate and produce offspring.

The Pack

Dogs were born to live in social units referred to as packs. The pack works as a team in hunting for food, defending its territory, and accomplishing the various tasks connected with survival. Pack behavior establishes the need to be with other creatures. When they live as pets, this need is transferred to humans, provided that the dog was "socialized" with people at the seventh or eighth week of life. This is

Komondor puppies

known as the *critical period*. The human family is then viewed as a substitute pack by the dog, even if there is only one person in the family. This explains why dogs are constant and loyal companions.

There can be no doubt that the purpose of the dog or wolf pack is to enable this relatively small animal to hunt for large game. As a pack they have the ability to track and attack moose, deer, wild sheep, reindeer, etc. One dog or wolf alone could never tackle animals of this size. Smaller animals are brought down by one wolf.

As wolves become older, at about two years of age, they become less and less tolerant of newcomers joining the pack. This often leads to dangerous fights, sometimes to the death. Although this behavior does not exist as such among dogs, there are traces of it in some of the more territorial breeds, especially among very aggressive males. Among dogs many of the working and herding breeds are more territorial and tend to protect their families, especially the children. Visitors, even young ones, must be introduced to this type dog lest they be met with suspicion and/or hostile behavior.

There are few mammals that live in so highly established a group as do wolves and wild dogs. The dog, it would seem, is a domesticated version of these wild animals and fits neatly into the fabric of human society. Not even the domestic cat blends so well into the life-style and behavior of human social patterns. Pet cats live somewhat apart from humans while dogs participate in every imaginable activity if allowed. Humans and dogs have much in common.

Social Attachments

Within a pack society social attachments develop as a matter of course. It is the dogs' need to be with other creatures while enjoying all the contact involved that makes them so lovable and suitable as home companions. All members of the pack remain secure so long as challenges are not made to the established order of rank, privilege, and performance. Very meaningful relationships can develop because of a dog's need for a pack structure and a child's desire for emotional contact that is unchallenging and unqualified. Both child and dog share a natural curiosity and dependency, each giving something, each getting something.

The pack is a social unit that really stems from pairing, where one female and one male stay together for the purpose of sharing the tasks connected with survival and procreation. This behavior still exists in the dog's other cousins, the fox and the coyote. It is a kind of economic and social system, the pack, much like those that exist in human societies, holding groups of related families together with a loose but efficient system. A "pair bond" develops between males and females, making it possible for litters of cubs or pups to be produced and reared. New packs are formed when males and females pair off to mate, whelp young, and establish their own lives independent of their parents. We could almost be discussing postadolescent humans. The domestic dog has as great a need for social attachments as its wild cousin. If humans become involved with puppies at the *critical period,* the social attachments become directed toward humans as well as toward dogs. That is the ideal situation for a pet dog.

Need for a Leader

The dog or wolf pack requires a minimum of conflict within its ranks in order to function well. This stability is achieved with the inherited factor of dominant or subordinant tendencies programmed into every wolf or dog. A "leader of the pack" always emerges, along with other dominant and subordinate pack members who manage to sort themselves out in some order of rank. It helps all of the dogs or wolves living in the wild to survive. Dogs continue to function on this level even if they do not live with a pack. The need for leadership is primary if the group is to survive.

If you carefully observe the behavior of the most timid or aggressive house dog you will see this pattern in action. Every dog requires that someone assume a leadership position. Your family pet will accept the position of command if no one else will. Dogs are insecure without a leader and have been known to take charge of complex households. Conversely, they accept leadership from those with dominant personalities or who behave with some degree of authority. Once you assume the position of leader, your dog will accept it for the rest of his life. Many children have difficulty being dominant over the family dog. There are many variable factors at work. The child's personality, age, and experiences affect this. The dog's size, temperament, breed and early influences play an important role as well. The answer lies in teaching the child how to train the dog. See Chapter 6, "Teaching Parents to Teach Their Kids to Train Their Dog."

In the wild, dominant dogs or wolves have first access to food, shelter and mates. The original pair that formed a new pack are its leaders (for a while) and they are referred to by researchers as *alpha males* or *alpha females*. The position of rank begins to form early in puppyhood and can be witnessed during the later stages of breast-feeding and episodes of puppy play-fighting. If the youngsters remain with the litter beyond sixteen weeks one can observe totally dominant and totally subordinate dogs. From twelve to sixteen weeks of life in the pack or litter one begins to witness hostile encounters involving aggressive displays and combats. Fights ensue but end quickly, with the establishment of rank being the result.

In the center of every pack is the alpha male, behaving with a brooding dominance that is feared and respected by all. All members of the pack look to him for the first reaction to anything out of the ordinary, such as the invasion of their territory by an intruder. The alpha male usually leads all chases and accepts nothing less than total submission on questions involving hunting, feeding and mating. In a sense, the alpha male is an absolute autocrat. When a wolf asserts its dominance over another he stands straight, with his ears erect and tail in a horizontal position. The teeth are bared with a frightening upward wrinkling of the lips, and a deep growl is given. The lesser wolf assumes a lower posture and flattens his ears as his tail lowers between his legs. "Top dog" is established when the dominant animal stands over the submissive one with his head over the other's neck and abdomen. This ritualized behavior helps to avoid many fights and disruptions of pack routine.

In the home, domestic dogs will forever attempt to display dominant behavior unless taught otherwise. With a puppy of normal temperament there will be at least one "showdown" situation where the child will either assert dominance and establish the dog's subordinate rank or be ruled or even bullied by the family pet. The opportunity most often presents itself during the first or second session of obedience training when the dog insists on walking in one direction while the child insists on another. With firm, intelligent use of the leash, without abuse, the child wins out and sends a loud and clear message to the dog. Of course, a dominant manner on the part of the child reinforces the newly established order in the mind of the young dog.

Territory

Dogs, like other meat eaters, instinctively require an area for hunting and within that area a place for sleeping. These activity zones are referred to as *territory*. The hunting area is the dog or wolf pack's *range*, which is shared with other animals. The sleeping area is the *den*, which is also used as a nest for whelping newborns and as a lair for the youngsters' safety. A den may be a cave, a tunnel or even a hollow log.

Although dogs and wolves regard their hunting range as territory, they will seldom fight to defend it. However, the den or resting place is guarded with vigor. In our homes the dog may consider the entire house or apartment as the den or simply his small section of it. His range may be a backyard or an entire neighborhood. It depends upon the individual dog. Certainly a doghouse or collapsible wire crate (a form of traveling cage) or anything resembling it is considered a den. The place your dog rests is an element in his life that provides comfort and security. It is very important to him. Dogs feel best when enjoying the peace and comfort of the den.

There are three important aspects of the domestic dog's behavior that stem from canine territorial instincts. First, many pet dogs respond aggressively when a stranger approaches their territory. This could mean your entire grounds or your house or simply where the dog's food bowl is placed. It happens if the dog is somewhat dominant. Obedience training plus a dominant demeanor help to keep aggressive behavior to a minimum. Second, all dogs *mark* or *scent-post* their territory for the purpose of claiming it as their own. Marking is accomplished with urine and feces. It is sometimes marked by scratching onto the ground with the front paws. Dogs will try to do this on cement surfaces as well. Although no one is absolutely certain if a dog is claiming territory with its urine or leaving a message for other dogs, this behavior ties in with the subject. Life is more livable when the human family directs the dog to scent-post outside the home at specific locations. Here, housebreaking is served by intelligent manipulation of this instinct. (See Chapter 5: "Housebreaking and Other Delights.") Third, a *den* or inner core is required. Without one a pet dog can become quite stressed. Emotional stress can easily be prevented by providing your dog with a man-made den. This can be a collapsible wire crate manufactured with a door in front, a solid floor and a wire roof. It can be made quite comfortable with a mat or blanket on the bottom and a blanket spread over the top affording tentlike privacy. This area should be exclusively the dog's, where he can rest or retreat without being disturbed. It is an act of intelligence and kindness to make the dog's den area, wherever or whatever it may be, off limits to the children. As a child needs the refuge of his own room, so does a dog.

Hunting

Although domestic dogs do not hunt to survive, some of the hunting behaviors remain as instinctive reactions to certain stimuli. Most hunting is a pack activity, particularly when the prey is a large animal. It requires the utmost of cooperation and team effort to succeed. Wolves and wild dogs hunt in the open and never stalk or ambush as do cats. The prey, if it is large, is almost always a herd animal and one that is too weak to stay with its herd. The method of hunting is to give chase through long-distance running, with one wolf attacking the hind quarters as the others attack from the front.

All of the combined hunting skills of wolves and wild dogs can be seen in individual domestic dog breeds, but in a diluted and separate form. Here one comes to understand that each breed has been refined as a specialist rather than an all-around general practitioner. Through selective breeding one or more of the various hunting skills have become emphasized, with a deemphasis on all the other skills. For example, sheep and cattle dogs have developed their herding and droving skills as an outgrowth of hunting techniques that involve moving a prey animal toward waiting members of the pack. Hunting dogs have developed either their sense of smell or sight to assist the human hunter. Retrievers have been bred to carry home downed birds without biting hard, thus preserving them as food for the human. Working breeds guard, protect, haul, or attack on command. These skills all contribute to the survival of a wolf or wild dog pack.

The pet owner is best served by reading about the skills of their breed and how they are utilized. Then that individual dog can be compared to his wild cousin and seen in a more understandable context. It becomes abundantly clear that no adult or child should behave in a manner that elicits a dog's aggressive or hunting instincts. A child darting quickly in front of a family dog is enough to set in motion deeply buried and seldom seen reactions such as running, jumping, growling, or even attacking. The same is true of tug-of-war games with a towel or dog toy. Do nothing that encourages a dog's dormant instincts for aggressiveness.

Mating and Producing Offspring

Dogs are at least twice as fertile as wolves. They are capable of mating twice a year (wolves mate once a year) and producing much larger litters of pups. It is thought that this has evolved through domesticity. Large wolf packs do not function well and have difficulty maintaining a food supply for all, considering their need to live off the land. Because a high fertility rate among wolves would be undesirable, nature has provided automatic checks and balances. There is a limitation of food and increased competition for mates, leadership and dominance. The net result is a huge population of domestic dogs and a much lesser population of wolves. Of course, the encroachment by society upon the environment and the killing of wolves to protect herds and flocks of food animals has done more to decimate the wolf population than anything nature had planned. That notwithstanding, there would always have been more domestic dogs than wolves.

The sexual behavior of dogs, it is thought, is simply a modification of the sexual behavior of wolves. The alpha male of the pack has greater access to females in estrus (heat) than others, but not exclusive access. Other dominant males, while showing preferences for certain females, are still subject to being chosen by more dominant females and do not mate until the female has indicated her readiness.

There is little or no sexual behavior among dogs until the female enters estrus. The normal estrus period lasts twenty-one days. The first sign of estrus is a slight discharge of blood from the vagina. The female gives off an odor (imperceptible to humans) that alerts males in the vicinity. The entire period of receptivity by the female to the male dog is only six to twelve days. The pattern for canine copulation involves mutual investigation of the genital areas. The female moves her tail to one side while standing still. The male mounts from the rear while clasping the female with his front paws. Once the penis is inserted, the male thrusts his pelvis forward in rapid succession. The tissue within the penis becomes engorged with blood, causing it to swell. This creates a "tie" or lock that holds the two dogs together until ejaculation. While still locked together the male dismounts and turns in the opposite direction forcing the two dogs to stand, tail to tail. It may take several minutes before they are able to release from the "tie." It is a noisy encounter and frightening to the uninitiated. It is best for young children to avoid seeing this.

It takes nine weeks (sixty-three days) for a female dog to whelp a litter of puppies. This is an estimate because ovulation takes place approximately seventy-two hours before the end of receptivity. It takes three weeks for the fertilized egg to become implanted in the dog's uterus. When the puppies are born it is possible for them to be delivered up to twenty-four hours apart, although that is not common.

THE CRITICAL PERIODS OF PUPPY DEVELOPMENT

Pet dogs have much to tolerate, especially if they are going to live with children. There is one thing a dog needs if it is to survive three kids, a Frisbee and a bag of potato chips, and that is an even, easygoing temperament. This is not too difficult to find in a dog if it was "socialized" at the critical period of its puppyhood. A dog of good temperament is one that is adaptive to living with human beings without fear or hesitation. Unfortunately, some dogs have difficulty adjusting from life in the puppy litter to life in the human litter. These are the dogs that are more likely to be shy, timid, nervous, overly aggressive or downright dangerous. Apart from any inherited genetic behavior and breed characteristics, the problems may stem from a lack of "socializing" during puppyhood.

There is a specific period of time in a puppy's life when the slightest experience has the greatest impact on future behavior. These specific times are the "critical periods." They last for a short time and achieve the greatest effect on the dog the puppy will become. Few serious breeders in this country are unaware of the techniques of "socializing" and its importance during the critical periods of puppyhood. I cannot urge you strongly enough to be certain that your next puppy be one that was "socialized" at the proper time. It can make the difference between a great dog and a so-so dog.

From Birth to the Thirteenth Day (Neonatal Period)

During this period the newborn puppy is completely dependent on its mother for everything. Its eyes and ears are closed and its ability to move about is restricted to a slow, forward motion. The puppy's nervous system is at a primitive stage of development and it cannot even maintain its own body temperature. It is the mother dog that provides milk, warmth and even the process of digestion through stimulation of the outer abdominal area with her tongue. There is no discernible learning during this period. Life for a neonatal pup consists of crawling about in search of warmth and nutrition.

The Thirteenth to the Twentieth Day (Transitional Period)

A rapid transformation begins at this time in the puppy's life. His eyes open and he begins to walk instead of crawl. Exploration of the world beyond the mother's teat is the most notable change. At the end of this period the puppy is capable of leaving the nest for the purpose of independent urination and defecation. With the further development of the motor and sensory capacities, the little dog begins to interact with its environment. The tail begins to wag and the pup tries to satisfy its own needs. At the end of this period the ears open, allowing for responses to loud noises. At this stage it can also experience pain. On the twentieth day the teeth begin to erupt from the gums. The sleeping puppy is easily distinguished from the puppy that is awake. Almost all sensory and motor abilities are in place and functioning. The dog is about to enter a period of learning about creatures other than itself.

The Third Week to the Seventh Week
(Beginning of Socialization)

It is difficult to pinpoint the exact time when one phase ends and the next begins, but the times stated are very close. Because the pup's sensory and motor capacities are not yet fully developed, he is still somewhat clumsy and uncoordinated. During this period the most important development is the beginning of social behavior. Over the next four weeks the brain and nervous system develop to the point of adult maturity. At the same time the puppy begins to socialize with its mother and littermates. This canine socialization is extremely important. During this time the young dog learns to adjust to other dogs. Without the experience of this period the dog will always be distrustful of other dogs and constantly pick fights with them as an adult.

At this time the process of weaning away from breast milk to whole food has begun, along with more sophisticated urination and defecation behavior. The areas used for this purpose become well defined and farther from the nest. A sleeping puppy can refrain from eliminating for many hours. Also, puppies are learning to holler for help when they need it. If they are separated from the mother or other littermates, they will cause a racket. Play and play-fighting with littermates is apparent, along with intense investigatory behavior. The puppy will respond to the sight or sound of people or other animals with tail-wagging enthusiasm.

Up until this period the puppies engage in independent movement. But after the fourth week they begin to follow each other around and by five weeks move together as a group. It is the beginning of pack behavior as adults.

By the seventh week weaning is complete. The mother refuses the puppies access to her breasts and threatens them when they try to nurse.

It is at this time that humans intervene and "socialize" the puppies. When a puppy is handled for short periods of time by humans, from the fifth week of puppyhood on, that animal grows to be highly adaptive to living with humans. However, it is extremely important that these short spans of affectionate handling be limited to once a day and that the dog remain with its litter for the rest of the time. This assures the puppy's socialization to both humans and dogs.

The Eighth Week to the Twelfth Week
(Final Phase of Socialization)

The puppy is now capable of vocalizing with greater variety and maturity. Although pups tend to cry less, when they are in strange places they will bark, which indicates an assertive attitude. Coordina-

Photo courtesy of Dan Farrell

tion is much improved and with it one sees the ability to run developing. Most of the social development that began in the fourth week becomes much more pronounced in the eighth, such as pack movement and antagonistic tendencies. Combative play becomes more intense as a means of developing the ranking order of dominance and subordinance. This has a lasting effect, resulting in timid dogs, even-tempered dogs or overly aggressive dogs.

For this reason researchers have concluded that a dog experiencing human handling as a socializing technique should be removed from the litter and taken to its new home with a human family no later than the beginning of the eighth week. This, of course, is a matter of opinion. Some breeders disagree and feel the puppies should remain with the litter until the end of the twelfth week. By removing the puppies at this time the last vestiges of weaning are automatically ended but the effects of a developing dominance order are avoided. Assuming the puppy has been handled since the fourth week, it is now ready to make the transition to living as a pet and accepting some small amount of obedience training including the beginning of housebreaking.

At this stage of the dog's life he has the capacity to become an engaging, well-trained companion providing he is allowed to develop self-confidence as an individual dog with worth and value. This can be achieved by not allowing the young dog to be alone or isolated for long periods of time; by giving the pup a great deal of positive attention; and by short obedience training sessions that allow for the opportunity for much-needed praise. At the end of the twelfth week your dog enters his juvenile period, ready for complete obedience training and all the pleasures of being an adult dog.

Four

The Dog and

Your Family

I once asked a psychologist, "Who needs children, anyway? What is the point to it all? Do human beings really feel incomplete if they fail to become parents?" The older man smiled warmly and replied, "No, not necessarily. But a child gives us one more person to love and feel better for doing so." Now that I have three children I no longer ask such foolish questions, because the good doctor's answer is more valid than ever. And you know what? The same is true about dogs.

Once a dog is taken into your home it is an integral part of the family whether you planned for that or not. Looking for the essence of family life is like peeling away the layers of an onion. It is not until we get to the tiny piece in the center that we recognize that the peeled layers are the true essence of the onion. Whatever exists within and around your family are the parts that make up the whole of it. For better or for worse, the dog you have taken in, like the child you have borne, the spouse you have committed to or the parent you live with, is a part of your life. It adds or subtracts, strengthens or weakens your day-to-day existence. It cannot be ignored. Even though the dog was gotten for the kids, its impact on every member of the family is quite great. The friendship, love and responsibility of a dog are a shared experience.

WHOSE DOG IS IT?

It really doesn't matter for whom the dog was purchased. Dogs are independent creatures in that they will focus their attention on one or more persons as they desire, and there is no controlling that. There is a misconception that the dog will belong exclusively to the one who feeds him or pays the most attention. Certainly, the one offering the essential goods and services has an edge, but not at the exclusion of everyone else in the family. It has sometimes been the case that the person offering the least encouragement received the most attention. No one knows for sure why this happens. Some dogs are attracted to the strong, silent type. It could simply be that the dog likes one person's odor more than another's.

The point is that a new dog's presence sets in motion a rippling effect in the family structure. The focus will certainly change, at least for a while, and spotlight everything the dog does. If there is more than one child, the youngest may not garner all the concern and fuss that he or she is accustomed to receiving. The dog takes some of that away, at least temporarily. Some relationships will be altered, creating new alliances and dissolving old ones. Emotions can run high. It's as if a new baby were brought home from the hospital, causing joy, concern and thinly veiled anxiety.

Getting a dog for one child when there are others in the family is not recommended for many reasons. This sets up a potential situation for dissension leading to deeply felt resentments. Anyone who has ever lived with more than one child knows that peace in the family rests on very shaky treaties between siblings. Arguing over the use of the telephone or a favored toy is bad enough in its own shallow futility. But the overlap of emotions connected with a love object creates intense feelings that can shake boulders. No, I suggest that you acquire a *family* dog rather than a personal possession of one child over another. For this reason alone dogs make poor birthday gifts. If one insists on giving a puppy as a gift then do it at holiday time so that the dog can be a gift for all.

Often a new dog will attract a member of the family with an intense need for exclusive attention, love and companionship. But the dog must be considered as a member of the family, belonging to himself. Activities involving care of the dog can be considered exclusive time spent with him. It will help get feeding, grooming, training, and walking chores accomplished and satisfy a desire for exclusive attention from the dog. You'll get two for the price of one. Even if you have one child, it is still a good policy to refer to the new dog as a member of the family rather than a personal possession of the child. If your child has a psychological need of things that are exclusively his or hers for identity (and most do), let it be an object, a room, or a monogrammed item of clothing. But allow the dog to be *the family dog.* It's a matter of mental hygiene for humans and canines.

NAMING THE DOG

The first activity connected with a new dog is selecting a name for him. It should be a very pleasant task, although for some it leads to the first of many conflicts. I would make this a family decision rather than the choice of one child. The one who selects the name can very easily take possession of the dog in his or her mind and get off to a bad start. Although choosing a name for a dog seems to be such a simple, innocent task, it really is important. The objective is to avoid a major conflict.

Choosing a name right away promotes self-confidence in the dog as well as facilitating training procedures and all activities pertaining to him. Everyone has to refer to the animal by the same name lest the dog suffer from an identity crisis.

One should convene a family council and agree to a shared decision. You could make a game of it by having everyone in the family participate in the selection. Each person can think of a name category, such as TV cartoon characters, historical figures, Greek mythology, geography, or names of friends, relatives or celebrities. Once a category is chosen, subdivide it into other categories, such as dates, time, nostalgic or contemporary, etc. Allow everyone to choose one or more letters to create a name or spell someone's name backwards. The point is to allow each person to have chosen one element of the process. Then it can be truthfully stated that everyone named the dog. It sets the right tone.

Suggestions for Naming Your Dog

The dog's characteristics lead to good names

Curly	Cocoa	Sorrowful	Flicker
Whiskers	Spike	Slick	Blinky
Smoothie	Toes	Spud	Lightning
Flappy	Sparks	Jigger	Chief
Wings	Blackie	Flash	Pearl
Birdie	Red	Slats	Pickles
Silver	Coffee	Bubbles	Lovelady
Goldy	Cinnamon	Wag	Macaroon
Spot	Chum	Wheezy	Sailor
Patches	Splash	Big Boy	Gloves
Tangerine	Jazzy	Big Girl	Spats
Peaches	Chips		Lemondrop

Favored cities make unique names

Boston	Tulsa	Memphis	Levittown
Albuquerque	Tucson	Wichita	Daytona
Cleveland	Denver	Albany	Atlanta
El Paso	Altoona	Boise	Bismarck
La La	Cheyenne	Toronto	Nashua
Buffalo	Wayne	Calgary	Missoula

Miami	Nome	Houston	Brooklyn
Toledo	Honolulu	Pittsburgh	Paducah
Portland	San Juan	Providence	Sandusky
Washington	San Jose	Independence	Reno
Manhattan	Fayette	Salem	Baltimore

And who says you can't have two or even three names?

Johnny Carson	Lady Macbeth	Mr. T
Clark Kent	Olivia Newton-John	Twyla Tharp
Scooby Doo	Michael Jackson	Big Bird
He-Man	Kermit the Dog	T. J. Hooker
Wonder Dog	Ronald McDonald	Donkey Kong
Ralph Waldo Emerson	Gary Coleman	Pac-Man
Miss Piggy	Mickey Mouse	Superdog

There is educational value in naming a dog from the classics.

SHAKESPEARE

Henry IV	Richard II	Dogberry	Portia
Coriolanus	Titus	Puck	Cato
Julius	Titania	Petruchio	Montague
Romeo	Pericles	Kate	Capulet
Juliet	Macbeth	Hotspur	Horatio
Cymbeline	Othello	Gloucester	Polonius
King Lear	Mercutio	Brutus	Gertrude
Antony	Prospero	Cordelia	Yorick
Cleopatra	Ariel	Macduff	Banquo
Timon	Pistol	Iago	Benvolio
Hamlet	Falstaff	Laertes	Calpurnia
Troilus	Sir Toby	Ophelia	Cassius
Cressida	Beatrice	Roderigo	Caesar

GREEK MYTHOLOGY

Zeus	Echo	Pygmalion	Odysseus
Prometheus	Poseidon	Midas	Psyche
Athena	Heracles	Narcissus	Achilles
Hermes	Typhon	Medea	Andromeda
Pandora	Dionysus	Phaedra	Icarus
Helius	Jason	Hippolytus	Pluto

Hades	Cupid	Centaur	Proteus
Titan	Theseus	Uranus	Helen
Olympus	Aphrodite	Medusa	Telemachus
Apollo	Orpheus	Tyro	Troy
Artemis	Atlas	Eurydice	Agamemnon
Pan	Orion	Perseus	Nemesis

POETRY

Glory	Tara	Deever	Kangaroo
Tiger	Joy	Mandalay	Prufrock
Lamb	Nightingale	Fog	Sweeney
Sweet Afton	Barefoot	Trees	Just So
Skylark	Raven	Gulliver	Sonnet
Milton	Bells	Seven	Naughty Boy
Lochinvar	Rubaiyat	Quangle	Walrus
Kubla Khan	Captain	Cummerbund	Shadow
Xanadu	Jabberwock	Guppy	Frankie
Charms	Boy Blue	Peekaboo	and Johnny
			(for a brace)

Entire books exist about naming pets and show dogs. Hopefully these suggestions will help in the family decision on naming the dog. The lists are merely to stimulate the imagination and give you an inkling of the possibilities. One could look for a dog name in the days of the week, months of the year, types of food (radish, berry, pizza, hambone, soufflé, hot dog, spaghetti, etc), from crossword puzzles or any other source that the human imagination can land on. The point is to allow everyone to get involved in the process, and that certainly includes all the kids.

THE DOG AS BEST FRIEND

Although it is very rewarding for a child to feel competent enough to assume the responsibilities of dog care, they must not be thrust on anyone. If you get a dog for the kids, it should be fun. Making a chore out of it right away is a mistake, as is making it a success or failure situation. Allow the kids to enjoy the animal without assigning responsibilities. This permits the development of relationships between the kids and the dog. The pet should be introduced to the family and then be allowed to play with them (in a way that isn't overly tiring). This will allow initial feelings to emerge without added negative factors.

Far too many parents set up rules and regulations governing the dog's care and the children's responsibilities before the animal even enters the picture. These preconditions may or may not work out because of the dog and because of the kids. It takes a potentially light-hearted, mirthful occasion and casts a needless, serious shadow on the event. Giving the kids a dog can be a meaningful experience and still be fun at the same time. Allowing your kids to have a good time with their new dog is more important than any "educational" or "growth-development" factors. That all comes later. As a matter of fact, most kids begin to set their own rules and limitations on matters pertaining to the dog. Allow for the possibility of the children themselves sorting out which responsibilities they want. That's a much more meaningful development for both dog and children.

Their relationship with the dog will grow and deepen quickly as it occurs to each one what he or she wants to do for the family pet. Most children that I have seen in this situation want very much to be involved in everything that affects the dog. The wise parent will sit back and let it happen. As a child volunteers for a chore (hooray!) he or she must be praised, encouraged, and helped so that a feeling of successful accomplishment is experienced. This will create the proper motivation for continuing along these lines. Do not be disappointed if the child becomes bored or loses interest in any one aspect of the dog's care. When that happens it is time to suggest a different chore. The success of dogs and kids together lies in the development of their relationship. It is desirable for a child to be a dog's best friend and, to a lesser degree, the other way around. This can only happen if the initial contact is pleasurable.

THE DOG AS RIVAL

A dog, like the arrival of a new child, can inadvertently become the symbol of established friction. Most brothers and sisters compete with one another for parental attention and favor. The competition can be comical, serious or totally absurd in its forms and directions. Absolute equality and parity are demanded of harassed and hassled parents by the bickering siblings. The combination of one dog and several kids has the makings of a potential nightmare for a mother and father who have had it up to here.

It would be wise always to walk the dog out of the competitive storm at the first sign of clouds on the horizon. Only a psychotherapist could use the outcome of such conflicts as clues to the underlying meaning of this behavior. At this point it is best for the dog not to be the focus of your children's anger. It's not really good for the children or the dog. Without getting involved in their argument you can inform them that they are upsetting the dog (not to mention their bedraggled parents). Although the problems between siblings vary, this one has something to do with the ability to share. The children must be told that the dog is to be shared by the entire family and they mustn't tear the animal apart. Schedules, appointments and the ability to take turns with the dog are essential. You might even convince them to play with the animal together.

Sometimes, unwitting parents find themselves the rival of the dog for the children's attention or, more serious, the children competing with the dog for a parent's attention. These are situations that are easy to adjust but must be taken care of before serious emotional problems develop. It is inevitable that jealousy develops where family dynamics are concerned. But remember, dogs will accept whatever attention you decide you can give them. They start out neutral and can be brought back to neutral from any imbalance that grows. If the dog figures into any feelings of jealousy between the kids, it is time to sort it all out by having a family talk and clearing the air. Just keep pointing out that the dog belongs to himself and is to be enjoyed by everyone in the family.

THE DOG AS PROTECTOR

There was once a situation where a Labrador retriever kept diving into the family swimming pool and rescuing the young swimmers whether they wanted it or not. Some dogs are much more territorial than others and regard the people in their lives as part of their work. On the whole, it is a good kind of problem. Dogs that will protect home and family are worth their weight in gold. They are the kind of dog we all dream about . . . well, almost all. Even the small terriers and, believe it or not, some of the toy breeds offer a great deal of protection. Terriers and some of the toy breeds are highly sensitive to the comings and goings of strangers in their territory and will alert the family at the slightest irregu-

larity. Often this is a nuisance because of the barking and yapping it causes at any hour of the day or night. Don't expect a ten-pound dog to knock a burglar over while you call the police. But I have heard of situations where some of these mighty mites have opened arteries in the ankle, thus driving off would-be assailants. That's the good news.

The bad news is when a dog attacks strangers who are in your home on business or for some other legitimate purpose. And then there are the visits from relatives, friends and neighbors. There is nothing worse than a twelve-year-old kid getting attacked by your dog when coming to your house to see a friend. An overly protective or highly territorial dog will cut down on everyone's social life and could even provoke the Postal Service to discontinue delivering your mail.

If you have a dog of this type you must become aware of the awful possibilities. Dogs can make protection decisions that are irrational and deadly. This is especially true of breeds of the Working Group, which include collies, Bouvier des Flandres, boxers, German shepherd dogs, Great Danes, and some of the Hounds and Sporting Dogs, such as Weimaraners and Chesapeake Bay retrievers. Occasionally an overly protective dog comes from a breed not noted for this characteristic.

must pay careful attention to a dog and learn to recognize this trait for what it is.

There are several courses for the owners of such dogs to take. First and foremost is to have the dog obedience trained by a professional. I would not recommend a training class (more than one dog being trained at a time) or a course given at home by a member of the family. This is a job for a skilled obedience trainer giving hands-on, one-to-one training. At the end of the training the dog must obey members of the family instantly. The next step is to become diligent about using the dog's leash outdoors and whenever a stranger comes to the house (unless the dog is confined to another room). Never allow this kind of dog out of the house, free to roam. Last, do not allow anyone, especially children, to engage in play that encourages, teaches, or provokes aggressive behavior. This includes tug-of-war, biting games, chewing and mouthing games, excessive chasing, and cornering. Use your common sense.

THE CHILD AS PROTECTOR

A seldom-considered aspect of pet ownership is protecting the animal. It is all too obvious that small puppies and even young dogs need protection. They are just babies and totally dependent on us for everything from warmth to food to shelter. But, adult dogs need various forms of protection too, and they can be helped in part by children. To some degree, they can be saved from their own self-destructive behavior. For example, dogs that chew on their own paws cause skin problems and infections. Here a child can make the dog stop it with a command to do so (assuming the dog is obedience trained). Getting into things for the purpose of snacking can be detrimental to the dog. Rooting through the garbage is not only disgusting, it is also bad for digestive stability. Swallowing a splintery bone has the potential for internal puncture wounds. Some human foods are not tolerated by a dog's sensitive stomach, indeed they are barely tolerated by the human stomach. Because children pay more attention to dogs, they are far more capable of observing their behavior and stopping them from hurting themselves.

The worst thing a dog can do to himself is get embroiled in a fight with another dog. Although males are more likely to fight other males, do not discount the female penchant for this destructive activity. Dogs can become severely wounded or even lose their lives in such skir-

mishes. Moreover, a human trying to stop a dog fight can also be wounded seriously in the process. Fights can and should be avoided and children can help.

When children handle dogs they must be made aware of the possibilities for fighting when one dog meets another. It is simply a matter of education. Inform your child about dog fighting and the need to try to avoid it. Tell him or her that strange dogs meeting for the first time are quite likely to challenge each other to determine who is "top dog" and whose territory they are in. The dogs must not be allowed to get close to each other if there seems to be the slightest bit of aggressive behavior, such as hard staring, pricked ears, cautious and deliberate body language, low-throated growls, and bared teeth through snarling lips. Two dogs meeting on the street, at the end of their leashes, may start out sweetly. In an instant things can change and they may go for each other's throats. Children can protect their dogs from these incidents by watching for the first signs of aggressive behavior toward other dogs and pulling the dog away while they keep on walking. If two dogs begin to fight, children should only pull them apart with the leash. No one should step between the dogs or place their hands *anywhere* on either dog's body. Holler at them, give corrections and commands, even douse them with water. Parents must advise children to avoid getting bitten by avoiding physical contact with fighting dogs. It's a good idea for a child to leave his dog at home when playing at a friend's house, especially if the friend also has a dog. Separating two fighting dogs is not an easy or safe task for a child.

Prevention can save the dog from himself, and even a child can do it. Part of a child's love of animals is a desire to protect them. That should be encouraged to blossom.

YOUR CHILD'S ATTITUDE ABOUT DOGS

What is it about animals that is so attractive to children? Some grown-ups believe that animals are disguised human beings to young children, thus making it "safe" to express their true feelings:

"The bear [Daddy?] is ferocious and will eat me up unless I get away."

"The bunny [Mommy?] is soft and feels nice. It will love me and be my friend."

"Puppies [young brother?] are dickens and should be punished."

"Kittycats [himself?] are naughty but too smart to get caught."

"My dog [big brother?] likes me and will bite you if you try to be mean to me."

Occasionally a child will trade places with a pet and then be free to say what's really on her mind:

"I am going to jump all over you and lick your face and then you'll have to look at me."

"I'll bite your fingers off and that'll teach you not to spank me."

Sometimes a pet dog is regarded as a strong protector controlled by the child, ready to do his or her bidding as the master. This may allow the child to feel more secure with those who are frightening or more dominant, as with an older brother or sister.

Obviously, there is a great deal of fantasy connected to a child's attitude toward a pet dog. First, dogs make incredibly dynamic *huggies* or love objects. A sweet-natured dog that will curl up with you is infinitely more effective and attractive than a stuffed toy or old baby blanket. A dog can make a terrific substitute parent, one that can be cut down to size or easily controlled when desired. Some dogs are even thought of as superheroes who can save the child from danger or feelings of loneliness and despair.

Try to tell a small child that his dog doesn't have the same feelings he has and you'll be regarded as a lunatic. As a matter of fact, most children believe that their dogs know exactly what they are thinking. Children often endow their pet dogs with magical powers that enable them to fly away at night and live out incredible adventures, returning home in the morning as conquering heroes.

When my oldest boy was four he believed his dog could speak to other dogs in what he called *Doglish*. For a year he tried to learn that language. I believe he succeeded. When children feel bad they often believe their dogs feel the same way. The reverse is also true. What it all seems to mean is that children identify with small animals much more easily than with complex humans who "have their own problems." Sometimes a very young pet owner sits her dog down, pours him a miniature cup of tea, and holds a thirty-minute conversation with the charitable guest. Only a dog will sit still for that. A smart parent will try to eavesdrop on such a conversation. He may learn how his daughter feels about the quality of his parenting.

It is much easier for a child to express affection to and receive it from an animal. Young boys regard hugging and kissing from their moms as "mush." However, a dog can plant a kiss and it's called "licking the face." Dogs are so direct in their pursuit of contact with humans that they cut through the typical barriers set up by children.

DIFFERENCES BETWEEN DOG AND CHILD BEHAVIOR

The only similarity between dog behavior and child behavior is the powerful impact of early experience on adult behavior. What young dogs are exposed to will definitely affect such elements of adult behavior as adaptability to humans and animals, learning abilities, emotional stability and self-confidence. The same could be said about young children.

With the exception of dog guides for the blind and other serious workers, dogs at twelve to eighteen months of age are pretty much what they will be for the rest of their lives. This, of course, is not the case for children. They are in a constant, ongoing state of intellectual, emotional, psychological and physical growth for many years. Every week seems to bring a new development in the life of a child, and that is important to understand, particularly as it relates to living with a dog. Parents must expect constant change in a child's relationship with a dog. A child may begin a week loving the dog with enthusiasm and wanting to do every single thing connected with the dog's care. By the end of the week he may be totally disinterested. It's difficult to know why this happens. I do not believe it is as simple as a "limited attention span" or "boredom." I suspect that the child has experienced some transitional phase of growth and has refocused on another aspect of his or her life to the exclusion of the dog. This does not mean that the love affair with the animal is finished. It means that the dog has been placed on *hold* for a while, and parents should be tolerant. *Do not get rid of the dog.* Some parents might take over the care until the child is ready to relate again. Some feel it's correct to insist that the child continue with some of the chores, such as walking and feeding. It depends on the emotional state of the child and the parental point of view.

It is worth mentioning that dog behavior is very different from human behavior. Dogs cannot function without a "pack leader" and function best when that leader maintains a dominant manner. Children, on the other hand, must be encouraged to strive for their maximum potential, and that requires self-confidence, independence, a healthy self-image and the ability to risk failure. It is paradoxical that dogs reach their potential as human pets from an environment that is detrimental to children. Dogs accept the world as they find it and seek their place in it. Children look for new worlds in order to create their place. Each, in his way, is correct. It is the wise parent who relates to dogs and children in the manner needed for each. They are, indeed, separate creatures.

THE HUMANE CHILD

If your child respects his dog as a living creature with a right to live a life free of pain and oppressive behavior, he is what the world needs the most of. Do not underestimate the power for good that lies in the hearts of humane children. Loving animals and respecting their needs for a decent life follow children into adulthood, and isn't that a fine thing for them and the rest of us?

It is not farfetched to believe that humane and kindly behavior toward animals can become a way of behaving toward all. But the values of decency must be taught and promoted by a child's parents in word

Boy and dog with roller skates

and deed and example. What you say and what you do have an enormous influence on your child. If you hit a dog, your child will hit a dog. If you are abusive, then your child will learn to be abusive. Although children love animals because they identify with their innocence, they also experience moments of anger, rage and a desire to strike out. It is a parent's responsibility to see to it that these irrational bursts of minor violence are never directed at the family dog, just as they are not tolerated against any other member of the family.

Those of us who are in the trenches, trying to raise children to be upstanding, decent human beings, never forget that the kids are watching and learning from what they see and hear. It isn't easy. Being nice to your dog as an example for your children is not hard and goes a long, long way to make the world a better place.

THE FAMILY DOG AS TEACHER

By bringing a dog into your home, you are introducing children to a living thing with needs corresponding to those of humans, i.e., food, water, shelter, and love and affection. But your pet dog also serves as a

121

valuable teaching tool, capturing and holding a child's attention far longer than books or diagrams. There are endless possibilities for parents, as the partners of teachers, to apply dog-related lessons to the personal and academic development of their children. With the help of a fine reference entitled "Professor Pet," written and produced by the American Pet Products Manufacturers Association and distributed by the Pet Information Bureau, I give you many examples of ways to use your dog as a stimulus to learning.

Defining right and wrong.   Children remember best what they have learned through experience or direct observation. Although a dog's actions are not necessarily indicative of proper human behavior, certain situations can draw attention to lessons to be learned from them. When a larger dog dominates a smaller dog, a natural instinct, the child may be taught how unacceptable this is among humans. Animals are motivated by instincts while humans additionally function on the basis of complex reasoning powers.

Getting along with others.   Through observation, kids can be taught how animals interact with each other — those of the same species and those totally unrelated to each other. Promote a discussion of how animals behave with each other with an emphasis on *why* they do what they do. The next step is to compare that behavior with the children's own personal relationships, illustrating how different people are from animals.

Sex education.   When a child asks, "Where did I come from and how did I get here?" questions that are inevitable, you may find the answers easier through the analogy with your pet.

Life and death.   Just as birth is a mysterious subject to small children, death is a concept even fewer children can begin to comprehend. The natural death of a neighbor's dog can become an ideal opportunity for a parent to begin a discussion on the subject, explaining what caused the aninal to die, the physical realities of dying, the naturalness of death, etc.

Survival.   Even domesticated animals preserve their keen instinct to survive. They rely on a system of defense mechanisms when their security is threatened. A discussion could be generated concerning the natural defenses of dogs compared with the deliberate actions humans take to preserve their well-being.

Independence.   Animals exert their independence from their mothers much earlier than humans do, and although a dog remains dependent on its owner for basic essentials, it still displays a sense of independence. Parents can lead a discussion of the ways a dog takes care of itself, and how children can display their independence at home and school.

Companionship, affection, love.   As children care for and play with a dog, they will develop emotional attachments to the animal that can be related to their feelings for other people. Discussions could center on what love means to each child, how his or her feelings for the pet differ from feelings toward parents and friends, how the child imagines the dog feels about him or her, etc.

Working with basic shapes.   Have your child observe the dog and pick out basic shapes from various parts of the body and coat pattern — circles, rectangles, squares, etc.

Decorating the dog's space.   Make a project of drawing pictures and/or constructing a mobile with dogs on it. The pictures could utilize all aspects of the dog's life, including his bowl, leash, pillow, etc. Use the artwork as a way of decorating the walls around the dog's corner of the room.

Mural painting.   Cover a wall with paper and all the kids can draw themselves playing with their dog; have them illustrate elements of responsible pet ownership, feeding, affection, etc.

Drawing from live models.   There is no better model for drawing than the family dog. Wait until he is taking a nap and then set your child up with paper and crayons or paints.

Animal environments.   After discussing what a dog's environment is like in the wild (you may draw from the wolf), have the kids draw their

dog in the woods, the mountains, along the timberline, or in the African jungle.

Dog collage.   Look for materials from old magazines, box tops, string, leaves, etc., that relate in some way to the children's dog and his life. Encourage the kids to crate their own collages on some form of cardboard, with a drawing or photograph of the dog on top.

Making gifts for the dog.   For Christmas tell the children to make a stocking for the dog or for the dogs of friends and neighbors and fill them with homemade toys for them.

Writing stories.   Suggest to your children that they write a story about your dog and the adventures it has had or may have had. "A Day in the Life of" your dog is a perfect story to write. An interesting and possibly revealing story for your child to write is what it would be like if she traded places with the dog and lived his life for a while.

Dog poems.   Ask your kids to write some poems about their dog. Having them read aloud can be fun, especially if there is an audience. You might want to read aloud some famous dog poems to the children. Look through the works of Ogden Nash, A. A. Milne, Don Marquis, Stephen Foster, etc. Talk to your librarian.

Read a dog story.   Help your child select a book about a dog and tell her to read it as part of a quiz game later. If your child does not read, then read it to her. When the child has read the book, provoke a discussion summarizing the story and identifying the most important information she obtained from it. Ask questions about the book, as in a quiz show, and award prizes. You can use the book for a spelling bee or even to help identify verbs, nouns, and other parts of speech. The dog story will make it more interesting.

Animal role-playing.   Ask your kids and their friends to put together a play in which they take the part of animals, including the family dog, portraying their feelings and thoughts, imitating their actions and interactions. It should be great fun.

Pet photography.   With the help of a simple camera, perhaps a Polaroid instant, have your kids photograph the dog. There are many ways to go about this. First, you can take a photo of the kids and the dog together. Next, have the children operate the camera, snapping the dog as he engages in his daily activities. You could start a photo album of pictures of the dog. When a large quantity of snaps exist, hang them on a wall and hold an exhibit inviting friends, relatives and neighbors. An opening of a dog photo exhibit makes a wonderful social event for the kids and their friends.

Foreign language and culture.   If you take the trouble to read the history of your purebred dog, you will find that in all likelihood it originated in another country. You may use that as a springboard to using the language of that country and any other aspect of that particular culture. This could start a discussion of which dogs came from which countries, thus taking the opportunity to introduce French words, Italian words, etc.

Animal origins.   Just as different races of humans originated in various countries, dogs too came from areas all around the globe. Have the kids research where your dog (and their friends' dogs) originated, what year they were first mentioned in history books or logged in science books, what other animals the dog is related to, what its ancestors were like, etc. It could be done as a quiz with a prize for the one who answers the most questions correctly.

Pets' service to mankind.   Many animals were first kept as pets because they provided a service to some kind of humans. Try to learn what type of service your dog (and other animals, too) may have provided. It could also be part of a quiz.

Working dogs.   Many dogs are actually "employed" by their owners to perform a specific job, such as guard dog, seeing eye dogs, hearing ear dogs, etc. Explore with your kids the possibilities for other dog jobs and what the training is like for them.

Pets and climate.   Discover the different weather and temperature preferences of various dog breeds and discuss what characteristics enable them to live in the climates they do. This can be related to human adaption to climatic conditions and/or to other animals.

Pets in history.   Famous people often had famous pets, from the royal dogs of Chinese emperors to the many dogs of George Washington and Teddy Roosevelt. See how many dogs (and other pets) you can uncover in historical situations and compare their role with famous pets of recent years, such as Morris the Cat and Lassie.

Table of measurements.   To teach children about units of measure, illustrate with the amounts used in feeding the family dog, growth measurements, size of living quarters, etc.

The metric system.   All the measurements used in maintaining the dog can be converted to metric amounts. Help the kids create a chart of conversion formulas and equivalent measurements. Many metric weights and measurements can be found printed on the bags and boxes of dog food.

Introduction to accounting. Lessons in accounting can be illustrated by the amount of time and money needed to care for the family dog. Explain the basics between debits and credits, and keep an accounting ledger for the costs involving the dog.

Working with graphs. The older kids can learn how to work with graphs by monitoring weight gain or loss, food intake, costs to maintain the dog, growth of the dog, etc.

Health care. By introducing children to the proper nutritional requirements of their dog they will develop a better understanding of their own bodily requirements. Have them make a poster of basic foods that their dog needs to remain healthy and then have them design a poster with the basic food groups humans need to remain healthy. It is yet another opportunity for educational discussion.

Grooming care. Some pets, such as cats, groom themselves, while others need to have their owners do it for them, and that includes the family dog. Discuss what is required to keep the dog groomed and cleaned. You can also talk about how cats groom themselves. Add to the discussion the benefits of keeping a dog well groomed and clean, and relate this to the importance of children's personal habits in cleanliness.

Your dog's senses. All dogs have the same senses as humans. However, some kinds of dogs have greater proficiency in one or more senses than others. For example, bloodhounds, beagles and dachshunds have a greater sense of smell than other breeds. Greyhounds, whippets and salukis have a more efficient sighting ability. These added sensory abilities are important to these animals for survival in the wild, where they must hunt for their own food. Lead a discussion on dogs, senses, and then talk about human senses. This exercise can be further illustrated by showing various objects and having the kids close their eyes and use alternately their sense of smell, touch and taste to determine what the objects are.

Investigating locomotion skills. In studying the area of motion and locomotion, dogs make an excellent visual aid. Take the dog out for his walk and bring the kids with you. On leash, have the dog run, walk, stop, sit, lie down, etc. In the summer, if the opportunity presents itself, have the dog swim. Have the kids describe each of the animal's methods of locomotion and determine how the body facilitates each one.

Protection. Start a discussion about how dogs protect themselves from the harsh elements, or predators if living in the wild. Add to this the way they prepare for the seasonal changes with such physical changes as shedding in the summer and growing a new coat in the winter. Include in this talk how the dog would defend itself if it were in its natural environment.

Anatomy. With the aid of illustrations in books, explore the anatomy of the dog and make a diagram, labeling the parts. Compare the dog's body structure to that of humans and other animals, pointing out distinctive characteristics, such as the dog's tail, the length of this body, and his snout.

Communication. Communication is a vital part of any creature's existence and dogs have the ability to communicate with or without sound. Discuss how your dog communicates with other dogs and with

128

humans. Compare these methods of communication to the advantages of human language skills.

These are some of the very many ways that you can use the dog itself as a helper in your children's education. More than that, these various activities have a play value that will serve you and the children quite well on a rainy day when kids "have nothin' to do." It's all part of the dog and your family.

Five

Housebreaking and

Other Delights

Children and dogs have much in common when it comes to toilet training. When both species are very young they cannot control themselves to any degree because of a lack of development of the muscles opening and closing the floodgates. *Sphincter* control does not begin to develop in a child until the third year of life, earlier for some and later for others. Thank God, those muscles in a dog develop far earlier. A three-month-old puppy can go eight hours, through the night, under the right circumstances, without eliminating. If the puppy is confined in a dog crate (a wire enclosure with a door, roof and floor), is not given food or water at bedtime, and is not disturbed, he will not soil because his body won't have the need. There are other reasons, which I will come to. Neither infants nor puppies have a concept of using a specific place that is more desirable than others to relieve themselves. Housebreaking and toilet training are both learned processes based on environmental control, eating schedules, instruction, repetition, and, to some degree, imitative behavior. Most child experts tell us not to rush the toilet-training process at all and to begin somewhere around two and a half or three years of age. Pediatricians are famous for saying, "No child ever wet his pants at his college commencement." However, puppies and young dogs must begin housebreaking at a much earlier age. In terms of physical development, a three-month-old puppy is possibly the equivalent of a three- or four-year-old human. Besides, no one

130

bothers putting diapers on a dog, so housebreaking is an aesthetic necessity. To wait longer is to make the task more difficult.

In our society one's sensibilities seem to be assaulted by the sight of or even the mention of our bodily wastes. We choke with inhibition, embarrassment, anger or inarticulateness over this subject. Some giggle while others regress to "Boop-boop-a-doop." It provokes a wide variety of emotional responses in people, both expressed and suppressed. And yet, mothers (and some enlightened fathers) have been dealing with the subject in their dear children for many years with resignation and dignified good humor. It would be irrational to raise one or more children from infancy on and yet feel upset about dealing with a dog's eliminative realities.

Once parents understand they are going to have to change soiled diapers for a minimum of two or three years per child, they settle down and accept the situation. It would be unthinkable and quite destructive to express great anger or hit a child for "having an accident" during toilet training. Well, the same is true for puppies and young dogs. If you want a healthy, housebroken dog that is a pleasant creature, not cowed or frightened of you, then the housebreaking technique, coupled with a basic knowledge of canine eliminative behavior, is important to you.

There are some very distinct differences between children and dogs as to what elimination means to each. Obviously, toilet training for the child and house training for the dog are quite different in approach and technique. Children toilet train, if handled properly, because they want to be like mommy, daddy, brother and sister. Dogs appreciate house training because they are programmed genetically to eliminate as far away as possible from where they eat and sleep. Nature has provided this behavior as a means of avoiding detection in the wild by predators. The nest in which newborn puppies snuggle is kept clean because the mother ingests what little waste matter there is. As the weeks go by, the young puppies instinctively crawl out of the nest to relieve themselves, and ultimately return to the same spots they have already soiled.

When a child finally begins using the toilet and gives up diapers for training pants, it is a source of pride and accomplishment. It is one of those milestones in a child's life that tells him he is becoming a "big boy." From then on, going to the toilet is simply an aspect of human digestion. Not so for a dog. As dogs leave puppyhood they begin to do something that is known as "marking" or "scent-posting." It is a way of claiming one's territory, proclaiming dominance (without the actual presence of another dog), and a means of communication between males and females. So one can see that urine and feces are extremely important to dogs and have far greater use than mere elimination of waste matter.

There are two facts of canine elimination that are of vital importance to the family that wishes to house train a dog. First, confining the dog to a small area when not closely supervised utilizes his instinct to avoid soiling his nest. Second, by carefully selecting "scent-post" areas outside the house you will be using to great advantage the dog's attraction to the posted odors of canine body waste. The dog will return to the same spots to eliminate time and time again because of the scent, even if it is his own. Dogs in the neighborhood will "mark" the same spots and then your dog will "mark" over theirs in a sort of battle-by-proxy. It's all quite harmless and very useful for housebreaking purposes.

When housebreaking your dog, you may wish to consider allowing the children to become involved in the process. Whether or not that is a good idea really depends on the age of the child, his or her attitude toward urinating and defecating, and how much responsibility he or she can handle. Certainly all children can learn something by simply watching the process as it's carried out by the adults. I would say a child of ten years or older can actually help out. Housebreaking a dog consists of confinement, a rigid feeding schedule, supervising the dog when he is not confined, walking the dog or taking him to his newspapers, correcting him and praising him. Which aspects of housebreaking your child can handle can be determined only by you. It would be a bad choice to allow a ten-year-old to walk a large, untrained dog in city streets. It would be a good idea to decide ahead of time which aspect of housebreaking your kids can handle and then stick with that, assuming it works out.

If your dog is past two months of age, he is biologically ready for housebreaking. Although training is not a voluntary activity, the dog will do much better if your emphasis is on praise for what he does properly rather than harshness for his mistakes. Do not misunderstand: a dog must be *corrected* when he does the wrong thing, but let us not make a losing battle for him. As with a child, the more the dog loses, the less confidence he has in himself. To be sure, much of dog training is behavior modification and conditioned responses. But we must not ignore the dog as an individual entity with a personality and perception of the world. To rub his nose in his own mess is to tear a page from the Joseph Stalin school of behavior. Even a dog that poops on the floor deserves to be treated with kindness and understanding. If your dog is a *sooner* (sooner mess the floor than go outside), don't take it personally. It has nothing to do with spite or the dog's teaching you a lesson for leaving him alone. Forget all that ill-informed nonsense.

There are only a few reasons why a dog messes on the floor. The first and foremost is simply that the dog has not been house trained properly or completely. The second reason is medical. A sick dog has no control over himself. This is true of dogs with worms, upset stomachs, viruses, infections or bladder problems. Many old dogs lose control. Another reason for incontinence is genetic. Some breeds or groups of breeds have a difficult job accomplishing a state of housebreaking. (See chapter 2, "45 Breeds That Love Children" section, for details about your breed of dog.) This is not to say that they cannot be housebroken. But it means that these breeds are more difficult to house train and require a rigid training program that is administered vigorously. Some of these breeds were developed to live outdoors on their own or outdoors in a kennel with a large pack. Such an animal is too busy minding the store to be concerned with the pantywaist activity of carefully avoiding house soiling. He must be conditioned for such behavior, and that requires more effort from the trainer than normal.

When a dog messes on your bed, the floor or under the carpet, it does not, in my opinion, have anything to do with spite. Revenge is a Mediterranean art confined to the madness of obsessed human beings. Dogs are much nicer than that. No, I hate to spoil all that funny cocktail party chitchat, but dogs soil the house when you are gone because they are ridden with anxiety and not with some form of primitive rage laced with the desire to get even. Your absence may give your dog a form of identity crisis in that he has no idea if you're ever coming back to feed him, to nurture him, to make him feel secure. It is quite possible that his urine and feces are a message-sending technique or simply a physicalized expression of fear. That would explain why some dogs, especially the toy breeds, pee on your bed when you're gone. It is the one locale with the strongest human odor. Although it is irrational, there is a sort of dog logic to leaving a message where your scent is the strongest. Dogs that are permitted on the bed are more likely to soil it. But, of course, understanding all this is of no comfort if your mattress is permanently stained. What is required here is a vigorously pursued housebreaking technique that is implemented until successful, no matter how long it takes. Another solution (as an adjunct to house training, not a substitute) is crating your dog when you leave the house. We'll come to that in a bit.

HOW TO HOUSEBREAK YOUR DOG

Basic Housebreaking

The object of housebreaking is to condition the dog to relieve himself outdoors when being walked. Housebroken dogs will conform to a walking schedule created by you or will give you signals about an urgent need for toileting. Your goal must be to have a completely housebroken dog and nothing less. Halfway measures are worse, in a way, than none at all because you can never be sure of what you'll come home to. Usually, a dog that is not housebroken at all is confined to one small location when the family leaves, and the mess is localized. That, at least, is easier to clean and far less upsetting.

To housebreak a dog you must deal with four elements. 1. Restriction of the dog's movements. 2. A feeding and walking schedule. 3. Control of the dog's scent-posting. 4. Praise and correction. None of these is complicated or even difficult to remember. Housebreaking is a simple training technique that conditions the dog's mind and body about where and when to relieve himself. It is based on the identical training principles discussed in chapter 6, "Teaching You to Teach Your Child to Train Your Dog." Once you have accomplished house training, your dog's mind-set will be geared for basic dog obedience. One last word before starting the training . . . *linoleum!*

Step One

Select a small room or portion of a room where you can restrict the dog's movements. The use of a portable gate that jams against both ends of a doorway can be extremely helpful. When you confine a dog to a small room or area, it is essential that you not close the door, thus shutting the dog out of family life. This is why the gate is so helpful. Check with a hardware store or dog equipment catalog for one. Some

The perfect portable gate for confining a dog

are better than others. They are quite common, though. *You must be resigned to the fact that the young dog must remain in this confined space all day and all night except when you walk him.* The dog may be removed from this area for play and socializing if you have the time to watch him carefully for the signs that indicate he has to "go." A puppy or young dog will have to "go" immediately after eating or drinking, upon awakening from a nap or deep sleep, after playing, or approximately every two hours of the waking day. The signs are sniffing the ground, squatting, turning in circles, trying to find the door, or a general hyperactive behavior. Eating, drinking or physical activity are the triggers for urinating and defecating. A three-month-old puppy can make it through the night without relieving himself because he has not been fed, given water, or allowed to run around.

When you restrict the dog's movement to one small area, you are taking advantage of his instinctive need to keep his den free of any odor that will reveal his presence to a predator. The smaller the restricted area, the less likely he is to have "accidents." If the dog is in the kitchen or bathroom, lay down several thicknesses of newspaper to facilitate a cleanup. It is of vital importance that the dog never think of the restricted area as a form of punishment. Although he will want to come out as often as he can, the confinement area must be pleasant. Hopefully there will be enough room to walk around a bit and see out to the rest of the house. Feed and water the dog in this area. Give him a nylon chew toy, but don't provide him with balls or play-provoking toys. That only triggers the need to eliminate. Taking your dog out to relieve himself is the next step.

Step Two

A word about the food you give the dog. Housebreaking cannot possibly be taught if the dog suffers from diarrhea or has a loose stool. If that is the dog's current condition, have him examined by a veterinarian for worms or other internal parasites. If the dog's bowel movements are fine, avoid introducing stomach upset. Maintain the present diet without changing it during the housebreaking period, which, under normal circumstances, should not last more than two weeks. A well-balanced canine diet consists of protein, carbohydrates, fats, vitamins and minerals in the proper proportion as recommended by the National Academy of Science and can be achieved by feeding a premium commercial dog food. I recommend a meat diet mixed with dog kibble.

It is now time to consider a feeding and walking schedule that will be adhered to rigidly. Your dog's body will regulate itself to accommodate the schedule. Put nothing in the dog's body unless it is dictated by the schedule. A crucial point: *Every time you feed or water the dog he must be taken out for a walk soon afterwards so that he can urinate and/or defecate.*

The following is the correct procedure for *all* dogs, whether they live in apartments or homes with fenced yards or acreage to run around in. Select a location that is suitable and acceptable for walking your dog. It must be a place that will not upset your neighbors when they see your dog relieve himself. Naturally, you will be prepared with the proper equipment and materials for cleaning up afterward. Scoopers and plastic bag-type products are for sale everywhere and by law must be used in most large cities. When you take the dog out he must be properly leashed at all times, not only for the sake of the law, the dog's safety and your neighbors' comfort but for the success of the housebreaking. You cannot train a dog that is not under control at all times.

Once the dog relieves himself in a specific location he is going to want to return to that location every time you take him out. He will be drawn to it by scent and by habit. Remember, during the housebreaking period (approximately two weeks) the point to the walk is for toileting purposes only. Do not make it a sightseeing excursion or a play-exercise period. There will be plenty of time for that in the years to come. Take the dog to the toileting area, make sure he relieves himself, and then return home. Some dogs need a longer walk than others before relieving themselves.

The closer you stick to the schedule, the faster you begin to regulate the dog's body in conformity with your needs. If your dog is between the ages of three and five months, he will be eating three meals a day. During the housebreaking period, do *not* leave water down for him at all times. Otherwise you will delay the success of the training. When you feed the dog make it a meal to be given at a precise time with exactly five minutes to eat it. If the dog hasn't eaten by then, remove the dish. Allow him another five minutes after you serve the water bowl and then remove that, too. If the dog indicates a great thirst between scheduled watering times, then give him an ice cube or two to tide him over. The following schedule must be strictly enforced.

Feed-Water-Walk-Return Schedule

Early morning	Walk the dog and return to dog's area
One-half hour later	Feed, water, walk, and return to dog's area
Midmorning	Water, walk, and return to dog's area
Past noon	Feed, water, walk, and return to dog's area
Midafternoon	Water, walk, and return to dog's area
Late afternoon	Water, walk, and return to dog's area
Early evening	Feed, water, walk, and return to dog's area
Before retiring	Walk and return him to his area for the night

During the day and evening you may remove the puppy from the restricted area for play and attention. Watch carefully for signs that he has to "go." If he does, take him out for a walk. That is the only part of the schedule that you may violate. Do not feed or water the dog at night during housebreaking. No between-meal snacks during housebreaking. How and when to praise the dog is extremely important and is discussed in the next step.

Step Three

Because a dog's instinctive need to live with and be part of a pack is so strong, he thrives on various forms of acceptance and feels dejected by firm criticism. The principle of praise and correction is based on this pack instinct. Notice the word *punishment* does not enter into it. Hitting a dog or scolding him too harshly for housebreaking mistakes may get the desired results to some degree, but the price in self-confidence and personality is too great. If you want a dog that is terrified of you, then you are reading the wrong book. Fear in a dog builds walls between the animal and his young companions. It can also create shyness and the biting behavior that goes along with it. An abused dog sooner or later gets back at the abuser.

When you praise a dog you are instilling in him a desire to do what you want him to do and to work hard for your praise. The reward is greatly appreciated. If the dog does something properly, don't hold back. Tell him how wonderful he is. Praise is a verbal compliment given with enthusiasm. "Good Girl" or "Attaboy" are good examples of this.

A *correction* on the other hand is the exact opposite. If the dog fails to obey or does something wrong, *correct* him. Corrections are a form of rejection. They have the exact opposite effect from the praise and teach the dog what *not* to do. The important word is *teach*. Although corrections are negative in nature, they are not punishments per se.

The dog feels the correction when the choke collar tightens for an instant around his neck. The trainer has given a quick tug on the leash that is hooked to the choke collar. It is not painful, but it is uncomfortable and somewhat of a surprise. The tug must always be accompanied with a firm "NO" from the trainer. (See chapter 6, "Teaching Parents to Teach Their Child to Train Their Dog.") In housebreaking, a noisy shaker can is also a useful correction tool. If you take a clean, empty soda can, insert five pennies or other metal objects into it, and tape it closed, you have a terrific noise-maker. By shaking the can vigorously and saying "NO" in a very firm tone of voice, you can effectively correct the dog from across the room without the help of the leash and collar. The effect is to startle the dog and get his immediate attention while delivering the negative message.

In housebreaking you correct the dog when he is in the process of making a mistake. During the puppy's play periods when he is not in his restricted area he will run around the house. If he begins to urinate or defecate you must correct him by shaking the can and saying "NO" in a loud, firm tone of voice. Then immediately scoop him up, grab the leash, attach it, and walk him to his proper toileting area, outdoors. Once there he will probably relieve himself again. When he does, give him heaps upon heaps of praise. You must always do this during the housebreaking period. It takes many repetitions for the dog to understand what it is that earns him your praise or your rejection. However, if you do not correct the dog *as he is in the process of an "accident"* the correction has no meaning to the dog. It will have been a wasted effort.

Do not underestimate the importance of your response to the dog. Praise is the most effective reinforcement of the training there is. It is absolutely vital that you lavishly praise your dog every time he relieves himself outdoors in an acceptable location. Every time you walk the dog, be prepared to praise him for doing the correct thing. It is an essential part of the training. Avoiding future mistakes is the next step.

Step Four

Just as scent-posting works for the trainer in housebreaking, it can also work against her. When the puppy "lets go" on the floor, he has, for all intents and purposes, "marked" territory. No matter how thoroughly you clean the spot, an odor detected only by the dog will remain. This "scent-post" will always draw the dog back to it to further "mark" it. That means once the dog has peed in one location he is going to do it again and again unless you get rid of that scent. The same thing happens when the dog defecates.

Two things must be accomplished here. First, the odor or scent must be obliterated. Only an odor neutralizer can actually change the scent chemically rather than simply perfuming it away. Soap and water, ammonia, detergent, and other cleaning products cannot eradicate those odors. There are several odor neutralizers prepared commercially and sold in pharmacies and pet supply stores. The leading one is called *Nil-odor*. It is a highly concentrated liquid that requires no more than a few drops. The second thing to do is to remove the stain so the dog cannot see it. On a hard surface this is easy. Cold water or warm water and detergent will do the trick. On a washable carpet cold water and seltzer are effective. If the urine or feces causes a visual stain, use a 1:1 solution of cold water and vinegar. Once the spot is cleaned, apply the odor neutralizer. Its minty odor usually repels dogs.

Step Five

House training is accomplished within one week for some dogs and four weeks in others. The average dog catches on in about two weeks if the trainer has rigidly adhered to the regimen. You know your dog is housebroken when he keeps his own area spotless; has almost no "accidents" when allowed to run around the house; and begins to go to the door when he wants to be walked. At that time it is okay to give the dog more freedom and less supervision. It is still necessary to confine him to his area when you leave the house. You may test him by releasing him and leaving for fifteen minutes. Each day increase the length of time he is left alone without restriction.

If the dog should have a housebreaking failure after the training program has been successfully completed, you may repeat the process for one week. Another option is to hook the leash to his collar and walk him to the mess. In a very firm tone of voice say, "NO! NO! NO!" Force him to look at it as you clean it up. Immediately walk him to his toileting location, outdoors, allow him to relieve himself, even if it's only a tinkle, give him great praise, and take him back and pray.

WORKING PARENTS/SCHOOL-AGE KIDS

It is extremely difficult to housebreak a dog while no one is home. Some will tell you it has been done, and indeed they are probably correct, but it is very difficult. It depends upon the individual dog's physical and emotional needs, plus the animal's temperament. An hysterical, anxiety-ridden puppy is simply not going to respond to house training when left alone for four, five or eight hours during the day. Neither is a typical specimen of a breed noted for being difficult to housebreak such as a Siberian husky, a beagle or a Bichon Frise. These are examples of breeds that do not thrive when left alone, especially at an early age. No puppy feels good about being alone, to be sure, but some breeds take it harder than others. Your individual dog's temperament also has a bearing on housebreaking when he's left alone during the day. A hyperactive dog, a highly nervous dog (or one that has been made nervous) simply cannot control its bladder or need to defecate. Dogs express their anxiety as well as their submissiveness through their eliminative activity. One must understand that there can be no guarantee that a puppy left alone during the day can be housebroken properly.

The requirement to schedule a puppy's body with food, water and walk when housebreaking is necessary in all but very rare cases. All that can be suggested for working parents/school-age kids is to acquire the dog at the beginning of a long holiday period, such as spring break or summer vacation, so that the puppy is not alone for the first week or two. If it's too late and you already have the dog, pay someone to come to your home during the day and maintain the proper schedule for you. It is in this situation that a wire crate is extremely useful. However, it is very bad for a puppy or a grown dog to spend its entire day in confinement. It is altogether possible for a pup to become depressed and fall into bad health and even develop a personality disorder. No matter what anyone tells you, a puppy spending its entire day alone in confinement will never be totally housebroken and will never realize its potential as a happy, joy-giving pet.

If you observe the Feed-Water-Walk-Return Schedule on page 137 you will notice that there are eight walks a day recommended. Some breeds (and individual dogs within a breed) could conceivably adjust to a tighter schedule and still be housebroken. You might be able to eliminate the midmorning walk along with the midafternoon walk if you can persuade a friend, neighbor or paid individual to come in at noon and feed, water, walk and return the dog to his crate or area of confinement. If you do this, it is absolutely essential that the animal not be left with a bowl or food or water while you're not there. Food and water simply stimulate the digestive reflex and create a need to eliminate.

I suggest you leave a radio on with soothing music or an all-day talk show. Leave chew toys with the dog, a favored blanket or other reassuring object. It will still be a compromise, but perhaps one that will work. If none of this works, someone is going to have to come in and stay with the dog at various times during the day. Unfortunately, there is no other solution, in my opinion.

PAPER TRAINING

There is much difficulty and confusion on the subject of paper training. Most training courses along with most dog trainers tell us that you must decide whether or not you want your dog housebroken or paper trained. Paper training means that the dog has been taught never to soil anywhere in his home except where the newspapers are spread out and only when he asks to "go" or is told to "go." We're further told that trying to teach your dog to use both newspapers indoors and the street outdoors leads to confusion in the dog and ultimate disaster. Confusing the issue even further is when those same trainers tell us to spread papers down on the floor in the dog's confinement area during housebreaking. If you do that, it would seem that you are still teaching the dog to use papers and the street.

The truth is that some dogs can learn to use newspapers indoors when necessary and the street as well without dumping on your couch, carpet or stairway. It is true that many cannot. So what do you do? If you have a toy breed or even a small-to-medium-size dog, paper train him. A large male dog lifts his hind leg to urinate and just may create a new design on your wallpaper. If you are adventuresome, train for both. First housebreak the dog and then paper train him. It may work out. If it does, it's really great. You can use the street in nice weather and paper the dog indoors when it rains or is too late or too cold or too scary to go out.

When you are housebreaking the dog it is a good idea to spread some newspapers on part of the floor of the dog's confinement area. He is definitely going to eliminate in his area during the early stages of the training and the papers help clean it up. Most dogs hit the papers most of the time. But this has nothing whatsoever to do with paper training. You are simply using some paper for the sake of convenience.

When you paper train your dog, you do everything exactly the same as in the housebreaking technique, with a couple of exceptions. The place you choose in which to restrict the dog should be the place you are always going to use as the dog's newspaper area for toileting purposes. Instead of walking the dog after each feeding and watering, you change the newspapers (see the schedule in Step Two of Housebreaking). On the first day cover the entire floor of his restricted area with papers. When you change them the first time save out one soiled sheet and place it on the spot farthest away from the doorway, under fresh paper. This will attract the dog to that spot for his next squirt. Always do this to get the dog to eliminate in the same general area of the papers. On the next day do not cover the *entire* floor with paper. Leave one small area of the floor uncovered. On each succeeding day use slightly less paper. Hopefully, the dog will confine his toileting area to the paper only. Watch the dog carefully and use the shaker can accompanied with a firm "NO" if he starts to use the uncovered floor. It takes only five days to complete the training but count on more than that. The dog is paper trained when he goes only on paper even though most of the floor is uncovered. It is important to read all of the housebreaking section to better understand what to do for paper training.

USING A COLLAPSIBLE WIRE CRATE FOR HOUSEBREAKING

For those who are willing to go to the expense, I recommend a collapsible wire dog crate as an extremely effective tool for housebreaking and as a sanctuary for the dog. This bit of classic dog equipment is meant to appeal to the dog's instinct to live in a den. A dog crate is a wire rectangle with a metal or wood floor and can be purchased in sizes suitable for all dogs. It only *looks* like a cage with a door. If used properly, it ties in directly with your dog's desire to maintain an inner core territory similar to a doghouse or, if he were in the wild, a cave.

When housebreaking your dog, you do everything the same as outlined in the housebreaking section. However, the dog crate is the area of confinement rather than your kitchen or bathroom. This is a better method because the dog is not under foot and he is in a place that will always be his exclusive domain. Once the training is completed, the crate may be used as a doghouse with the wire door open. Most dogs go in and out of the crate at their own discretion.

Puppies accept the crate in a short time if not forced into it or placed there for punishment. Set it up in an area near family activity, such as the hallway. Be certain it is placed away from sources of direct cold or heat. If you place a few toys and a mat or blanket inside, it will be a friendly sanctuary for the dog. If you drape an old sheet over the top, it becomes more like a doghouse, offering much privacy.

The dog's asociation with the crate must always be a positive one. Never use it for punishment. Some trainers place a food reward in the back of the crate before confining the dog inside. This creates a pleasant association with entering. Except at night a dog should never be crated for more than three or four hours at a time.

The crate will prove useful in other ways. When traveling with your dog the crate becomes a portable den providing security, comfort and safety. Depending upon the size, it can fit into the back seat of a sedan or station wagon. Confined in the crate, your dog cannot stick his head out the window or distract the driver. It is also valuable during periods of chewing, begging, jumping, nipping, etc. It can be used as part of an overall obedience-training program or simply as a way of confining the animal and preventing him from getting into trouble. At no time nor under any circumstances should the crate be used as a punishment area.

The crate you buy should be long enough to permit your *grown* dog to stretch out and high enough for him to sit up without hitting his head. Construct a wooden partition for your puppy so there is just enough room to lie down or sit up. It must never offer more space than necessary or it loses its denlike quality. As the puppy grows, increase the space by moving the partition back. This equipment is useful, humane and appreciated by most dogs.

Six

Teaching Parents

to Teach Their Kids to

Train Their Dog

The most important goal of this book is to encourage a meaningful relationship between the family dog and the children who live with it. That is the true value of having a dog. Convince your children of the value of dog training and help them go about the process of doing it themselves. The objective of this chapter is not perfect dog obedience training executed by dog or child. Although obedience training is quite important in and of itself as a way of creating a pet dog you want to live with, it is not the reason for this mini-obedience course. Getting involved with training creates a communication between dog and child that deepens the bond of love and respect on both ends of the leash.

The child cannot accomplish the training without the full participation of an adult. The course represents a twenty-minute teaching lesson once a week and a twenty-minute daily practice session. At each lesson the parent must first read the various steps involved in the teaching of a given command and then tell the child what to do. The parent takes the child through each lesson, step by step, with book in hand, just as a pro teaches a novice adult anything. This training course includes one or more children, one parent and one dog at all times. For some older children it may not be necessary for the parent to be involved with the daily practice sessions. If more than one child is going to be involved, the teaching lesson must be repeated for each child on a separate day for the sake of the dog's sanity.

Please do not be concerned if your dog does not respond *perfectly* to the commands your child learns to give. And do not be upset if your child's form is less than perfect. The most important element here is *contact* between dog and young person. It is wonderful if they look at each other and respond in a positive manner. This training program should offer a blue ribbon to both dog and child. In this course they are a team.

Although the best age for children to be involved with formal dog training (or AKC-sponsored Junior Showmanship) is approximately twelve years old, that does not apply here. We all know that some six-year-olds are more mature than some fifteen-year-olds. It isn't really a question of physical stature. *Training a dog requires that the child learn to become the animal's leader.* This activity will help develop leadership qualities in your child. Leadership has nothing to do with being a sergeant in the army or making a commencement speech. It is the ability to be responsible, to make decisions, to risk failure. If you are fortunate enough to attend an AKC-sanctioned dog show, watch the professional dog handlers. They are *masterful* but not abusive. They do not even speak loudly to the dogs, much less harshly. What does exist is an immediate communication between dog and human. The human knows what he or she expects from the dog and that gives the dog self-confidence. In the show ring, obedience training is not really a factor. It is the crystal-clear dog–master relationship that helps achieve the blue ribbon. That is a goal worth going for.

Dog training requires some physical strength, and that places a child at a disadvantage. But with training techniques and inner strength, anyone can be a dog's leader. The miracle of dog/human communication comes from a brief understanding of dog behavior and simple obedience training (See chapter 3, "Understanding Your Dog"). Dogs understand very little of our language. Every pet dog develops a human vocabulary but, of course, they cannot repeat the words. This makes it a listening vocabulary. Mostly, they respond to the tone of your voice, your gestures and *the feelings behind your words.*

Dog training and dog psychology are based on the known facts of dog and wolf behavior. 1. They form social attachments and live in groups known as packs. 2. They require a leader. 3. They claim territory and create a den in the center of it.

Pet dogs are happier when given obedience training. Children living with pet dogs are happier when they have a reliable means of communicating with their animals. Training brings order out of chaos and appeals to the dog's need for pack security. The canine mentality thrives on family life, leaders and followers, and a safe place to live. An obedience-trained dog sleeps better in the knowledge that all his needs are satisfied.

Obedience training is based on the dog's acceptance of the human's position of dominance and the animal's need to have someone, anyone, leading the pack. After teaching the dog an obedience command he is *praised* for executing the command properly and *corrected* when he does not. This establishes the trainer as the leader.

Praise or reward is usually in the form of an enthusiastic verbal compliment such as, "Good girl. What a good dog!" Do not hold back on your enthusiasm except in the case of a highly excitable dog, where you would be a bit more subdued. Sometimes an affectionate pat on the body does the trick. Many trainers use food tidbits for this purpose, but I do not recommend that practice in a situation involving children. It can easily turn the training session into a play period, and that would be counterproductive.

When a dog is being obedience trained he works for your praise or reward. It tells him that you are pleased and reinforces the teaching of each command. Most breeds of dog, in various degrees, work for your approval. Some are stubborn and must be handled with more firmness than others. Some are on the shy side and must be handled in a gentler manner and given lavish praise. The same gentle manner and lavish praise are needed for a nervous or frightened dog. Puppies can be trained at two months of age or older but they must receive a modified version of obedience training. Think of puppy training as kindergarten. That means going much slower and having greater sensitivity for their youth. Praise, as a reward, may be given lavishly to any age dog but should not be squandered. When training your dog be certain he has earned the reward. Every time you praise your dog you are teaching him to do whatever he did just before the reward was given. It is wrong to praise your dog immediately after he jumps on you, tracking mud on your clean dress. That would be to teach him to jump on people. Correct him, show him the proper behavior, and then praise him.

A correction is a signal to the dog that he did not obey a command or execute it properly even though he was taught what to do. The traditional correction is a tug of the leash, which is attached to a training collar. This communicates a negative message because it is usually accompanied by an authoritative "NO" from the trainer. There must never be any pain or abuse connected with this gesture. It is simply a means of communicating to the dog that he was wrong. Some trainers advocate the use of a noise-maker (an empty soda can with pennies) for this purpose. Corrections must never be mistaken for punishments. Punishment is not humane nor is it an effective teaching method. When you hit a dog he may become cowed but not really trained. Besides, it is difficult to predict how your child will relate to the idea of punishing the dog. Some children will identify with the dog and resent it, while others may be encouraged to become abusive. In a classroom one doesn't punish a student for learning slowly or for forgetting the previous day's lesson. A teacher may look a student in the eye and firmly tell him his answer was wrong, but she will not yank him across the room or call him a dummy. The same applies to dog training.

If you can teach your child when and how to praise or correct your dog effectively, the child will have at her fingertips the primary means of communicating with him. It is the language of dogs and people. The child will feel confident in what she is doing and the dog will know he is loved and cared for. You'll know you are doing something right when you see the dog and the child share moments of mutual affection and concern.

YOUR CHILD'S FRAME OF MIND

Before starting any dog-obedience course with a child, it is necessary to make a few ideas understood. Explain that the purpose of this activity is to create a language between the dog and every member of the family. You are about to teach her to teach the dog how to understand what is expected of him. The child must think of herself or himself as a teacher and not a student. Although teachers are firm and the ones in charge, they are not mean, harsh, insulting or unkind in any way. The child, as teacher, is the one in charge. This is essential. The dog will never learn a thing from the child unless the child becomes the leader the dog craves. *Being the dog's leader simply means teaching him what to do and insisting that he do it when commanded.* Do not push too far. Every child has limits and will quit if the pressure is too great.

The dog's teacher should be warm and loving but demanding. No one should lose his temper when the dog or the child fouls things up. Keep your sense of humor. You're going to need it. Anger delays the effectiveness of the training and most certainly cuts off communication. The child's tone of voice and physical manner with the dog are the keys to the effectiveness of the activity. Although training should be plea-

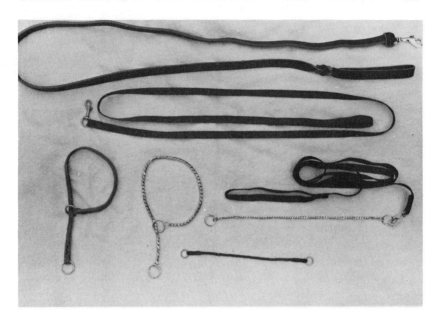

surable, it must not be a play session. Therefore, expect of the child a somewhat serious attitude. When she speaks to the dog it should be in a somber-yet-warm tone of voice. There must be an obvious change in the teacher's attitude so that the dog begins to take her seriously.

When speaking to the dog do not use long sentences and meandering statements. Use short, concise words that are consistent in their meaning. Always use the same word for the same command. "Let's go," is not a good command when you mean "Heel." "No" will do instead of "Hey, stop walking; come back here."

TRAINING EQUIPMENT

To train a dog you need a six-foot leather leash of good quality so there can never be any possibility of its breaking while outdoors. Dogs are pretty strong, so the leash must be dependable.

You will also need a training collar. They are referred to as *choke collars*. This is a short length of chain or nylon with a large ring at each end. The best ones are made of small, metal links that are welded together. By looping the chain through one of the large rings you form a slip knot that is wide enough to slide over the dog's head and onto the neck. Measure the diameter of your dog's neck and purchase a chain or nylon collar that is three inches longer than the neck size. The leash then snaps onto the outer ring. For puppies and fragile dogs it is best to get a nylon choke collar. It is also ideal for dogs with long, silky fur, to avoid damaging the coat.

PRAISE AND *CORRECTION*—THE TOOLS OF COMMUNICATION

During the actual training sessions there are only two means for conveying your pleasure or displeasure to the dog. Dogs are pack animals that require a leader. In order to remain members of the pack, they must please the leader. Your child is now the leader. If the dog pleases his leader, he must be praised. If the dog makes a mistake, he must be corrected. Very quickly the dog begins to work for the praise and avoid the correction.

Praise. It is absolutely essential that the dog receive verbal praise at the successful conclusion of each and every command given. His leader's approval is what the dog should be working for. Give a command such as "Barny, heel," wait till he starts off properly, then tell the dog what a good boy he is. Do not add any physical reward to the verbal one. If you have an excitable dog or one that is too exuberant, the tone of your voice must be toned down a bit lest the session turn into a play period. Gear the enthusiasm in your voice to the temperament of your dog.

Correction. Correcting your dog requires a tug of the leash causing the training collar to tighten around his neck, which delivers a mild but unpleasant sensation. The teacher must release the leash immediately so the collar loosens quickly. When the correction is given, the teacher also says, "NO," in a very firm tone of voice. Immediately following every correction the teacher must praise the dog to reward him for discontinuing his mistake. Here, we always give the dog the benefit of the doubt because he must never feel that he has lost your goodwill. All dogs are sensitive and will take it to heart if you do not reassure them. A happy, confident dog is always best. The praise following a correction gives the dog that vital reassurance. Its importance to training cannot be emphasized enough. Eventually, you will be able to correct

This is the correct way to hold the leash before correcting the dog with a tug of the leash. It is easier for youngsters to hold it with two hands, but eventually it can be done with one hand.

the dog without any tug of the leash by simply saying "NO" in a firm tone of voice. The proper sequence for a correction is this: Pull the leash so the choke collar tightens for an instant around the dog's neck. At the same time say, "NO," in a firm tone of voice. Then immediately praise the dog with "Good girl." When you give praise and deliver corrections, you are engaging in behavior modification based on *negative reinforcement* and *positive reinforcement.* Dogs, like most animals (including humans), tend to repeat behavior for which they are rewarded and avoid behavior for which they are not rewarded or for which they are corrected. All dog training rests on this principle. However, if the reward is too great or the correction too severe, the principle disintegrates as a means of training dogs.

WHERE, WHEN AND HOW TO TRAIN

Assuming your kids attend school, training should be a Saturday, Sunday and after-school affair. The place you select to have the dog trained should offer no distractions and as little noise as possible. Both dogs and kids need all the help they can get when it comes to concentration. A backyard, vacant lot or empty schoolyard will do. Actually, your

To correct your dog, you tug the leash firmly but gently to the right and allow it to release instantly. When the correction is given the teacher says, "NO!" in a firm tone of voice.

basement, garage or living room will also suffice. When you first teach a command, there should be no noise or distraction. Once the dog learns the command, the learning can be reinforced by executing the command in busy, outdoor areas such as the sidewalk or at a shopping mall. *Always allow your dog to relieve himself before starting a lesson or practice session.*

This training course is divided into lessons. Each lesson is meant to teach a new command to the dog. However, one must not go from one lesson to the next without many practice sessions in between. If you teach Lesson One on Sunday, the entire week should be spent in practice sessions. Each lesson should take no more than twenty minutes. The same applies to the practice sessions. More than that will tire the dog and make training something to dread. Puppies should have two ten-minute sessions each time with a break in between for relieving themselves.

Once a command has been taught, the practice sessions become ex-

152

The slip collar. Allow the chain to drop through the bottom ring so as to form a slip knot while still holding the top ring with your other hand.

tremely important. Dogs learn through repetition. That is why each command taught must be practiced once a day for a week before moving on to the next command. *Each practice session must include every command the dog has been taught, in the order it was taught.*

HOW TO USE THE TRAINING COLLAR AND HOLD THE LEASH

Stretch the chain-link collar in a vertical position with one hand holding the top ring and the other holding the bottom ring. Allow the chain to drop through the bottom ring so as to form a slip knot while you still hold the top ring with your other hand. The ring and chain in the top hand go over the top of the dog's head with the ring pointing to the dog's right. It is important to slip the collar over the dog's neck properly. When the leash is pulled it causes the collar to tighten around the dog's neck. If properly applied, the collar should smoothly slide back to

153

Practice placing the collar on your wrist and be certain it forms the letter P *so that it will loosen instantly when released.*

its loose position once the leash has been eased. When placing the slip knot over the dog's head, you are applying it correctly if it looks like the letter *P* around the neck. When incorrect the slip knot forms the number 9 and will not slide back and forth as it should.

You are now ready to attach the leash to the collar. The teacher must always stand on the dog's right side for the sake of consistency and face the same direction as the dog. Drape approximately two feet of the leash across the child's legs and have her hold her *right* hand out, thumb up. Place the loop at the end of the leash over the thumb of her right hand as if it were hanging on a hook. With the leash lying across the open palm, gather up the slack into the right hand so that there is only a slight drape across the knees. This will give her just enough leash to pull to her right in giving the dog a correction around his neck. The leash must be returned to its original slack position immediately for the sake of the dog's comfort. The tug must not be so hard as to knock the dog off his feet. But it must be firm enough to tighten the training collar, delivering a mild, corrective sensation.

For an absolutely firm grip on the leash, place the loop over the thumb of the right hand as if hanging it on a hook.

Show your child how to practice the tug by placing the choke collar around her left wrist (slip chain on top, ring moving to the right) and pretending it is the dog. Do everything as described so that the child gets a sense of how hard to pull the leash in a correction without hurting the dog. Do not allow the child to become overzealous. *Never correct your dog unless it is justified. Too many corrections will ruin the training and make the dog leash-shy.*

A WARNING

Your child must never do anything to make the dog aggressive. Never hit the dog, not with your hands, a rolled-up newspaper or, God forbid, a stick. Before beginning any training, impress your child with this cardinal rule. Apart from any humane considerations and how it encourages violence in the child, hitting the dog will eventually become dangerous to you and the children. This goes for everyone. *Never hit your dog.* When you do you are cutting off the lines of communication that we are so hopefully trying to establish. In most homes where the dog has been a resident for more than a month, a certain amount of hitting has already taken place in the belief that it has something to do with dog training. Without feeling guilty, it is now time to establish a

155

resolute nonviolent attitude and cut it out. If you hit your dog over a period of time, eventually he will start hitting you back . . . with his teeth. Once he begins, it is difficult to stop. Every time one of your children raises an arm to throw a ball or express a feeling, the movement may set in motion a defensive-aggressive response in the dog and he may attack.

Direct staring at your dog, eyeball to eyeball, has one of two effects, depending upon the dog. Large, aggressive dogs interpret the stare as a test of dominance or a challenge about territory. It can provoke an attack or a threat of an attack from an *adult*, aggressive dog. Do not encourage children to stare into the eyes of such dogs. It can be dangerous. However, staring into the eyes of a puppy is different. From a practical view it gets and holds the little dog's attention for the purpose of teaching him. Some puppies will accept the stare as an indication of dominance over them and behave in a submissive manner, most typically to roll onto their backs and urinate. (Some very timid adult dogs behave the same way.) Staring directly into a puppy's eyes just before and during training may help establish the trainer's authority. If staring upsets the little dog, then discontinue the practice.

Other actions that provoke aggressive behavior in dogs are cornering the animal (especially under a bed), using a threatening tone of voice, or pushing the dog in a threatening, abusive manner. These are definitely not acts of leadership and can actually teach the dog to become dangerous and unfriendly. Remember, most dogs and children start out with curiosity and innocence. Your job, as parent and dog owner, is to promote trust, friendship and affection in dog and child, and a quality of leadership in the child.

LESSON ONE — "SIT"

[*It is important to understand that the leash must always be used in this obedience training course. Off-leash training requires a different set of instructions not offered in this book. Before beginning Lesson One with the dog, try out all the hand and foot positions with the child, the leash and a lamppost or a stuffed dog. It cuts down on confusion. Especially concentrate on Steps 2 and 5. Do this before beginning each new lesson. It will help. Allow the dog to relieve himself before he begins each and every lesson. This is very important.*]

Before each training session practice all hand and foot positions with the child, the leash and a stuffed dog. It eliminates confusion without tiring the dog before the session begins.

Tell Your Child (the Teacher) to:

Step 1.   Place the training collar and leash on your dog and back away from the dog as far as the leash allows. Kneel down and in a very friendly way call the dog by name, enticing him to come to you. When he does, praise him but maintain control as the teacher. You may even rub him on the head and pat his chest. Not too much, though.

Step 2.   With the leash in your right hand, rise from the kneeling position and stand on the dog's right side with his body parallel to your knees. Gather the leash to all but twelve inches or less, so that it is *almost* taut. In a firm but friendly voice say, "SIT." Do not say the dog's name when giving this command. His name is used only for commands involving forward motion, such as "COME" or "HEEL."
   With your left hand apply pressure to the dog's rear end and gently push him into a sitting position. As you push with your left hand, pull

With the leash held taut above the dog's head, place your left hand on the dog's rump.

the leash upward with your right until it is taut but not uncomfortable for the dog. The effect is to push the rear end down and pull the front end up. Congratulate the dog with great enthusiasm.

If you are working with a puppy, do not push his rear end down. Rather, with a flat hand behind his rear legs push gently forward at the joints. This will also put the dog in a sitting position. Then praise him without touching him.

Step 3. Repeat Step 2 ten or fifteen times. The dog learns from this repetition.

Step 4. Give the dog a rest. Allow him to relieve himself, but do not engage in play activity. He has not yet been released from his training session.

Step 5. Repeat Steps 1, 2 and 3. You are now ready to correct the dog if he fails to obey the command SIT. You should not have to push the dog's rear end down now when you say, "SIT."

With your left hand, apply pressure to the dog's rear end and gently push him down into a sitting position. At the same time say, "SIT!"

If you give the command and the dog does not obey, tug the leash firmly but not abusively to the right side, tightening the training collar and then releasing it instantly. At the same time say, "NO." Then push the dog's rear end down, pull the leash taut above his head until he is in the SIT position and then praise him. Repeat Step 5 five, ten or fifteen times.

Step 6. It is now time to end the session. It must always be a definite conclusion decided by the teacher. Say to the dog, "OKAY," and then walk away in a definite manner. Your dog may want a walk or he may be tired and simply desire to go home and take a nap.

Step 7. Repeat this session every day for six days. Practice sessions are vitally important to the learning process. Once the dog obeys the command SIT without being placed in position by you, discontinue pushing him in place with your hand.

159

LESSON TWO — "SIT-STAY"

[*Before beginning Lesson Two with the dog, go over all the hand and foot positions with the child, using the leash and a stuffed animal. Concentrate especially on Steps 2, 3, 4, and 5. Allow the dog to relieve himself and then begin.*]

Tell Your Child (the Teacher) to:

Step 1.   Always begin the training lesson with a review of the previous week's lesson. Go through the first three steps of SIT before beginning the new lesson.

Step 2.   You are now going to teach the dog to STAY in the SIT position until you release him from it. This will involve a *hand signal* as well as a verbal command. The dog and the teacher should be standing side by side, facing the same direction, with the teacher on the right side of the dog. Hold the leash in the normal manner, with two or three feet draped across the teacher's knees. The leash is held in the right hand.

Step 3.   Look straight ahead, not at the dog. Give the verbal command "SIT." If the dog does not obey, give him a leash correction at the same time saying "NO." He should then go into the proper position. If he does not, go back to Lesson One, repeat the first three steps, and then begin Lesson Two again. Assuming the dog did obey the SIT command, then give him ten or fifteen seconds to get comfortable. Don't forget to praise the dog if he obeys the command. Praise him immediately after giving a correction, too.

Step 4.   Now give the command "STAY," without saying the dog's name but using the hand signal. Flatten your left hand as if for a salute and place it in front of the dog's face with the palm turned toward his eyes. If the dog moves, correct him with the leash, saying "NO." Don't forget to praise the dog after every correction.

Step 5.   Hold the leash straight up, above the dog's head about twelve or eighteen inches. As you do so, turn around and face the dog while keeping him in his SIT-STAY position. To do this, swivel on the ball of the left foot as you slowly move the right foot into a position that allows

Teaching the command SIT with the proper hand signal.

you to stand in front of the dog. Once the right foot is in place, bring the left foot to meet it. You are now facing the dog, holding the leash above his head to keep him in position. The leash must be taut. In a subdued tone of voice congratulate the dog for not moving (despite the fact that he was held in place). It is your leash control that teaches the command. Repeat Steps 3, 4, and 5 ten times, keeping the dog in the STAY position for fifteen seconds each time.

Step 6. While still standing in front of the dog as in Step 5, back away a few paces, allowing the leash to extend but always in a taut position. The dog will probably try to move toward you. Say, "NO," quickly return to your original position by the dog's right side, and maintain a taut leash extended above the dog's head. Again, swivel in front of the dog, using the verbal command "STAY," with the flattened hand signal in front of his face. Wait ten or fifteen seconds and try to back away several paces. Repeat Step 6 until the dog holds his position.

*To move in front of the dog as he remains in SIT-STAY, swivel on
the ball of the left foot as you slowly move the right foot into a position that allows you to stand in front of the dog.*

Step 7. Place the dog in the SIT position, using the verbal command
and giving him praise. Place your hand in front of his eyes and return it
to your side quickly while saying "STAY." Repeat Step 6 but try to go
to the end of the leash. Repeat Step 7 ten times.

Step 8. Repeat Step 7, but this time try walking half way around the
dog's right side. Once he allows you to do that without leaving his position, then try walking around his left side. Start over every time he
leaves his STAY position. Try walking a complete circle around the
dog as he holds his STAY position. Once he is holding his position,
place him in SIT and then STAY, move in front of him and then turn
your back. Another reinforcement of the STAY command is to command him to SIT and then STAY, drop the leash, and slowly walk away,
perhaps going around a corner. Always correct him if he breaks, and
start over again. If you are really bold, give him the command in the

162

Teaching SIT-STAY. Walk halfway around the left side of the dog while holding the leash tautly over his head.

presence of another dog. Remember, give the command and then the praise. If he does not obey, correct him and then praise him and start again. The more you practice this command, the longer the dog will be able to remain in SIT-STAY.

Release the dog from the session, saying in an enthusiastic tone of voice, "OKAY," and then walk him home.

Step 9. Repeat this lesson every day for six days.

LESSON THREE — "HEEL"

[Before beginning Lesson Three with the dog, go over all the hand and foot positions with the child, using the leash and a stuffed animal. Concentrate especially on Steps 3 and 4. Allow the dog to relieve himself and then begin.]

Once the dog has learned to hold the SIT-STAY position, move in front of him, drop the leash and slowly walk away. Correct him if he breaks and start over.

Tell Your Child (the Teacher) to:

Step 1. Put the dog through the paces of the first two commands. It is no longer necessary to teach the commands. The dog should be able to obey them once given. Practice SIT and then practice SIT-STAY. Praise the dog lavishly for performing well. This will prime him for the next teaching session.

Step 2. The teacher and the dog should be side by side as usual, facing in the same direction. Give him the command "SIT," and then "STAY." Hold the leash in your right hand in the normal manner, ready to execute a correction if necessary. Never correct the dog until *after* he has been taught a command. Allow enough slack in the leash so

Always begin the command HEEL by saying, "Johnny, HEEL," and start walking with the left foot, which is closest to the dog's line of vision.

that it drapes across the knees. In the verbal command for HEEL, the dog's name is used. HEEL is a forward-motion command, and the dog's name is what gets him going, along with the movement of the teacher's left foot.

Step 3. Give the command "JOHNNY, HEEL," and start walking with the left foot. No doubt the dog will run ahead. Allow him to get to the full end of the leash then make a hard right turn in a forceful march. As you turn, give the command "JOHNNY, HEEL." Then reverse directions, again giving the verbal command. Each time you change direction say, "JOHNNY, HEEL" in a very firm tone of voice. Praise the dog immediately after turning and again when the dog catches up with you, or at least tries to. Naturally, you must be gentle with a puppy or an extremely sensitive or fragile dog. But this is the

Teaching HEEL. Reverse directions by turning to the right. Each time you do it, tug the leash to the right and say, "Johnny, HEEL," in a very firm tone of voice. Praise the dog immediately after each tug of the leash.

moment of truth between dog and teacher. It is this lesson that firmly establishes the order of dominance in the dog's mind. Even if you do not execute HEEL perfectly, it will have a profound effect on both dog and teacher.

Step 4. Continue as in Step 3. Do not stop walking. Maintain a steady march rhythm until the dog catches up with the teacher. When he does, adjust the leash to the normal two feet across the knees. It is important for the teacher to talk to the dog, giving encouragement and praise even though she is being quite firm in her manner.

Every time the dog moves ahead of or behind the teacher, the teacher should turn right and march in that direction. On each turn say,

166

"JOHNNY, HEEL" in a very firm tone of voice and then praise the dog for catching up.

This lesson will be very hard on the dog but it is absolutely necessary. Praising the dog every time his head stays even with the teacher's legs or when he catches up will give him a sense of what is expected. Do not be surprised if you become entangled in the leash once or twice when turning. It is more likely to happen when you try to turn left, when the dog is even with your body. To do this you must tug the leash to the right, as in a correction, say, "JOHNNY, HEEL," and use your left leg to move the dog in that direction as you continue to make your left turn.

Step 5.   Take a five-minute break. Both you and the dog will need it. Allow the dog to relieve himself but do not engage in play.

Step 6.   Place the dog in the SIT-STAY position as before. Give the command "JOHNNY, HEEL" and start walking with the left foot. It is quite likely that the dog will be somewhat reticent and lag behind. Talk to the dog and encourage him to keep pace. "Come on, boy. Keep up, keep up. What a swell guy." The objective is to keep his attention fixed on the teacher and nowhere else when walking in HEEL. Once the dog has learned HEEL, he should pay a great deal of attention to whoever walks him in the future and gives the command "HEEL." After fifteen minutes end the lesson by saying "OKAY," and then walk the dog home for a well-deserved and much-needed rest. But the lesson is not over yet.

Step 7.   After an hour's rest, return to the training area with the dog. It is now time to teach him to stay even with the teacher's legs as he walks in HEEL. As in the first lesson, call the dog by name and let him run to the teacher. Review SIT and then SIT-STAY.

Step 8.   Place the dog in SIT-STAY. In the first part of this lesson the dog ran ahead and then lagged behind. Now his execution of the command must be sharpened. Because leash corrections will be necessary, it is desirable to hold the leash with both hands. Give the command "JOHNNY, HEEL," and start walking with the left foot. It is important now that the dog keep his head even with the teacher's knees. Whenever the dog is too far forward or too far behind, do the following: Correct the dog with a quick tug of the leash to the right and a quick

The objective is to keep the dog's attention fixed on the teacher when walking in HEEL.

release; say, "JOHNNY, HEEL"; turn right; and walk in the opposite direction. Praise the dog for following and catching up. Do not show any anger, only a firm sense of being in charge. Keep reassuring the dog that he is doing the right thing every time he catches up and keeps his head even with the teacher's knees. Keep repeating this action until the dog is walking evenly with the teacher's knees. Walk quickly, turn suddenly and with precision. It is almost like dancing, and masterful, graceful body movement communicates to the dog that this is important work. The teacher must be lively and in charge. This, more than any other command, gives you a sense of leadership and competence. The teacher is to take the dominant position and hold it for life. The dog will not mind at all.

Step 9. Conduct at least one twenty-minute practice session every day for six days. Take a break after ten minutes and practice for ten minutes more. Two practice sessions a day, one hour apart, are even better.

LESSON FOUR — "HEEL/SIT"

[Before beginning Lesson Four with the dog, go over the hand and foot positions for Step 3 with the child. Allow the dog to relieve himself and then begin.]

Tell Your Child (the Teacher) to:

Step 1.   Repeat everything the dog has learned thus far.

Step 2.   The objective of Lesson Four is to teach the dog to SIT without being given a command, every time the teacher stops walking with him in HEEL. It is accomplished by giving the dog an indication that the teacher is going to stop walking. The teacher simply slows down before coming to a halt. Slowing down is the signal for the dog to get ready to sit automatically once there is no more forward motion. This is one of the reasons it is important for the dog to focus on the teacher when walking in HEEL. Begin with the dog in the SIT/STAY position.

Step 3.   Give the command "JOHNNY, HEEL," and start walking with the left foot. Walk in HEEL for at least one minute and then begin to slow down. The following action should be done only during the teaching process and then abandoned forever. Come to a gradual halt. Give the dog the command "SIT." If he complies, as he should by now, give him much praise. If he does not, deliver a leash correction and say, "NO!" He should go into the SIT. When correcting the dog, never use the command word. You do not want the dog to have an unpleasant association with the command word. If the dog does not respond to the correction by obeying the command, you must teach him the SIT command all over again as described in Lesson One.

Step 4.   Repeat Step 3 over and over for at least twenty minutes. You may give the dog a break after ten minutes and finish up after the next ten minutes. End the session, as usual, by saying "OKAY," and then walk home.

Step 5.   Conduct one twenty-minute practice session every day for six days. Always review everything the dog has been taught in each session.

LESSON FIVE — "STAND"

[*Before beginning Lesson Five with the dog, go over the hand and foot positions with the child, using the leash and a stuffed animal. Concentrate on Steps 4, 5, and 6. Allow the dog to relieve himself and then begin.*]

Tell Your Child (the Teacher) to:

Step 1.   Repeat everything the dog has learned to this point. Remember, reviewing his other lessons does not mean teaching them all over again. It should be thought of as a quickie refresher.

Step 2.   The objective of Lesson Five is to teach the dog to STAND and to STAY without sitting or walking away. This will be useful when grooming or bathing the dog. It is also a blessing when you take the dog to the veterinarian's office for an examination. What makes this command difficult to teach is the dog's inclination to SIT whenever you stop. Remember, we taught him to do that.

Step 3.   Place the dog in SIT/STAY. Standing on his right side give the command "JOHNNY, HEEL," *and at a slower pace* start walking with the left foot. After four or five steps begin to stop and say, "STAND." It is important to say the command word before you stop or else the dog will automatically SIT.
Place the left hand lightly on the right side of the dog's stomach where it meets the right thigh. The dog will stop instantly because of the instinct to stand still when two dogs investigate each other. The dog should stand for as long as you keep your left hand under the rear section of his body. Wait a few seconds and remove your hand. Place the dog in SIT/STAY and then give the command for HEEL. Repeat this step fifteen times and take a five-minute break.

Step 4.   Place the dog in SIT/STAY. Standing at his right side, give the command "JOHNNY, HEEL," *and at a slower pace* start walking with the left foot. After four or five steps begin to stop and say, "STAND." Be certain to say the command word before you stop. Place the left hand in front of the dog's right hind leg. Incidentally, the teacher's hand should just barely touch the dog's body. Remove the

When teaching STAND, place the left hand on the right side of the dog's stomach where it meets the right thigh.

left hand and place it in front of the dog's eyes as was done for SIT/STAY and say, "STAY!"

Step 5. Remove your hand from the dog's eyes quickly, then swivel on the ball of the left foot and slowly move the right foot into position so you are standing in front of the dog. Once the right foot is in place, bring the left foot to meet it. Because the dog has been taught SIT/STAY and because the teacher has been giving the command in every training and practice session since the course was begun, the dog theoretically should STAY without any further instruction. If that is the case, then the teacher can slowly step backward, allowing the leash to extend as she does. If the dog holds the position, there is no need to keep the leash taut.

If the dog breaks he should quickly be given a leash correction accompanied by a very firm "NO!" This will mean that the teacher must move forward as she quickly gathers up the leash, so it can be jerked to the side and then released. Remember, do not repeat the command word when correcting the dog. Say, "NO!" After the correction praise the dog for taking the correction. Start from Step 4 over again if the dog does not return to the STAND/STAY position. If the dog obeys the command correctly, heap lavish praise on him and repeat the command fifteen times.

171

Step 6.   End the teaching session by saying "OKAY," and walking home.

Step 7.   Conduct one twenty-minute practice session every day for six days. Always review everything the dog has been taught in each session.

LESSON SIX — "DOWN" AND "DOWN/STAY"

This is the most difficult of all commands to teach a dog. Going into a DOWN position is the ultimate act of submission for a dog. Not only does he feel vulnerable to attack but it is the most complete acceptance of the teacher's domination. If your dog is one year old or more, if he is a very stubborn, very nervous or very aggressive animal, then it may be best to skip this command until an adult or professional dog trainer can teach it. The dog may balk and become uncooperative. If the child is gentle but firm, if the dog is young and has been properly obedient throughout the training and if the dog is of even temperament, then proceed to teach this command.

[*Before beginning Lesson Six with the dog, go over the hand and foot positions with the child, using the leash and a stuffed animal. Concentrate on Steps 2, 3, and 4. Allow the dog to relieve himself and then begin.*]

Tell Your Child (the Teacher) to:

Step 1.   Repeat everything the dog has learned to this point.

Step 2.   The command DOWN means exactly what it says. Upon verbal command plus a hand signal the dog should drop to the ground and remain there with his head held high and his front paws extended from his body.

Teach the dog this command on a smooth surface, such as a linoleum or hardwood floor. It is easier to get the dog into the correct DOWN position even if he is unwilling at first.

A word about the vocal intonation of the voice command "DOWN." When saying the command, extend the midddle sound of the word so that it comes out in an exaggerated manner. "DOWWWWWnnnn." It somehow helps the dog do what you want, but I'm not really sure why. Perhaps the trailing sound of the voice gives it a sort of body English.

Step 3.   There are two effective techniques to teach DOWN and the one chosen must be determined by the nature of the dog involved. The techniques are (1) pulling the dog by the front paws into a DOWN position as you give the command or (2) pushing the dog into a DOWN position by applying pressure to the leash with the bottom of your foot.

The most direct and uncomplicated technique is the first, pulling the dog's paws forward. However, a large dog may be too difficult to maneuver in this manner. An aggressive dog may bite when pulled at the paws. Technique Number Two, applying pressure to the leash with the foot to lower the dog to the ground on command, is the most practical one for training a large or uncooperative dog. It is also the safest method for the child.

Technique Number One. Place the dog in the SIT/STAY position. Stand beside him as in HEEL. Hold the leash with the right hand. Leave a small amount of slack so it drapes. Pivot with the left foot and place the right foot in front of the dog. Bring both feet together once you are facing the dog. The leash should be held above the dog's head to keep him in position. Kneel to the ground and take hold of both front paws with one hand, if you can. Say the command, "DOWWWWWnnnn," and gently but firmly pull the front paws forward. For puppies, small dogs and even-tempered dogs there is no choice but to slide into the DOWN position. Once the dog is in the DOWN position, heap lavish praise on him. Repeat this teaching procedure at least fifteen times and give the dog a ten-minute break. Allow him to relieve himself. After the break repeat the procedure until the dog offers no resistance whatsoever to being pulled into the DOWN position. You are now ready to teach the hand signal for DOWN.

Technique Number Two. (If you have used Technique Number One, go on to Step 4.) This is an alternative to the above if the dog is large, stubborn or aggressive. Place the dog in the SIT/STAY position. Stand beside the dog as in HEEL. Hold the leash with both hands. Allow a little more slack than usual so it drapes closer to the ground. Raise the left foot and place it on top of the leash at the center of the drape. Say, "DOWWWWWnnnn." As the voice descends in tone,

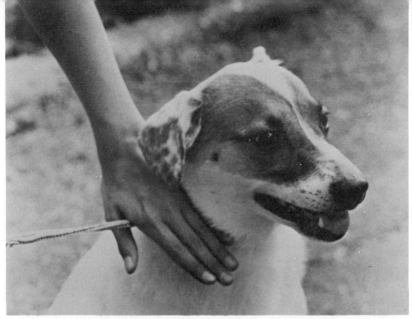

Use this hand-on-leash method for placing the dog in the DOWN position when teaching the hand signal for DOWN.

press the leash down with the left foot. This will force the dog to go down. Even a large, stubborn dog will slide down if the floor is somewhat slippery. As you push down with the foot, you must slide the leash upward across the bottom of the shoe. Do not pull up on the leash too quickly or too harshly. As the dog descends, pull the leash upward in a slow but steady manner. When the dog reaches the ground, praise him enthusiastically. Allow him to remain in the DOWN position for ten seconds and then say, "SIT." Praise him and then say, "STAY," using the proper STAY hand signal as taught in Step 4 of Lesson Two. Praise him again. Repeat this procedure fifteen times and give the dog a ten-minute break. Allow him to relieve himself. After the break repeat the procedure until the dog offers no resistance to going into the DOWN position. You are now ready to teach the hand signal for DOWN.

Step 4. Whether you used Technique One or Two to maneuver the dog into the DOWN position, you must now add the use of your hand as part of the command. Place the dog in SIT/STAY position. *Kneel* next to the dog at his right side facing in the same direction as the dog, as in HEEL. Hold the leash with the right hand across your chest and keep it taut. With a tight leash he can do nothing but SIT. Flatten your left hand as if for a military salute. Raise the left arm above the dog's head.

174

Once you get the dog into the DOWN position, give a great deal of enthusiastic praise. This may be the most difficult command to teach. Patience, kindness and firmness are required.

Say the command, "DOWWWWWnnnn," and lower the left arm so that the dog can see it coming down, past his eyes and onto the top of the taut leash at the clip. By now the dog should be lowering his body in response to the voice command. While you are still saying "DOWWWWWnnnn," your left hand should be pressing the leash all the way to the ground. Repeat this fifteen times. The objective is to associate your lowering hand with the command DOWN in the mind of your trained dog. Once this is accomplished you will be able to stand a good distance from the dog and simply give him the hand signal to which he will respond as he should. This could save his life in an outdoor traffic situation. If the dog does not respond properly or resists the teaching of this part of the lesson, place him in SIT/STAY position and begin again.

Once the dog is accustomed to seeing the hand come down onto the leash from the side, it is important to acclimate him to the hand coming down from the front. Place him in SIT/STAY with the dog at your left side, as in HEEL. Pivot around so that you are standing in front of the dog. This time hold the leash with the left hand, keeping it taut, as before. Kneel on one knee, flatten the right hand, raise the right arm above your head, keeping it straight, and then say the command "DOWWWWWnnnn." As you say the command, you must lower your arm, in full sight of the dog, landing on top of the leash, palm facing down. You may or may not have to apply pressure to the leash to force the dog into the DOWN position. At this time the dog should be moving into position at the sound of the command. Repeat this fifteen times or until the dog obeys both voice command and hand signal. Do not tolerate playfulness or any other avoidance behavior. When this happens, start over from the SIT/STAY position.

If the dog is not yet exhausted, take him through this one last step. The objective is to teach him to respond to the voice command and the hand signal for DOWN without the teacher's kneeling or applying pressure to the leash with the hand.

Stand in front of the dog from a distance of two feet. Allow as much slack in the leash as possible and hold it with the left hand. Give the command "SIT," praise the dog for obeying. Give the command "STAY," using the proper hand signal, and praise the dog for obeying. If the dog does not obey these commands, deliver a correction by tugging the leash quickly and releasing it while saying "NO." If the results are still not satisfactory, start over at the dog's side, as in HEEL. Repeat this procedure after making a pivotal turn to face the dog, as you have been doing throughout this lesson.

Assuming the dog has obeyed properly, you are ready to continue. He should be in a SIT/STAY position while you are standing in front of him. Flatten your right hand as if for a salute. Raise your right arm above your head in a straight line. Say the command "DOWWWWWnnnn," and lower the right arm onto the leash at the same time. The dog will probably obey the command and go down without any pressure from the right hand. Praise him and start over again without moving from the frontal position. Give him the SIT and STAY commands and then the DOWN command, repeating the above procedures fifteen times. Do not forget the very important hand signals.

You may try repeating this procedure from greater distances. At first, give the commands from the end of the fully extended leash. If the dog continues to respond properly, try it from six feet away without

Teaching DOWN/STAY is quite similar to teaching SIT-STAY. If the dog remains in STAY in the SIT position, he should repeat this behavior in DOWN. Bear in mind that some dogs feel more vulnerable when stretched flat on the ground in the DOWN position. Be patient.

holding onto the leash at all. Be ready to step in quickly to grab the leash and deliver a corrective tug if the dog moves or bolts from the proper position. If you are still experiencing success, try the command from two, three or even six feet away from the dropped leash. Always be prepared to make a quick grab for the leash if the dog bolts. End the session by saying "OKAY," and then walk home.

Step 5. Teaching DOWN/STAY should not be very difficult once the dog has learned to obey the command DOWN. After giving the command DOWN with the proper hand signal, give the dog his customary praise. Then say, "STAY," and use the appropriate hand signal (which is the flattened hand several inches in front of his eyes). Remove it quickly and once again praise the dog. Remember, he must be praised after executing each and every command. If the dog does not respond properly to DOWN/STAY, then review Steps 4, 5, 6, 7 and 8 from Lesson Two but in the DOWN/STAY position.

Step 6. Conduct one twenty-minute practice session every day for six days. Review everything in each practice session.

177

LESSON SEVEN — "COME TO ME"

COME TO ME is an extremely valuable command, one that could some day save the dog's life in traffic. On command the dog must discontinue any action and come running to the one who called. Once at the child's feet, the dog goes into the SIT position.

The verbal command is extremely important to the successful teaching and execution of this command. The child's voice must communicate to the dog that something wonderful is happening. Because this command involves forward motion, the dog's name is always said just before the word *come*. To further convey an exciting feeling, we use the word *okay* in front of the dog's name. The command, therefore, is *"OKAY,* JOHNNY, COME," with the stress on the word *OKAY*. If you always use the command in this manner, the dog will never be confused and will want to obey.

Never correct the dog while teaching this command. Never correct the dog after he has obeyed this command. When the dog comes to the child on command he should receive nothing but the highest praise, so that he will always obey the command with enthusiasm. This is extremely important. No dog will run to a human if he has experienced something unpleasant for his trouble.

[*Before beginning Lesson Seven with the dog, go over the hand and foot positions with the child, using the leash and a stuffed animal. Allow the dog to relieve himself and then begin.*]

Tell Your Child (the Teacher) to:

Step 1. Repeat everything the dog has learned up to this point.

Step 2. *On-leash.* Place the dog in SIT/STAY. With the leash in the left hand, stand in front of the dog, facing him, five feet away. Allow a slight slack in the leash.

Step 3. Call the dog with the proper command, *"OKAY,* JOHNNY, COME," in an extremely exuberant tone of voice. Because of your enthusiasm, the dog should move forward and come when called. If he does, give him heaps of praise for it. Repeat Step 3 fifteen times. If he does not come, then add more excitement to the tone of voice. Almost any dog will respond.

Step 4.   Once again place the dog in SIT/STAY. Stand in front of the dog, facing him, five feet away, with the leash in the left hand. Give the command *"OKAY,* JOHNNY, COME," while gently snapping the leash forward. The gentle snap of the leash should be on the word *OKAY.* When the dog moves to your feet, give him lots of praise. He should be thrilled and delighted about obeying this command. Repeat Step 4 fifteen times. Take a break.

Place the dog in SIT-STAY with the leash in the left hand. Call the dog with the proper command, "OKAY, JOHNNY, COME," in an exuberant tone of voice. Gently snap the leash forward on the word okay. *When the dog gets to you, heap loads of praise on him.*

Step 5.   *The hand signal.* This gesture is quite simple. One raises the right arm from the side and swings it around and across the chest. It is the same gesture one might make to call someone from afar.

Place the dog in SIT/STAY. Stand in front of the dog, facing him five feet away, with the leash in the left hand. Give the command *"OKAY,* JOHNNY, COME," as you gently snap the leash forward, *and then give the hand signal.* Remember, the leash is snapped on the word *okay.* The dog should be praised deliriously when he gets to your feet. Repeat Step 5 fifteen times. Rest a few minutes and then repeat it fifteen times again.

Step 6.   It is now time to teach the last phase of this command, and that is the SIT. Place the dog in SIT/STAY. Stand in front of the dog, facing him, five feet away with the leash in the left hand. Give the command *"OKAY,* JOHNNY, COME," gently snapping the leash on the word *okay.* Immediately after giving the hand signal, but as the arm moves forward, grab the leash and begin to pull it in, first with one arm and then the other so that it is held above the dog's head tautly when he gets to your feet. The dog must have no choice but to SIT once he is directly in front of you. Then give the command "SIT," praise the dog lavishly, and then give the command, "STAY," accompanied by the proper hand signal, and once again praise the dog. Repeat Step 6 fifteen times.

Step 7.   End the teaching session by saying "OKAY," and walking home.

Step 8.   Conduct one twenty-minute practice session every day for six days. Always review everything the dog has been taught in each session. Essentially, the dog is trained.

Practice every command at every opportunity, to reinforce the training in the dog's mind. Whenever the dog is going to be left alone, review all his commands for ten or fifteen minutes. It can make a difference between a dog that becomes destructive when left alone and one that does not. If you are going to travel with your dog or if you expect him to behave when company calls, review his commands for ten minutes beforehand. It makes a big difference in his behavior when you want him to be good.

*   *   *

Once the dog has learned COME TO ME, reinforce the training with a round robin game.

Allow me to repeat what was said at the beginning of this chapter. The objective here is *not* perfect dog obedience as commanded by the child and executed by the dog. This course is meant to promote communication and harmony between the dog and his family. If you desire a very well trained dog, I suggest you engage the services of a professional dog trainer, most of whom are proficient and quite helpful. An alternative is to purchase a book offering a complete dog training course and do it yourself. If you have the time and inclination, it is well worth the effort.

If you discover that your children are interested in dog training activities and demonstrate a desire to go further, on a more sophisticated level, there are options.

JUNIOR SHOWMANSHIP

The American Kennel Club sanctions and regulates an activity for youngsters that has become as popular as it is wholesome. Junior Showmanship is organized by local or regional kennel clubs, breed clubs or other AKC-affiliated associations. Essentially it is a class of competition at dog shows judging boys and girls between the ages of ten and seventeen years on their handling of dogs in the show ring. The prizes, awards and trophies are given for the skills of dog handling and have nothing to do with the show qualities of the dog. The dogs used, however, must be eligible to compete in dog shows or in obedience trials and that means AKC-registered purebreds. There are many local

Once the dog has been obedience trained he has the basis for many skills, including dog tricks. By learning a dog's natural inclinations one can develop exhilarating activities utilizing obedience commands with a sense of fun. It also makes for good mental hygiene. Refer to the Suggested Reading List for a good dog tricks book.

and regional competitions for youngsters to aim for. The most sought-after "wins" are at the Westminster Kennel Club Show in New York's Madison Square Garden; the Kennel Club of Beverly Hills; International Kennel Club of Chicago; Ottawa Championship show in Canada; and others in the southern and western regions of the United States. For information about Junior Showmanship, contact your local kennel club or write to American Kennel Club, 51 Madison Avenue, New York, New York 10010.

THE 4-H CLUB

Nationally, every 4-H Club offers a dog care and training project that teaches obedience training, dog handling and everything pertaining to a dog's well-being. These projects are among the finest activities for

youngsters in 4-H Clubs, which, of course, are found all over America. Development of the child is also part of the dog program, with an emphasis on assuming responsibility. There is another program that the 4-H Club offers, but only in nine areas of the United States. They have a puppy-raising project that comes out of the various dog guide schools for blind people. Children receive two-month-old puppies, bred by the schools. The children keep them for one year, socializing them by providing a loving atmosphere and general home-living conditions in preparation for the day when the dog will live with a blind person. The kids teach the dogs simple obedience training. At the appropriate time the kids turn them back to the school, where they begin guide dog training. To become involved with a local 4-H Club, look in your phone directory under your county government listing and look for: *County Extension Service*. For literature and information, write to National 4-H Council, 7100 Connecticut Avenue, Washington, D.C. 20015. The 4-H Club is sponsored by the United States Department of Agriculture.

For other youth organizations offering further training and education on the subject of dogs, write to any of the following organizations:

BOYS SCOUTS OF AMERICA
P.O. Box 61030
Dallas/Fort Worth Airport Station
Dallas, TX 75261

GIRL SCOUTS OF THE U.S.A.
830 Third Avenue
New York, NY 10022

BOYS CLUBS OF AMERICA
771 First Avenue
New York, NY 10017

GIRLS CLUBS OF AMERICA
205 Lexington Avenue
New York, NY 10016

NATIONAL ASSOCIATION OF GIRLS CLUBS
5808 16th St. N.W.
Washington, DC 20011

CAMP FIRE GIRLS
4601 Madison Avenue
Kansas City, MO 64112

Seven

Dog/Child,

Child/Dog Problems

Most problems are solvable. If a dog has a problem with a child or the child has a problem with a dog, it must be confronted and dealt with in a sensible manner. Although few parents would consider getting rid of the child, unfortunately the dog, for some, seems more expendable. To simply "throw the dog away" is not only foolish, it is a terrible example to set for a child. It would create the false value that life is cheap, nature is unessential, and that we humans are not a part of the natural world. It is to teach alienation. Children should understand that we are as vulnerable as our dogs. To get rid of a dog because one cannot cope with a behavior problem is an insensitive act that ultimately leads to a dog's destruction. Old-age homes are filled with persons who have been "thrown away" by children who were given that value. In relation to solving problems concerning your family pet, I can only quote Theodore Roosevelt: "Take your place and hold your ground."

THE-FIRST-WEEK-HOWLING-CHEWING-SOILING-BLUES OR "HOW DID I EVER GET INTO THIS MESS?" SERENADE

Not even the first day with a first baby is as rough as the first few days with a new dog if you've never been through it before. To be honest, it is almost impossible if the adults are away all day at a job while the kids are at school and there is no one to be with the new dog. That is a situation best avoided.

Whether or not the first week with your new dog is the most miserable time of your life depends on knowing what to expect and what to do about it. Expect a new puppy to pee or defecate indiscriminately wherever and whenever it wants to. You can also expect crying, howling and whimpering into the wee hours of the night along with scratching to get out of whatever enclosure the dog is behind. If the dog is left alone and not confined you will come home to puddles, piles and chewed-up possessions (yours). An unconfined puppy, left alone, can be expected to leave behind a wake of destruction not to mention the crying and whining. You'll know it whined because of the petition slipped under your door signed by all your neighbors.

What to Do

An even-tempered puppy adapts to change better than a submissive one. However, going from the security of the breeder's kennel, the pet shop environment or humane shelter is such a drastic change that few puppies take it in their stride. Therefore, the first element you and the kids must deal with is the little dog's deep insecurity and fear of the new home. This can be helped only by approaching the problem with sensitivity and common sense.

Do not worry about dog training, obedience or proper behavior the minute the pup walks into the house. There will be plenty of time for that later, once the newcomer adjusts to the new surroundings and people. Adults should not holler around the puppy, no matter who the object of wrath is. An hysterical human can most definitely create hysterical behavior in a dog. Try to remember that the puppy is all input and absorbs all the elements in your environment like a sponge and will be greatly influenced by them. The children can cause problems that only add to the difficulties in getting through the first week.

Do not allow rough handling of the dog, arguments about who gets to do what with it and the length of time spent with the animal. RESTRICT THE KIDS' TIME WITH THE NEW PUPPY TO FIFTEEN-MINUTE INCREMENTS SPACED ONE OR MORE HOURS APART FOR THE FIRST DAY OR TWO. This will give the dog the rest time it needs, as well as not getting it too stimulated. The more a puppy runs around, the more frequently it will pee! However, puppies and kids can

develop meaningful relationships early on if the adult in the situation supervises them. When pup meets kid it should be in a relaxed atmosphere, with nothing more than a cuddling exchange between the two or a gently rolled ball. Uncontrolled fits of giggly hysterics may seem like fun but it does not help you get through the hard night ahead.

As discussed in chapter 5 ("Housebreaking and Other Delights"), you must select an area of confinement for the new dog and allow that to be his sanctuary. Choose a small room or a portion of a room and fence the dog in with the help of a wire gate that jams against both ends of the doorway. The kitchen is the place most often used for this purpose. You may consider going to the expense of a wire dog crate that is suited to your dog's size. It must not be too big or it will lose its denlike appeal for the dog. Outfit the dog's area with a soft bed of some kind. One can purchase a formal dog bed, use a carton with a cushion or blanket in it, or simply use a folded blanket on the floor.

Puppies start eliminating the minute they trot into your home and necessitate the early stages of housebreaking (see chapter 5, "Housebreaking and Other Delights"). This means that you will have to develop the outdoor toileting areas immediately for the dog and place her on a feeding-walking-confinement schedule right from the start. This will take most of the unpleasantness out of your life immediately. I would caution you to maintain an awareness that you are housebreaking a very young dog who has just experienced the most important change in her life. That means being very gentle about anything that resembles training and the way the dog is handled or related to. Read chapter 5 very carefully.

Under close supervision, allow the puppy to explore her new home from room to room, giving her an opportunity to gain much-needed confidence that she is in no danger. Introduce the kids and adults to her ONE AT A TIME, maintaining a relaxed ambience. The objective is to alleviate her fears and give her a sense of security. By the same token it is helpful to gently develop in the dog her place in the social structure. She must be subordinate to the human members of the family, and that includes the kids. This can be achieved by having each member of the family, if he or she is old enough, cradle the dog in his or her arms on its back for a few minutes several times each day for the first week. This places the puppy in a submissive position and helps establish human dominance, which will make your life infinitely more pleasant in the years to come. After a few minutes place the dog on the floor and congratulate her for accepting this. Pet her and tell her what a good girl she is. This will reinforce the concept that accepting human dominance is rewarding and inevitable. If the dog resists being cradled on its back, insist with endearing entreaties and soft-spoken praise.

The most difficult time during the first week will be the nights when the dog will want to be free to roam and alleviate his fears. Most puppies cry and howl, whimper and whine and then try to claw their way out of their confinement. There are a limited number of things to do about this that may or may not be effective. However, understanding that this is a very temporary form of behavior helps get everyone through the night. If the dog was recently parted from his mother and littermates, he is howling for them. If he came from some other environment, he is in a state of confusion and fear. It all boils down to anxiety.

One must find a balance between rewarding whining with attention, thus promoting it as a general form of behavior, and alleviating fear with petting, stroking and soft-talk. I find that talking directly to a puppy in a loving tone of voice throughout the day establishes the gentle line of communication needed so that a firmer tone of voice (not harsh or abusive) is not terrifying when needed.

When a new puppy cries in the dark during the first nights, there are some things to try. Fill a hot water bottle with warm water, wrap it in a towel, and place it next to the puppy in his bed. This sometimes soothes the animal because it is like lying next to his littermates. We've all heard this one before, but it can be quite effective — place a ticking alarm clock near the dog so that it simulates the beat of his mother's heart. Believe it or not, one can even purchase a 33⅓ rpm recording of a heart beating. A low-playing radio can also be effective in soothing an anxiety-ridden puppy coping with his first nights in your home. Some puppies respond better to music and others are comforted by the human voice on an all-night talk show. Whether you tune in to rock, classical or elevator music is strictly between you and your dog.

FEAR OF DOGS

Dogs can be very frightening to some kids. This should come as no surprise. What with so many stories about "the big bad wolf" in books, movies and TV, the dog, a close cousin, can be viewed as a ferocious beast that will bark and bite and pretend to be Grandma after swallowing her whole and hopping into her bed just to fool Little Red Riding Hood. The child who is afraid of dogs is somewhat overpowered by this strange-looking animal's energy and seemingly uncontrollable behavior. If there has never been a bad experience with a dog, then the child's fear is irrational and must be dealt with in a soothing, gentle manner. The irrational things that frighten people are as real to them as those that are truly justified. It is wrong to foist a dog on a child who is terrified of them. It is far better to try ending the fear with talks about dogs and with photographs and stuffed toy dogs. A visit with a benign dog (not too close in the beginning) is a better way to introduce the child to real dogs than suddenly bringing one into your home. Do not join the sink-or-swim school of behavior wherein one throws a frightened child into the deep end of the pool and says, "Swim or drown." That is not only cruel, but terribly destructive. The child who can overcome his fear of dogs will benefit greatly. But it must be accomplished slowly and patiently and with loving understanding of the child's problem.

PREVENTING PROBLEMS BEFORE THEY START

Soiled carpets, all-night howling and scattered garbage from the pail are part of the puppy experience and quite normal . . . for a while. These are typical puppy problems and will end in time with some basic obedience training and diligent corrections. But has your dog drawn blood from your finger yet? If so, are you all still on speaking terms? What are you doing that is reinforcing this behavior for a lifetime?

Does the dog flinch when you raise your hand? Does he run from you the minute you enter the room? In some respects these are more serious problems than what the dog has done. These are the results of hitting and hollering. A frightened puppy grows into a shy dog, and that leads to more problems than you can imagine at this stage of the dog's life. Shy dogs relate only to their owners, sometimes only one member of the family. They cower at everything and everyone. They bite the minute your back is turned. They bark irrationally and indulge in every bit of behavior that has been labeled neurotic. Shy dogs are, for the most part, antisocial and not a lot of fun. An hysterical person very often creates a "hyper" or hysterical dog. A household that is chaotic makes a dog chaotic — we all know that a dog functions best in a consistent routine. As we temper our behavior for our relatives, friends, employers and fellow workers, we must try to do the same for our dogs. Most behavior problems are preventable. We hardly ever realize what our contribution was in creating these behavior problems.

All the hollering you are capable of and all the smacking and swatting you can muster will never get an animal to behave the way you want it to. First, you must understand that dogs can never be like people. Ideally, a house pet should be required to behave itself, but in canine terms. This comes about through instruction, leadership and determined insistence. Obviously, an obedience-trained dog behaves much better than one who isn't. But such puppy problems as nipping, biting, chewing, jumping and excessive barking are too often the result of humans' unwittingly encouraging, and even teaching, such behavior.

It is safe to say that the lack of obedience, training is not the sole cause of problem behavior. The way we relate to our puppies teaches them how to behave positively or negatively. Your new puppy adores you and everything else connected with you — including your shoes, socks, carpets, garbage bags and your most valuable possessions. How do you feel when you come home to find your most valuable property gnawed and mangled by your young dog's young teeth? Own up to it. Don't you feel a surging, hot rage that borders on hatred, laced with a desire for revenge? But think about it. Did you or did you not give your sweet and adorable puppy an old sneaker to gnaw on or one of those stupid toys shaped like some object in your house, such as a latex pork chop or a plastic rolled-up newspaper? Well, that's probably where the chewing habit became generalized.

Your new puppy adores you and everything connected with you, including your shoes. Beware.

Chewing problems begin with a young dog's teething or his anxiety or his boredom. Once the dog finds solace in chewing and gnawing away on something, anything, it quite easily becomes a habit. From the habit stage it turns into a generalized behavior pattern that is indulged when experiencing any and all forms of emotional upset. In the first year of a dog's life it experiences gum irritations and itching sensations from the eruptions of new teeth or the settling into place of those that have been in for a while. The answer lies in veterinary attention. Sometimes a few ice cubes or a half-frozen, bone-shaped toy soothes the discomfort and prevents the problem before it begins.

Anxiety and boredom are problems that have obvious solutions. Do not scare the dog and do not leave him alone for long periods of time. Here, your most effective device is a collapsible wire dog crate. First, it prohibits the dog's ability to destroy your property or even develop the habit. Second, it eases anxiety by appealing to the dog's *denning* instinct. Even boredom is somewhat alleviated because the crate encourages the dog to sleep while you're gone. Do not misunderstand. A dog crate is not the complete answer to a dog's anxiety and boredom problems. Exercise, attention and other forms of mental and physical stimulation are the answer. But the crate helps a great deal. Having another dog or even a cat might help.

If you want to prevent your dog from chewing, never give him anything to chew if it resembles in any way your personal belongings or valued objects in the house. How on earth can a dog distinguish between an old towel and a new one, an old sneaker and a new pair of pumps from Bonwit's? And never give the dog some of your child's old toys to play with. You will be teaching the puppy to grab the new ones and munch them to shreds. By the way, many objects not meant for chewing can cause serious medical problems for the dog. Teething dogs can chew on ice cubes or a frozen cloth that was dampened. Rawhide bones are okay, but I do not recommend very small ones, not even for small dogs. They can be swallowed whole. The best chew toy is a product called "Nylabone."

Nipping and biting problems are intolerable and must be stopped the moment they begin. The nip of a puppy may tickle, but when that youngster grows into a dog it can tear a muscle or even break a human bone with its teeth and powerful jaws. Nipping often begins with teething or it may be related to the inherited temperament of the dog. More than likely it was behavior that was encouraged and possibly taught by humans during puppyhood. Keep your fingers out of the dog's mouth. It is not a proper way to play with a puppy. A finger in her mouth teaches her to bite. It can become a horror.

Bear in mind that fun and games and sweet-talk are rewards that actually teach a puppy to do whatever she was doing at the time the reward was given. When you allow your dog to sit in your lap whenever she is excited, you are not only teaching her to jump on you but also to sit on the furniture. We teach our puppies to jump on us by lifting them to our laps in response to their jumping on our legs. It is an unintentional reward for doing the wrong thing. Remember, it's cute as a puppy. But try to imagine this same behavior when the dog is full grown and behaving this way to guests in your house. It will be much more difficult to stop at that point. Don't expect a dog to refrain from jumping on visitors and strangers if she is allowed to do it to you.

Barking is another serious problem that must be stopped as it begins in puppyhood. The small yiping of a sweet baby dog soon becomes full-throated barking and howling and can get your neighbors quite angry. There are hundreds of precedents of judges ordering tenants to get rid of the dog or vacate the premises. Excessive barking is no joke. Sometimes dogs are encouraged to bark by receiving a favorable response to this behavior. It is bad enough if you have a breed with a predisposition

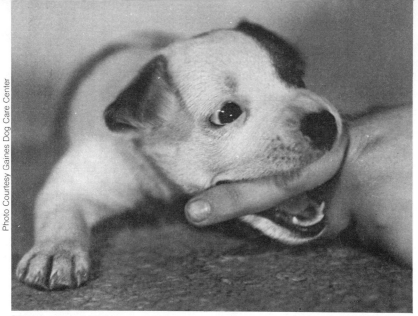

Nipping and biting problems are serious and must be stopped the moment they begin.

toward barking, such as the terriers. But to laugh when a puppy barks in response to your command is asking for trouble. You are then teaching a dog to bark, actually rewarding him for it, and also encouraging him to "talk back" when given a command. It is a violation of the dominant role you are supposed to assume. Avoid this at all costs. It is much easier to teach a dog not to bark as a puppy than to try to solve the problem later on. Vigorious daily exercise often stops a chronic barker from disturbing the neighbors when you're gone.

The typical dog is an animal very willing to please you. It is the fair trade for love, trust and kindness. It is not difficult to persuade a puppy to live in your home on your terms. Just remember to reward good behavior with praise and enthusiastic approval. Bad behavior is to be rewarded with physical corrections such as shaking the puppy while saying "NO" in a firm tone of voice or tugging the leash as explained in chapter 6, "Teaching Parents to Teach Their Child to Train Their Dog." Although there is no profit in abusing your dog, you must be consistent and insistent on what the dog can and cannot do. Puppyhood presents humans with the best opportunity to create the most desirable behavior in their dogs. Pay attention to your own behavior in front of your puppy. She's got her eyes on you and your children, and it's more than puppy love.

BITING

The reasons dogs bite are inherited aggression, aggression created by environmental influences (humans), or medical problems. It is based on fear and/or the aggressive defense of territory. Fear-biters or shy biters are essentially very frightened and timid dogs. They do their damage as a way of defending themselves against an anticipated harm. It is an uncontrollable response to something terrifying. It could be as simple as a visitor walking into the same room. Biters may also be dogs who have been hit or beaten, abandoned, tormented, or taught to be vicious. Some dogs chase and/or bite those they perceive to be intruding on their territory.

All dog owners should be observant and learn to spot the early signs of biting behavior. It is important for the safety of the child and the future of the dog. When a puppy snaps, nips, or bullies in any way, it must be dealt with firmly, effectively and instantly. Like some humans, some dogs have been genetically endowed with more aggressiveness than is good for them. Look for intense barking. The potential danger can be gauged by the ferocity of the barking. A dog who growls and snarls at you from deep within his throat; chases people, bicycles or cars; or maintains an aggressive body language is a potential biter. Some dogs and puppies snarl at anyone approaching their food bowl and even snap. This is not normal. This is not acceptable. A puppy nip is the equivalent of an adult dog bite. Take it seriously!

The Cure.   Obedience training and an uncompromising attitude toward this behavior are the only true answers. You could have a very aggressive male dog castrated and that will settle him down. However, it takes at least six weeks or more for it to become effective. That is the time required for all of the male hormone, *testosterone,* to leave the animal's body. A dog can be well trained by that time, in the hands of a skilled professional. Of course, in extreme cases it is best to do both.

The reason obedience training is the only effective method of coping with a biting problem is twofold. First, it firmly establishes dominance over the dog and gets him in a generally subordinate frame of mind. Second, biting behavior is stopped with enforced corrections and only a trained dog or a dog in training responds to corrections *if properly given.* One of America's most respected dog trainers, Captain Arthur

J. Haggerty, says, "When your dog bites someone, you ⸍
weeks late."

STEALING FOOD FROM YOUR CHILD

This is a bit of behavior that seems harmless from a puppy or young
dog but is quite serious from a full-grown one. It is more than annoy-
ing. If the child is young enough, it can be frightening and even dangerous. Some dogs have the audacity to place their front paws up on a
child's shoulders in order to get a good balance as they chomp at the
desired food. The child, out of fear, may pull away and make the dog
aggressive and snappy. Someone could get hurt, and it's bound to be
the child if he or she is small.

Make no mistake, all but the obedience-trained dogs will go for
something that smells good. There are two aspects to handling this situation. First, it must be a fixed rule that the dog is never *hand fed.* This
should especially apply to the kitchen and dining area, where the dog is
likely to beg for food. Begging for food is out completely. The dog
must always be fed from his bowl. Second, the dog must be consistently
and firmly corrected each and every time there is an incident involving
food.

How, you may ask, can this be accomplished unless the leash is attached to the collar at all times? If the dog collar is on (and it should be
at all times), you can make an improvised correction by tugging the
collar to the side in a firm manner and saying "NO." Once the dog is
down, be nice and say, "Good girl." Correction without praise immediately afterward is ineffective.

A more precise way of ending this problem is setting up the situation
under controlled conditions and then giving a proper correction. Place
the leash and training collar on the dog (see chapter 6, "Teaching Parents to Teach Their Child to Train Their Dog," *Praise* and *Correction.*)
Allow the dog to walk around with them on for fifteen or twenty minutes. Then send your child out toward the dog with a salami sandwich.
Watch from the other room. The instant the dog goes for the food, rush
in, grab the leash and tug it hard to the right, then release it instantly.
As you tug the leash say, "NO," in a loud, harsh voice. Once the dog
has recovered from the surprise, give him immediate praise. Then walk
the dog to his own food bowl and hold it up to him and once again offer

praise. This is a teaching technique as well as a corrective technique. A food problem must not be allowed to develop into a steady habit. Your child's safety is at stake.

SHOULD THE DOG SLEEP WITH YOUR CHILD?

Whether to allow the family dog to sleep on the bed or not is one of those issues that must be confronted directly. Decide how you feel about it before it becomes an issue, so you allow yourself a choice. For many, sleeping with their dog is the most pleasant part of owning a pet. There are those who merely yield to their animal's wishes but secretly agonize over the question. For those who have recently acquired a puppy, now is the best time to decide whether to allow it or not.

Is there any luxury greater than sliding between two crisp bed sheets, freshly laundered and pressed? But what about those grayish pawprints smudged across the clean pillows, trailing onto the blanket like wolf tracks in the snow? A dog of generous coat will certainly leave more than a few hairs on the blanket and perhaps a sprinkle of that night's dinner as well. A dog must, by some genetic echo, deposit onto the bedding whatever it was that he walked through or brushed up against that day. Expect more than a broken whisker.

Whether dog fur or tracks on your child's bed is good hygiene or bad depends on the life-style of the animal and the diligence of the parents

196

involved. But that has to do only with physical hygiene. Emotional or personal hygiene is also an issue.

From a special perspective one can view childhood as an ongoing process where the child slowly, sometimes painfully, learns to separate from the parents and become independent. Starting with infancy, children are continually learning to leave home and meet the world. However, this is a frightening challenge loaded with emotional ambivalence. Children, especially infants, become attached to a "huggy" or a "lovey" as an object to cling to during the emotionally stormy periods. Teddy bears and security blankets are fine for toddlers, but a dog is more acceptable for an older child.

If a youngster is lucky enough to have his or her own dog, sleeping with it should be permitted, provided the child wants to and Mom and Dad have no objections. Most animals will settle down at the foot of the bed and not want to be held throughout the night. However, if both child and pet want to nest together, that is fine. A living, breathing teddy bear can do more for a child striving for independence than parental strategy. A dog can be an object of affection without the child's losing ground in the striving for maturity. It is a more important form of hygiene than clean sheets. It can also be the answer if your child crawls into your bed in the middle of night and you find that unacceptable.

The most desirable life-style for a dog lies somewhere between the parameters of instinctive behavior and the needs and conditions set up by the human family. Adult human beings need the warmth and comfort of fellow creatures as do children and will often reach out to the family pet. Whether the dog curls up on top of your child's feet or actually snuggles under the blanket, it will make one feel less alone and somewhat needed. Fortunately, the animal feels the same about the child.

Sleeping with a dog in the same bed is one of the more loving, deeply gratifying comforts in life. But the idea of cleanliness where we sleep is an important one. Is it clean, hygienic or even healthy to allow our pets in bed with us? In truth, it is not, unless certain precautions are taken.

There is no avoiding some amount of superficial dirt on the animal's paws. This can be easily removed with a slightly damp towel before allowing the pet in bed. Make it a habit to brush your dog's coat each night. This will remove most dirt and debris as well as make the animal feel awfully good. Check between toes and clean them out if necessary. It is a favorite hiding place for fleas.

Clip the dog's nails every two or three weeks and check them constantly. There is nothing worse than getting scratched up because of the dog's bad dream or getting rolled upon. If you have recently sprayed or powdered your animal for fleas, do not allow him to sleep in the bed until the fumes of the insecticide have worn off. Many dogs wear an all-year flea collar. Remove it before bedtime. This is especially important.

Some internal parasites can be transmitted to humans, and all external parasites will definitely be transmitted. Therefore, veterinary examinations become an absolute necessity for dogs who sleep in human beds, as are frequent baths, brushings and combings. There are several *zoonoses* (diseases that can be transmitted from animal to human), but they are uncommon and not a problem if your dog enjoys reasonable veterinary scrutiny.

If your dog is indoors most of the time and has reasonable living habits, along with a clean environment, then sharing the bed is a great idea. When the world closes in, dogs and kids can cling to each other and set things right again.

WHEN YOUR CHILD IS ALLERGIC TO DOGS

Unless you've lived through it, you cannot imagine the fright connected with an asthma attack. Some attacks are merely terrifying, but others are actually life-threatening. When a child wakes in the middle of the night and gasps for breath, parents are ready and willing to do anything to bring relief. If an allergist concludes that your child's problems are connected to the dog, weigh the situation carefully before destroying the dog's life by moving him out.

If you have lived with the dog more than one month it is quite likely that the child will be emotionally shattered at the thought of giving it up. It could be exchanging a serious illness for a psychological scar that stays for a lifetime. It is too often an emotional impossibility to dispose of the animal as if it were a used paper cup. Not only are the feelings of the patient involved, but there are humane considerations as well. Finding a good home for a "used" pet is almost impossible.

The symptoms of allergy are varied. On the skin they are rashes, blisters, itchiness, hives (swellings similar to large mosquito bites). In the nose they are stuffiness, sniffing, sneezing, itching and a constant watery running. The eye symptoms of allergy are watery secretions, itchiness and red irritation from rubbing. Respiratory symptoms are coughing, wheezing, hoarseness, infection of the sinuses and even fainting spells and dizziness. Asthma is a chronic respiratory disease, often caused by allergies. It involves labored breathing, chest pain and a hacking cough. There are many other symptoms, but these are the most common.

One could describe an allergy as an uncomfortable or painful or life-threatening reaction to a food, a drug or a substance in the daily living environment that does not normally affect other people. The treatment of allergies is an extremely important, specialized field of medicine. Allergists sometimes save lives and certainly bring needed relief to those children and adults so afflicted. Many elements in the environment cause allergies in children, but here we are dealing with the allergic reaction to dogs as confirmed by clinical testing.

Most allergic children are sensitive to more than one substance. Merely removing a dog from the house may not rid the child of his or her allergic symptoms. Only a medical doctor specializing in the field of allergies can determine which allergies your child has. This is accomplished through the taking of a complete medical history plus extensive testing by the doctor in his clinic. Once it has been determined that your child is allergic to all dogs, or perhaps just your dog, then something must be done about it.

Sensitivity to animals is among the most common allergies in the United States, according to the Asthma and Allergy Foundation of America. The sensitivity is usually seen in the form of allergic rhinitis (sneezing, nasal stuffiness, nasal discharge and itching) or by bronchial asthma (cough, shortness of breath and wheezing). Unfortunately, no one is allergic to a substance the first time she or he comes in contact with it. Two years is a normal time to become allergic, although sometimes it may be much sooner than that and sometimes much later.

According to allergist Dr. Doris J. Rapp in her book *Questions and Answers About Allergies and Your Family,* it is not only the pet's hair but its dandruff and saliva that start allergic symptoms. Another source may be some proteins in the urine of animals. Cats and horses, however, seem to cause more extreme reactions than other pets. Dr. Rapp, who maintains an allergy practice in Buffalo, New York, states in her book that all humans, especially children, need love and understanding, which at times only a pet can furnish. If the pet's departure will cause more emotional difficulty than the allergic symptoms created, then the pet could possibly stay for a trial period. Dr. Murray Dworetzki, a New

York Hospital physician and clinical professor of medicine at Cornell University Medical College, says that it is best for people with any allergy history not to acquire an animal if they do not already own one. But he also says that if a person displays the same symptoms outdoors as he does at home, then it probably has nothing to do with the animal. Because a patient has asthma is not enough justification for getting rid of an animal. The doctor will want to know if the patient is worse when he is near the animal or if he feels better by going away for two or three weeks.

There *are* steps you can take to make it possible for an allergic child to coexist with the animal, and it may well be worth a try before making any final decision on whether to keep the pet. Observe the following suggestions:

1. Keep the pet outdoors if possible.
2. Or confine the pet to the basement or kitchen. Never allow the pet in the child's bedroom or on the furniture. Never let the child lie on a carpet the pet is allowed on.
3. Wash hands thoroughly after contact with the pet.
4. A dust mask may help the child when going into the pet's area or dealing with its possessions. The grooming and care of the pet should be carried out by some person other than the allergic child.
5. To reduce the air contamination, connect an air-filtering system to the furnace or at least use portable units (a high-efficiency particulate air filter, i.e., HEPA-type, is recommended by some doctors) in the rooms where the pet is allowed.

Dworetzki advises keeping the animal out of the allergic child's bedroom at all times. *Allow the bedroom to become a sanctuary with the door closed, and keep the room absolutely clean.* If a person spends a large portion of time in the bedroom, he or she may be able to tolerate an animal in the rest of the house. In conjunction with the animal-free sanctuary, immunization against the animal may be helpful.

There are only two conventional therapies for dealing with allergies. The first is to avoid the substance or the source of the substance. The second is to take a long series of injections that are meant to desensitize the patient to the substances causing the allergy. Desensitizing the patient does not always work. For a child with severe asthma caused by an allergic reaction to dogs there is no other choice than to observe complete avoidance of the animal and that, sadly, may mean the dog has to go.

Sometimes an allergen only causes symptoms when in partnership with other allergens. In some cases, dog allergens upset an allergic child only if they are combined with house dust, pollen, etc. It is worth investigating this. There are some allergists who take an inflexible position about keeping the animal, but more and more are working with the parents of children with pets to find better answers. Living in these enlightened times has made allergists aware of the intense feelings existing between most people (especially children) and their pets. Many are trying to find a way for allergy sufferers to go on living with their dogs without serious consequences. There is a great deal of research being conducted, and there is much hope.

INDIFFERENCE TOWARD THE DOG

The average life span of a dog is ten to fifteen years. If your child is between five and ten years old when she or he gets a dog, it means the two will be together for the better part of childhood. During those growing years the child will shift from periods of inner comfort to inner turmoil. It's to be expected. There will be periods when the dog is left on the outside wondering why his best pal doesn't show interest in him anymore. You, too, may wonder.

After one year the dog is pretty much who he is for the rest of his life. People are much different. Sometimes it takes an entire lifetime to figure that out or make it happen. Children are in a constant state of change (as the dog remains who and what he is). Consequently, the child's needs change. It is to be desired that children turn toward their friends for companionship, trust and sharing. As kids grow they reflect off one another to see who they have become and what they may do about the rest of their lives. The key issues become schoolwork and the ensuing grades, the opposite sex, clothes, suitable forms of entertainment, acceptance in the society of their friends, and much more. With all of that spinning around it is quite possible for the dog to get lost in the shuffle. If parents allow it, the growing child becomes indifferent to the entire family.

If the dog was merely the child's companion, then the transition and shift of interest is inevitable and must be tolerated. However, if the child is responsible for the dog's care and then neglects him, something must be worked out. A dog must always be fed, walked, groomed and given some attention. He doesn't want to hear about clearing up zits on the face and whether or not one should wear jogging shoes on a date.

If the dog is getting the cold shoulder, it may help to have a talk with your kid. During the ups and downs of preadolescence and adolescence the dog can be an important source of emotional comfort and stability. You can point out how the dog is being cheated and ignored and must get some of the kid's attention. Sometimes that solves the problem. If not, suggest a new schedule involving less responsibility for the dog's physical needs but assuming a few more of the dog's emotional needs. Five or ten minutes a day of "hands on" attention goes a long way for a dog. A brief period of obedience commands, as a practice or brush-up session, will make the dog feel wanted and appreciated. One could suggest that the child's friends might enjoy the dog's company if taken along on a few occasions. The name of the game is compromise. During this period other members of the family are going to have to share the dog if he is going to remain a tractable pet who is still nice to be with. It is more than likely that the child will eventually rediscover the dog as a valued friend and cherished member of the family.

BIRTH CONTROL

Dogs are not monogamous and will mate with any available partner if the female of the species is in heat (estrus). Dogs that are allowed to roam are the most likely to mate if the conditions are correct. Backyard breeding is a disaster in the making. Planned matings are complex and require knowledge and skill from serious breeders if quality puppies are desired. One must understand the mechanics of canine sex and possess a well-grounded knowledge of genetics and dogs.

The mating of pet dogs is considered undesirable by society in general and especially by those involved in humane activities. There are far more dogs than homes to place them in, a fact soon discovered by those with puppies to dispose of. Abandoned dogs and homeless dogs are victims of disease, traffic, human cruelty, animal attack or euthanasia when finally rounded up by animal control officers. The mating of most pets comes from carelessness or illusions of profit-making. It is very difficult to find takers for new puppies, for sale or for free.

Birth control is not a term usually applied to pets. But to the sophisticated dog owner the subject is of vital importance. The joys of puppyhood soon fade when the realities of sexual maturity become apparent some time late in the first year of life. Although males express this development differently from females, it is often a disturbing surprise to children experiencing their first dog. The various forms of birth control available for dogs can be of enormous value.

Male dogs are usually much more aggressive than females throughout the course of their procreative years, especially after having been mated. They tend to roam and are more difficult to train. When around a female in heat they are completely unreliable and quite often unmanageable.

Physically mature female dogs experience an estrus cycle twice a year. This is the period when mating, pregnancy and birth are made possible by hormonal changes in the body. To the uninitiated, these episodes can be upsetting. A vaginal discharge is apparent and the animal becomes restive and, in a word, seductive. Sometimes she appears to be in pain (although she is not) and may even howl or cry. The period of estrus lasts twenty-one days, but the female's receptivity to the male is only from six to twelve days.

Females of smaller breeds tend to reach sexual maturity earlier than females of the larger breeds. Puberty has been reported to occur in the beagle as early as six to eight months of age, while larger breeds may not express first estrus until nearly two years old.

The most important and effective form of birth control is surgical sterilization. In the female this is known as *spaying* or *ovariohysterectomy* and involves the removal of the animal's ovaries. For male dogs the procedure is known as *castration, neutering* or *having the dog fixed. Altered* is a term that applies to both genders. Contrary to popular belief altered dogs do not become fat, nor do they lose their personalities (although altered males lose some of their aggressiveness and other nasty traits). Surgical sterilization is the most popular form of birth control and 100 percent effective. The major drawback (if it is a drawback) is that it is irreversible.

There are other forms of birth control but they apply only to female dogs. There are two products available (and others may soon become available), both of which are administered orally and can be obtained only from a veterinarian. The first is a pill manufactured by the Schering Corporation and is called Ovaban. This product is given for eight days at the first signs of heat and eliminates the estrus cycle. When given continually for thirty-two days at a lower dosage it prevents heat for those specific thirty-two days.

The second product available is also administered orally and is called Cheque; it is manufactured by the Upjohn Company. This is a palatable liquid that is administered daily by placing a prescribed amount on a dog's food or directly into its mouth. Cheque is not recommended for dogs intended primarily for breeding.

According to Dr. Lloyd Faulkner, professor and chairman of the department of physiology and biophysics at Colorado State University, a device for animals is now in use that is similar to the IUD (intrauterine device). Although this contraceptive device is not quite the same as the IUD, it is being used with success. It is referred to as an intravaginal device. It does not combine any of the hormones, as do some of the newer IUDs for women. The new device does incorporate a copper band that contributes to the efficiency of contraception. This technique (as well as all the others) should be discussed with a veterinarian.

Other methods of birth control, for both male and female pets, are being pursued by various researchers. Implants, chemically treated pet food, chemical castration and hormonal manipulations are all being studied in universities and research laboratories in various parts of the United States, Canada and Europe. The prospects for a variety of birth control techniques are quite good. Until such time as the totally efficacious technique is developed, surgical sterilization, a closed door or a strong leash are still the best birth control devices around.

WHEN DOG MEETS BABY

It is hard to convince a dog that he is not the blessed event in the family even though a new baby has arrived. It is difficult enough when a new dog enters a home that already has a baby, but it can be much tougher if the dog was there first. When a dog moves into your home he establishes a sense of social structure, determining in his mind who fits in where in the pecking order. Even if he is subordinate to everyone there, he will regard a new baby as a subordinate animal. Some dogs will become very protective of the new baby while others may compete with the tiny creature for attention. Rarely does a dog become aggressive or dangerous to the newborn, but it can happen.

If you already have a dog and are expecting a new baby soon, there are steps to be taken that will help the dog behave when the infant comes home. First, have your dog obedience trained. If that was accomplished some time ago, it is important to give the dog a refresher course yourself. You can use the basics of obedience training that are outlined in chapter 6 of this book ("Teaching Parents to Teach Their Kids to Train Their Dog") for this purpose. The objective is to reinforce a subordinate role in the dog's mind. This will also give the existing family a greater control over the dog's behavior so that he will obey you at critical moments.

Second, invite to your home friends, relatives or neighbors who have a small baby. It will help your dog become acquainted with the species. In this case, familiarity breeds contentment. The smells and sounds of an infant are probably strange and new for your dog and it will help to expose him to them before the blessed event.

Third, make all changes in the house *before* the baby arrives so that the dog does not associate radical change with the newest member of the family. Bear in mind that change of any kind is difficult for a pet. This means the baby's furniture should be in place one or two weeks before the baby and the same for all the supplies, including blankets, clothing, diapers, powders and oils. If there is going to be any rearranging of furniture and decorating, get it done as far ahead of time as possible. Give the dog time to adjust to that aspect of things without having to cope with the newcomer as well.

If you have an aggressive dog, a shy dog or an overly exuberant dog, it may help to purchase a wire dog crate just to have an option of placing the animal out of harm's way during those very chaotic times with a newborn. Get out your old wire gate, the one that jams against the doorway of the kitchen, and have it ready so that the dog can be confined if necessary. However, you should understand that neither the crate nor the gated area is a permanent solution if your dog cannot be trusted with the baby. If your dog has ever bitten anyone at anytime, I would suggest the services of a professional dog trainer. If you can afford it, then professional dog training will help enormously no matter what your dog is like.

The Moment of Truth

When you come home from the hospital with the baby do not make the mistake of getting the dog out of the way. You are sending out a very negative message to your pet if you exclude him from the proceedings. Try to draw the dog into the situation in a controlled manner. Introducing the baby to the dog is almost as important as introducing the baby to your other children. Your reasons will be very different, however. The objective with the older children is to reassure them that they have not lost their mother and father's love and attention but rather have been given a reaffirmation of their parents' love and commitment to the children. Having another child only proves how much they are wanted. For a dog the idea is to get him to "claim" the baby as part of his territory . . . to take the baby under his wing, so to speak. It is possible to get the dog to view the child as a positive addition to his life rather than some strange creature wandering in where he or she doesn't belong, like a stray dog stealing food and shelter.

Allow the dog to be part of the welcome group and invite him into the circle to look at the newborn. Allow him to sniff or even lick the hand or face of the baby. If you can accomplish this, you have won half the battle already because he will forever associate the baby with his family (read: pack). This does not mean you are out of the woods, yet. UNDER NO CIRCUMSTANCES SHOULD YOU EVER LEAVE A BABY ALONE WITH A DOG. It is possible for a dog to harm an infant without even meaning to. The nails on a dog's paws are hard, blunt and dangerous if they swipe across the face inadvertently. Dogs pull everything with their teeth in an attempt to move an object from one place to another. Your dog must never have the opportunity to make that sort of mistake. Harm can come despite the best of intentions. When you deal with dogs and babies, your best tools are obedience commands or confinement in a wire dog crate or behind a wire gate in the kitchen,

allowing the dog full visual access to other parts of your home lest the dog be made to feel punished. Sometimes it is easier simply to shut the door to the nursery or control the dog with a leash.

WHEN DOG MEETS OTHER PETS

Introducing a new dog to the kids is no problem at all. However, if there is already another animal or two in the house, that has potential for trouble. Whether an established dog will accept the new dog or not depends on several variables. Were both dogs socialized at the right time during puppyhood? If the answer is yes, there should be no problem. Two even-tempered dogs will quickly establish who is dominant and subordinate and then get along very well. There is no question that a puppy will be dominated by an older dog, at least for a while. Variable factors pertain to breed characteristics, temperament, environmental influences, gender, etc. It is difficult to predict what will happen when more than one dog shares your home. Many experienced dog people believe that a male and a female get along best, but that isn't always the case. Sometimes an established female can be quite insane about another dog in the house. Some believe that a puppy and a mature dog get along best. No guarantee there either. It's not too different from mixing people at a party. Who can tell in advance whether two perfect strangers are going to get along? In the case of dogs you always have

207

obedience training to fall back on to make the situation tolerable. However, if two dogs constantly fight each other in a vicious manner, one of them will have to go.

What About Cats and Other Pets?

The most successful dog/cat relationships are developed when the animals are introduced to each other as puppies and kittens. Naturally, there are exceptions to this rule. Dogs and cats have needs that sometimes blend and sometimes clash at different periods of their lives and create the shifting sands of dominance and subordination. A teething dog or a cat in heat should be separated from the other animal until he or she is behaving normally. Many terriers and some hunting dogs should not be allowed near newborn kittens, as they are apt to mistake them for rodents or prey animals. Some dogs who are avowed cat haters will often develop a loving relationship with the family cat while still hating them as a species and attacking strays. A lactating queen (mother cat) will viciously attack a curious dog who gets too close to a young litter of kittens. An assertive unaltered male cat would not have the subordinate manner necessary to get along with a large, territorial canine.

Depending on temperament, early socialization, obedience training and a loving environment, most dogs will make some sort of peace with even the most impudent of cats. However . . . what about older cats accepting a new puppy? It is hard to know in advance. Certainly most cats are going to be apprehensive at the sight of a new animal, especially of another species. They will either arch their backs (with fur standing straight up), hiss and perhaps take a poke, or turn and run away to sulk under the couch for hours. More than likely these animals will eventually make peace with one another once they discover that there is no danger. It is here that human intervention can help.

First, do not try to force the situation. If you know anything at all about cats, you know that they must be allowed to calm down before you can affect their behavior in any way. An emotionally stressed cat cannot possibly respond to human coaxing, not even with favored food treats. Once the adult cat comes out of hiding (usually when it's hungry), try relating in a warm, indulgent manner. Place the cat on a table or other high plateau so that it is a good distance up from the floor. Stroke the cat (or cats, as the case may be) and offer it its favorite food treats. While you're doing this have someone release the puppy so that he will try to climb your leg. With the puppy on the floor and the cat on the table, they should be more able to tolerate each other in the same room without feeling threatened in any way. Try giving them both affectionate attention at the same time. This may go a long way in helping them accept each other. Do this as many times as necessary to reinforce their tolerance and help establish some kind of a relationship. Sometimes a dog rules the roost. Sometimes it's a cat. I've heard of a case where an older cat "parented" two new puppies. It is all influenced by the human sensibility. In this case getting along is a matter of survival. Bear in mind that the first Love Boat was the Ark.

As far as other types of pets are concerned, it is a good policy to keep them apart until you are ready to approach the situation with extreme caution and a wait-and-see attitude. Dogs and birds can be an engaging combination unless you live with a retriever, a setter, a spaniel or a mutt who has those instincts to hunt birds. Every dog has more than a few hunters in his family tree. Whether by scent, sight or sound, dogs are more than a little interested in all sorts of creatures that could make their day. Birds (especially out of their cages), turtles, lizards, snakes, and even fish could be viewed by some dogs as a delightful form of exercise and a snack as well. Keep them apart until you are absolutely certain the smaller pet is safe, and even then, do not allow the dog access when you're not there. Oh yes, explain all this to the kids and make it clear that they are not to take it upon themselves to play with both species together. That's a prescription for trouble. The family pets are not toys to be taken out like a set of blocks and a set of Legos and combined. Children are best served when given the value that the animals they live with are creatures of the earth like the rest of us and in the largest sense belong to themselves, with certain rights.

Eight

How to Take

Care of Your Dog

It only takes thirty minutes for you and the kids to realize that your new dog is more than a video game with fur. It is not a toy to be packed into the box and put away until you're ready for the next good time. That panting little furburger with the wet nose and wet bottom needs to eat, to run, to sleep (comfortably), to stinky-poo, to bathe and to see his doctor every once in a while. It is a rather complete involvement. Look at it this way: you haven't lost your freedom . . . you've gained a permanent houseguest. Your dog Spot is now a member of the family and there is no turning back. Ask the kids. That's what I did.

A while back I gave a talk about pets to a third-grade class at P.S. 41, the Greenwich Village elementary school. As a result I received many letters from that class. In order to give you some idea of what the young ones think about their dogs, I would like to share a few of the letters with you. They may make all the work and bother of a dog seem little enough.

A New Addition

Dear Mr. Siegal:

I'm going to have a puppy dog. I hafe Dobermint Pincher. Maybe I'll get it next week but I just need the liconse. It is going (to be) brown and white color.

Your truly friend,
Elias Galoway

Like a Brother

Dear Mr. Siegal:

I have a dog and I found him on the street and it deos what I won't him to do. I don't know what kind of dog it is but I love it very much. and I take it out a lot too. I give it food evry day and I tret my dog like my brother.

Yours truly
Zoe Bissell

A Puzzlement

Dear Mr. Siegal:

I have a fish and a dog. When I feed my fish sometimes he comes swimming over to me but sometimes he doesn't. I'd like to ask you a question if I can.

When I feed him why does he come swimming over to me? My dog likes to lick people everywhere.

Why does she like to lick people?

Her name is Beebee. She is partly black and partly white She is mostly black Beebee is a mut.

Your truly,
Jill Tolman

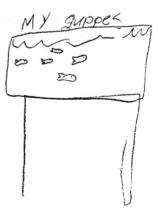

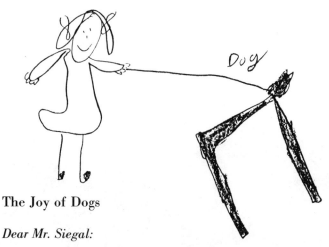

The Joy of Dogs

Dear Mr. Siegal:

Mr. Schuman read a story to the class today about pets and I want to know if you have any pets at home with you. I have a Labrador Retriever dog at home but my mother don't let me walk him at all because he pulled (me) in the street one day win I walk[ed] him last week with my flaimy and my mother has her best rug and my dog made a load.

Yours truly,
Veena

Watching the Watchdog

Dear Mr. Siegal:

I wanted to know if only german shepherds are good watch dogs? Because my dad says he needs a good watchdog and what I wanted to know is if collies are good watchdogs because thats what me and my brother want. One night my dad walked in the door with a dog the next day we took him to the vet because he had worms

Just after we got back he went to my mom's faviorte orinetal rug and made a little deposit on it. My dog's name was Tele because my dad found him while working with Tele Savales. I sort of felt sorry for him when my dad told us that kids were throwing rocks at her.

Yours truly,
Jocelyn Gecker

Obey the Light

Dear Mr. Siegal:

I have a dog. and When I take him out he looks at the red light. and when he looks am the red light he walks by him self and I always run after him. and when it says walk he does not walk but I walk

And I run back for him.

> *Yours truly,*
> *Barry Armond*

At our house we recently acquired a new dog. I asked my three children how they felt about their new relative. Jasper, my-three-year-old, said, "But she loves me and sleeps on my feet." Ida, age six, and TJ, age nine, wrote it down for me.

Didn't Catch the Name

Dear Daddy:

My dog is a vary good dod and her name is Feldlefa and a lot of peplla like her and I lover her vary match to and she is vary adorable and I think she is vary good.

> *Your daughter*
> *Ida Justine Siegal*

An Armful

Dear Dad:

I feel great about having philly. (short for Philadelphia.) It's a lot of fun having a dog just as big as a cat. She has red & white fur. I like philly because she is a dog I can hold in my arms. She is allso very cute.

> *Your son*
> *TJ Siegal*

FOOD — YOU'RE NEVER DONE WITH IT

It was not too long ago that a dog ate what was left over after his human caretakers were finished with their meal. A dog on his own had a much harder time finding food on a day-to-day basis. It was said that dogs in the wild had a much better opportunity to achieve a balanced diet than dogs fed in human society. That may have been so, providing a dog had the stamina, the health and the prey animals available for hunting, killing and then eating, not to mention the support of an entire pack to bring down the kill. Domestic dogs today under human stewardship have a greater possibility for sound nutrition than ever before. It may be true, as some claim, that certain commercial foods are better than others. It may even be true that some feeding styles are more effective than others. However, one can safely claim that few dogs will suffer the ill effects of malnutrition given the availability of quality commercial pet food. One could probably create an optimum diet at home, providing one knew the fundamentals of the nutritional requirements of dogs. And that information is available from the National Academy of Sciences in Washington, D.C., in a booklet entitled "Nutrient Requirements of Dogs." But realistically, few have the time or the inclination for such an involvement. Table scraps are enjoyed by dogs but can be harmful in the long run. For most of us that leaves commercial dog food as the feeding option, and, in my opinion, it is the best option.

Your dog's food should sustain life, promote growth, and help to maintain the quality of life by influencing good health. The introduction to "Nutrient Requirements of Dogs" (revised, 1972) by the National Academy of Sciences states, "Dogs can meet their nutritional requirements from proteins, carbohydrates, fats, minerals, and vitamins combined in a purified ration or from one of many combinations of natural foodstuffs. They can meet their energy requirements from plant materials if they have an adequate supply of essential amino acids. They can meet their protein requirements from many sources of proteins that supply the essential amino acids (the elements of protein). Dogs should have enough food to keep them in good condition. The amounts suggested in this publication are approximate. If the amounts suggested do not maintain satisfactory body condition, more food intake is indicated; if they result in obesity, food intake should be reduced."

The statements in this introduction only seem obvious. However, they are the logical result of sound scientific research and are not different from what most veterinarians will tell you. It is virtually impossible to formulate a type and quantity of food that will apply to every dog in terms of his needs for growth, sustenance and replacement of cells. Two identical dogs fed the same food in the same amount may not respond the same. One may gain weight while the other loses weight. The truth is that the metabolism of dogs varies from animal to animal and no two are alike. Therefore, feeding formulas must be regulated by the careful dog owner who determines when to feed more and when to feed less. There are fewer absolutes in the field of nutrition than in any other scientific discipline and that applies to human as well as animal nutrition. The dog owner is ultimately the one who must decide what is best. There are many conflicting points of view. Most of them are based on subjectively formulated theories that support one product as opposed to another. When selecting a dog food the average dog owner is pulled in many directions based on price, convenience, and a desire to do what's best for the dog.

The dog owner must decide whether "people" food is better than commercial dog food; if some commercial pet foods are healthier than others; if so-called natural pet food is better than conventional preparations; if food prescribed by and purchased from a veterinarian is healthier; and, finally, how much food to feed the dog. Each dog owner must face these issues alone and decide on the basis of what is affordable and what his or her convictions are concerning the vast array of food available.

Types of Commercial Dog Food

Dry type. Dog food that comes in a sack or box contains cereals, cereal by-products, soybean products, possibly meat or meat by-products, possibly poultry and/or poultry by-products, possibly fish and/or fish by-products, milk products, eggs, crude fiber, fats, added vitamins and minerals, and possibly chemical additives to retard spoilage and promote palatability as well as enhance the appearance. These basic ingredients appear in varied combinations depending on which brand is purchased. Not every brand, of course, uses all of these ingredients. Check the contents label on the package. Dry dog foods are considered to be the most economical since the moisture content is 10 percent or less, providing more solid nutrients than in other types. Premium dry-type foods offer approximately 1500 calories per pound of food.

It is difficult to predict which dry products are more palatable to any given dog. Some dogs refuse to eat the most expensive foods and actually prefer the cheaper ones. Many claims are made by the manufacturers of various dog foods, pertaining to quality, palatability and health-giving attributes. With few exceptions, it has been my experience that premium dog food products can be used safely and with confidence in that they sustain life and promote growth. Dry-type dog food is the preference of most professional dog people (breeders, trainers, exhibitors) because it is economical, convenient and good for dogs.

Soft-moist type. This type offers a highly palatable diet with a meat base (in combination sometimes with other protein sources) mixed with a complete and balanced formula. This type requires no refrigeration and comes in premeasured portions. It sometimes resembles hamburger or chunks of meat. It is usually odorless to humans but highly palatable to dogs. Often veterinarians will recommend this type for dogs that are dangerously undernourished and refuse other foods.

It is composed of 75 percent solids and 25 percent moisture and offers about 1300 calories to the pound in premium brands. The principal attraction of soft-moist food is its appearance of fresh meat despite its great protection against spoilage. It doesn't even require refrigeration. It contains meat and/or meat by-products, fats, oils, soybean products, carboxymethyl cellulose, vitamins, minerals, and chemical additives to retard spoilage, promote palatability and enhance its appearance. Soft-moist-type food uses large quantities of sugar and/or ingredients that produce sugar. The sugar acts as a preservative and makes the fresh taste and appearance possible.

Canned dog food. Premium brand foods of this type are extremely popular because they are highly palatable to dogs. The contents are appealing because of the resemblance to fresh meat in sight and smell. In fact, some brands use a high percentage of meat as the principal ingredient while others offer more cereals than meat and/or meat by-products. Read the contents on the label. According to FDA (Food and Drug Administration) regulations, the information panel on a dog food label must include a listing of ingredients in decreasing order by weight or percentage, and a list of guaranteed analyses (minimum crude protein and crude fat, and maximum crude fiber and moisture).

Canned rations are the most expensive because 75 percent of the contents of the can is moisture. It would take many cups of canned food to equal the same caloric value of one cup of premium dry food. The caloric content of a 14-ounce can of food averages between 400 and 600 calories depending on the brand. Canned dog foods with complete and balanced nutrition are blends of ingredients such as meat by-products and meat, cereal grains, vegetables, vitamins and minerals and possibly chemical additives to retard spoilage, promote palatability and enhance appearance. These foods are prepared by blending and cooking the ingredients, canning the mixture and sterilizing the sealed cans. With only a few exceptions canned ration is best when mixed with dry-type food.

How to Feed Your Dog

Puppies.   Puppyhood is the growth stage of a normal, healthy dog. During this extended period of early life the very young dog (between twelve weeks and one year) is going to experience its greatest rate of growth. Most breeds reach full size between eight and twelve months. The very largest breeds, Great Danes, Irish wolfhounds, etc., achieve full size between eighteen and twenty-four months of age.

Because of the high growth rate during this period, your young dog will require approximately twice the daily quantity of nutrients per pound of body weight to build bones, muscles and organs as will be needed later on for daily maintenance.

For three consecutive days feed your puppy a generous quantity of food. If he consumes all the available food in that time, the amount fed should be increased 15 percent. If food is left, the amount offered should be reduced by 10 percent. This formula for puppy feeding will take into account an individual dog's utilization of the food it eats, as it pertains to this important period of growth. You may elect to feed any of the described commercial products solely or in combination. Mixing dry-type food with canned ration is quite popular and recommended by some veterinarians although not required. Some dog owners like to slip into the ration a bit of "people food," although it can upset the nutritional balance so carefully formulated in premium dog foods. This is counterproductive if you are determined to have the dog eat one type of food exclusively, as many dog people are.

A twelve-week-old puppy should be fed three times a day (morning, noon and evening) and allowed fifteen minutes to eat what is in the bowl. At this time you may offer dry food because your dog will eat it without hestitation, thus getting him accustomed to this high-calorie, economical feed. You may reduce the feeding times to twice a day by the fifth or sixth month if you wish. The need for accelerated feeding terminates once the dog reaches near-full growth. The dog will indicate when to reduce the ration by refusing to eat all that is in his bowl. In this event reduce the amount of food by 10 percent each day until the dog eats everything in the bowl. You may then consider your family pet an adult and feed him accordingly (see "Feeding Chart for Adult Dogs" in this chapter).

A healthy puppy, fed properly, grows steadily in the first year and has a glossy coat with a slight looseness to the skin caused by a thin layer of fat just beneath the surface. A poorly fed puppy does not grow at a steady rate, shows a very dry, dull coat, has little spirit and sometimes exhibits a distended abdomen, depending on the degree of malnourishment. These may be medical symptoms indicating poor health.

Some dog foods have many more nutrients per pound than others. Therefore, the amount of food consumed by the dog is far less important than its nutritional content. It is altogether possible for a puppy to eat less and get more nutrition because of the food value of the ration given. Allow yourself to be influenced by the results of the food rather than the quantity consumed. If the dog is growing at a steady rate, looks good, is frisky and in good spirits, then you are doing the right thing, whatever that is.

Do not overfeed your puppy. This can adversely affect the animal's digestion and impair its ability to utilize the food. Chronic overfeeding can cause diarrhea or may result in obesity. If growth is accelerated beyond the normal rate, it could seriously affect the dog's health. A cute, fat puppy quickly turns into an unattractive, unhealthy fat dog. It is probably true that proper nutrition during the growth stage has a great influence on the health of the dog for his entire life.

Adult Dogs.   As stated earlier, the correct quantity of food varies from dog to dog because of the obvious differences in size, energy level, temperament, life-style, environment and rate of metabolism. For example, an aggressive, nervous watchdog, living outdoors in a cold climate, may need twice as much food as a similar dog living indoors with no specific job. Puppies, very small dogs, pregnant and lactating females and hunting dogs (those in training or working) require more calories per pound of body weight than average house dogs do. Few dogs have a similar rate of metabolism and therefore require different quantities of nutrition. Once the dog has reached his full growth he is an adult and requires a *maintenance diet.* The most practical method for maintaining a dog nutritionally is to establish an ideal or desired body weight and then feed a sufficient quantity of good-quality ration to maintain that weight. Weekly weighings are required during the time when this quantity is being established. After the appropriate quantity is established, monitor the dog's body weight monthly. Changes of more than 10 percent from the ideal should be accompanied by a change in the amount of food. With this in mind, a premium dry-type food can be given to a dog on a self-feeding basis. Unless the dog is sick or has a neurotic relationship to food, he will only eat his fill. The result will be a self-regulating diet satisfying all the dog's nutritional requirements. A self-feeding program simply means you keep the dog's bowl filled with dry-type food at all times.

The following chart is offered as a frame of reference for feeding adult dogs. It must not be taken as the last word. That is between you and your dog.

Feeding Chart for Adult Dogs

Dog's body weight in pounds	Calories needed for each pound of body weight	Daily rations of dog food		
		Dry food	Soft-moist	Canned
5	50	3½ oz.	5 oz.	10 oz.
10	42	5½ oz.	9 oz.	18 oz.
15	35	7 oz.	11 oz.	22 oz.
20	34	9 oz.	13½ oz.	27 oz.
30	31	12½ oz.	18½ oz.	37 oz.
45	28	17 oz.	25 oz.	51 oz.
60	26	21 oz.	31 oz.	62 oz.
75	25	25 oz.	37½ oz.	75 oz.

Modification of requirements of National Research Council recommendations by the Cornell Research Laboratory for Diseases of Dogs.

Older dogs.   Because of the nature of the aging process, each dog is affected in a somewhat different way, medically speaking. If one aspect of the body's system malfunctions as opposed to another, it could require a totally unique approach to a diet and feeding. It is within the province of a veterinarian to make such dietary changes when necessary.

In general, the older dog experiences certain body changes that radically affect metabolism and digestion. This in turn reduces his ability to use all the nutrients in the food given, in addition to making him intolerant of sudden changes in the diet. It has been suggested by some veterinarians and pet food manufacturers that this aging process begins somewhere in the seventh year of life for the average dog.

Aging most definitely alters the dog's nutritional requirements. Most house dogs become less active at this time and have fewer energy needs. This means they should have a reduction of caloric intake to avoid a large accumulation of fat, which only acts negatively on the body. Fat intake should be reduced so that the calories given can be used as energy rather than stored in the body. Fats also become more difficult to digest for the aging dog. They interfere with the absorption and use of calcium. All minerals with the exception of calcium should also be reduced but not eliminated.

As your dog ages it is best to consider reducing the quantity of food given. Assuming he has been fed a well-balanced diet, it is not necessary to change the diet except in terms of quantity. This is based on the assumption that the dog is healthy and without problems of the kidneys, liver, pancreas or heart. As the ability to digest slows down it is best to consult a veterinarian about the dog's diet.

Most veterinarians recommend a vitamin and mineral supplement that has been formulated for the geriatric dog. Norden Laboratories has developed a superior geriatric vitamin ("Geribits") containing high doses of vitamin A (for resistance to certain respiratory infections and weak, infected eyes); vitamin D (to maintain proper uptake of calcium and phosphorus); vitamin E (to help forestall aging and to balance the metabolic processes); and vitamin B_{12} (for the synthesis of red blood cells). These and other vitamins have been adjusted to minimize stress and to permit ready use by the dog's metabolism.

If your dog has been fed quality commercial dog food most of his life, it is best to continue with that diet but in reduced amounts. There are several commercial dog foods formulated specifically for older dogs and they are quite effective in supplying the same bulk but with fewer calories and less fat. Cycle 4 from Gaines is one such product (available in all supermarkets) as is Prescription Diet g/d (available from veterinarians only). These diets are meant to aid in preventing obesity, sustaining skin condition and hair coat, complementing normal blood flow, thinning secretions, absorbing nutrients and reducing excretory demands on the kidneys. They are even supplemented with needed vitamins and minerals.

If you are going to change your aging dog's diet, do it gradually. Begin by mixing a small quantity of the new food with a slightly reduced amount of the old food. Gradually increase the new food and reduce the old food each day until the dog is totally switched within one week. This will avoid stomach upset and emotional stress.

When Children Feed the Dog

If it is your desire to develop an active relationship between the family dog and the kids, then responsibility for feeding will certainly help. Many levels of communication develop between the dog and the human or humans who prepare the daily ration. When a dog is hungry she will often approach the one who customarily feeds her, look directly into that person's eyes, nudge him with a gentle paw and maybe even cock her head to one side in a manner that makes one want to hug her right away. It doesn't seem like much, but deep caring develops from such moments between dog and child. When a dog communicates with a child on any level, about anything, it is one of childhood's magical times that becomes etched in one's memories.

If your child is very young, up to six years old, he or she may help you with the feeding chore. It is important that the dog be made aware of the child's participation. Allow the child to hand you the bowl or actually pour a premeasured amount of food into the bowl. If the dog is not unusually aggressive, allow the child to place the bowl in front of the dog at the proper place, so it appears to the dog that she is feeding him. This must always be a supervised activity because the dog may suddenly dislike being fed by a child. This will be the case if the dog views the small child as a subordinate member of the pack (family). In that event allow the child to do everything but place the bowl in front of the dog. Feeding the dog is a dominant activity and good for both dog and child.

If your children are past seven they are old enough to assume the responsibility of feeding the dog on their own. I would caution you that children forget the most important things. For the dog's sake, make sure he is fed each meal, every day. Most children love feeding the dog because they know it is an important activity and appreciate your trust and confidence in them. However, household rules and boundaries must apply to this job as any other. Do not hesitate to present the chore as a privilege rather than as a drudge. Brothers and sisters will clamor to be the one who gets to feed the dog. You may have to rotate them on a schedule or make the job a reward for good behavior connected with homework, etc. This also applies to other aspects of caring for the dog, including walking, grooming, and bathing. Kids love it.

THE HEALTHY DOG

Maintaining a healthy dog is a two-prong affair these days, just as it is for human health. I refer to *treatment* and *prevention*. Of course, when a dog shows symptoms of illness or "is just not herself," it is best to take her to a veterinarian for an examination. However, we have all learned the great benefits of preventive medicine. All veterinarians believe in it. From sensible nutrition to vaccination to a hygienic lifestyle, it all contributes to keeping your dog in sound condition and in a reasonable state of good health.

Some dogs frequent the vet's office on a revolving-door basis, with far too many ailments, while others go once a year for a checkup. The objective is to keep your dog off the sick list as much as possible and not let her become one of the walking wounded. When a dog seems to be forever sick but she does not have a major disease, it may be something you're *not* doing.

Although there are no pat answers that apply to all dogs in terms of preventive medicine, there are some general guidelines that have a good effect. The areas of prevention sort themselves into several categories. These represent the foundation for good, basic dog care and should, in most cases, keep the typical house pet in fine fettle.

Annual Checkup

It is startling to discover how many pet owners are unaware of the necessity of a complete annual checkup for their dogs. During the course of the first physical exam, a complete vaccination program must be initiated. A typical examination should include checking both ears, the nose, mouth, teeth, throat, respiratory system, spine or musculoskeletal system, skin, legs, reproductive system, abdominal cavity, cardiovascular system and anal area. Laboratory tests involving stool samples and drawn blood are also part of a thorough exam. Anything less is not a complete annual checkup.

Some pets require more medical attention than others. Medical histories, health condition and age help to determine how much care is necessary. A physical examination for a pet is similar to that given to a human. The veterinarian may check your pet's temperature, pulse and respiration rate. The general appearance and weight of the animal is carefully noted. Notes will probably be made on the pet's diet, water consumption and a host of other factors that relate to the animal's health history. When your home companion looks or acts sick, do not try home remedies, do not listen to amateur advice. Make an appointment to see the animal doctor. He or she has met the same educational and licensing demands as any doctor of human medicine and perhaps more. Your veterinarian is your pet's best friend, next to you.

It is a good idea to allow the kids to accompany you to the veterinarian's office and witness the dog's medical attention unless there are going to be painful therapies and procedures. The animal's reasonable behavior sets a good example for the child when seeing his or her pediatrician. Often the child's presence is a comfort to the dog, who may have anxiety about being on the veterinarian's table. Every involvement with the dog's care, including medical attention, strengthens the bond between the family dog and the children. It also deepens the feelings of responsibility in the kids for the very dependent family dog.

Vaccination

The average adult dog should be inoculated for *distemper, infectious hepatitis, parainfluenza* (the two or three types of kennel coughs for which your vet is vaccinating), *parvovirus, leptospirosis,* and *rabies.* Vaccination types and schedules differ from doctor to doctor. In addition to some points of view, certain regions of the country are affected by statutes and local conditions. Local disease problems require regional modifications of immunization programs. *The single most important fact about vaccination is often missed by pet owners — an annual booster shot is required to maintain the animal's immunity.*

Symptoms of Illness

In general, the common signs of canine sickness are connected with the animal's eating habits, body temperature and moisture content. When a dog goes off his feed or eats more than usual, it could be symptomatic of illness. The same is true of water intake. However, if

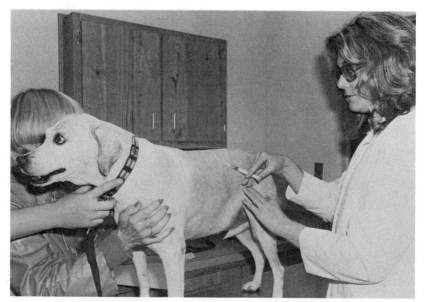

An annual booster shot is required to maintain the dog's immunities.

he refuses one or two meals, it is still not time to see the vet. It could be something quite mild and temporary. If the dog has no appetite at all for more than two days and sleeps most of the time, it is time to see the vet. Bear in mind, however, that hunger and energy could be related to finding his own food when you're not looking, the weather, exercise or emotional upset. Symptoms from these causes are temporary and not serious at all.

Normal body temperature varies from dog to dog between 101° F and 102.5° F. Large dogs run a slightly lower temperature (99° F). Veterinarians usually consider the dog to be running a fever at 102.6° F. However, an elevated body temperature is not necessarily fever. An exuberant dog or one that has just exercised vigorously will run a slightly elevated body temperature.

Taking a dog's temperature is accomplished by inserting a rectal thermometer (a dog's or a child's) into the animal's anus. With the dog lying down, raise the tail and insert the thermometer after it has been smeared with a small dab of Vaseline. For large dogs, insert the instrument to approximately half its length. Smaller dogs can only tolerate one-fourth or less. Allow at least two minutes for an accurate temperature reading. Be careful of the dog's movement while the thermometer is inside him. Make a note of the dog's temperature and the time for each reading and present that information to the veterinarian.

Excessive vomiting or diarrhea will cause the body to *dehydrate,* which is a significant loss of body fluids and electrolytes (minerals). This is an extremely serious condition. When more fluid is leaving the body than is going in, total dehydration is the end result. A loss of skin elasticity is a sure sign of dehydration. This is apparent if the skin does not fall back into place after grabbing a fold with your hands and letting it drop. Dehydration leads to shock, coma and death. Seek medical attention immediately if there is any suspicion of this condition.

The single most important aspect of treating a dog for illness is learning what is normal and what is abnormal for your pet. Annual checkups are important, but knowing your dog's normal behavior and body language can save his life.

Major Illnesses

Canine distemper.   This is the leading cause of virus-related death of dogs in the world. Similar to the virus causing measles, it is highly contagious and transmitted in the air, in water or on contaminated objects. Although it takes six to nine days to incubate, first symptoms are not apparent for two to three weeks after exposure. Initial symptoms range from a mild cough or sneeze, accompanied by nasal or eye discharge, to a severe attack of vomiting and diarrhea, with depression and loss of appetite. The outlook for infected dogs is grave though not entirely hopeless. Distemper vaccinations, though not permanent, are 94 percent effective. Vaccinations must be given early in life and boosted every twelve months throughout the entire lifetime of the dog. Distemper is not transmittable to humans.

Infectious canine hepatitis.   This very serious disease is caused by a virus that is not airborne but, rather, spread through direct contact with dog urine. It is highly contagious, but only to dogs. The symptoms can be similar to those of canine distemper. They range from mild to extreme and are expressed by elevated body temperature above 104° F, vomiting, discharge from the nose and eyes, diarrhea, depression, abnormal thirst, pain in movement, labored breathing and possibly spasms. Although this disease can be fatal, the recovery rate is quite high. Early immunization and annual boosters are essential for prevention.

Leptospirosis.   This is a bacterial disease that can affect dogs of all ages. It is characterized by listlessness, elevated body temperature between 103° F and 105° F, refusal to eat, vomiting, increased thirst and urination, bleeding from the mouth and blood in the stool. It is contracted through a break in the skin or by ingesting contaminated food or water. It is spread by the urine of infected animals, principally rodents. Although this disase is not common, it is to be taken seriously because it is contagious to humans as well as other animals. Treatment can be successful but is long-term. Prevention through vaccination is given as a matter of course by veterinarians and is highly effective. In areas where leptospirosis is seen, boosters are given more often than every twelve months.

Rabies.   Rabies is a serious virus disease that can affect all warm-blooded animals, including humans. Untreated rabies infection is fatal. The virus is transmitted through the bite of affected animals. It is carried in the saliva and can enter the body through scratches, cuts and other skin wounds or if given an opportunity to enter through the moist membranes of the mouth, eyes or other body openings. There is no treatment of this disease for dogs once symptoms begin. Prevention through vaccination is the only method available to protect the health of your dog. When a human suspects he has been bitten by a rabid animal, he must first find the animal and have it impounded as dictated by local statutes. Consult a veterinarian or physician. It must then be decided if the person must undergo a series of rabies vaccinations. The newest method calls for five injections rather than the customary twenty and is given along with an immune globulin when treatment is started. Most known cases of rabies are in skunks, raccoons and other wild animals, who may, in turn, pass it on to domestic dogs or cats. There have been far fewer cases in dogs, cats and humans than in wild animals.

   The symptoms of rabies are, in the beginning, personality changes, which are subtle at first. These are characterized by unusual shyness, crankiness, irritability and increasing aggressiveness. The next symptoms depend on the route the virus travels on its way to the brain. The "furious form" involves incessant biting of objects and those who approach, frequent urination and possibly sexual excitation. This is the form that has created the term "mad dog." The other form, which is the last phase before death, is the paralytic or "dumb" stage, in which the lower jaw is hung open and food or water cannot be ingested.

Every dog must be vaccinated to avoid this terrible disease. Immunization is totally effective. However, if you suspect that your dog has been bitten by a rabid animal, it must be examined and quarantined immediately for the sake of *all* humans and animals in the household.

Parvovirus.   Although this disease is not a threat to humans or other animals, it is quite serious and in some cases fatal. Puppies and older dogs are the most likely to succumb. The virus is spread primarily through contact with the feces of an infected dog. It can also be carried on the skin, clothing and shoes of humans. The virus is not killed by antibiotics (no virus is) and cannot be cleaned away by detergents or alcohol. It can withstand both freezing and extremely high temperatures. The symptoms of parvovirus are sudden illness, high fever, bloody diarrhea, constant vomiting. Stools are grayish to yellow, becoming bloody as the disease progresses. Dehydration and death ensue. This virus, along with corona virus (a similar disease with some variations), causes a condition known in veterinary medicine as infectious canine enteritis, which radically disturbs the gastrointestinal tracts of dogs, with acute diarrhea and vomiting. It is a very serious illness.

A vaccine for parvovirus is available which will protect dogs after a series of vaccinations and boosters. If a dog becomes ill with parvovirus, separate it from other dogs in the household or kennel and minimize traffic between sick and healthy animals. Clean all of the dog's areas with the following solution: liquid bleach diluted with water in a 1:30 solution. The virus is rapidly destroyed by this chlorine solution. Use this solution to clean the dog's crates, floor area, sleeping materials, food bowls, toys, plus human objects such as shoes and various items of clothing. Seek immediate veterinary attention at the first signs of this disease.

Parainfluenza.   This is another disease caused by a persistent virus that is spread through the air. It causes infection in the windpipe and large air passages of the lungs. This ailment is highly contagious among dogs (but does not affect humans) and is spread quite easily. It causes "kennel cough" accompanied by mild fever, nasal discharge, mild tonsillitis. Although the dog is otherwise in a good state of health, there develops a harsh, deep cough that ends with a hacking sound followed with gagging mucus. The real problem begins when more serious infections result from bacteria invading the cells damaged by the virus. The combination of viral and bacterial infection can cause extensive lung damage leading to pneumonia. There are now vaccines available that help prevent this condition. It is especially important to administer this vaccine if you plan to board your dog at a kennel, have him groomed at a shop, attend dog shows or bring your dog anyplace with other dogs.

Internal Parasites

Internal parasites (worms and one-celled animals) are common among dogs and must be treated as soon as possible. Treatment consists of deworming preparations determined by and administered by a veterinarian. A sound hygienic environment for the dog is an important preventive. The most common are roundworms, whipworms, hookworms, tapeworms and heartworms. Depending upon the degree of infestation, the condition may be mildly harmful or gravely serious; if caught, treatment in most cases is simple and 100 percent effective.

As the parasites are often detectable only with a microscope, samples of your dog's stool should be laboratory tested by a veterinarian two or three times a year. Heartworm tests require blood samples. Once a dog is tested and found to be free of heartworms, a preventive medication may be prescribed by the vet.

Most internal parasites are transmitted through fecal contact. Always walk your dog on leash and prevent him from coming in contact with other dogs' feces. Tapeworms are transmitted through intermediate hosts such as fleas, vermin or infested raw meat. Monthly wormers are not recommended, because they may be effective against one form of parasite but not another, plus amounting to a gratuitous ingestion of drugs.

It is quite difficult, if not impossible, to avoid some form of worms at least once in all puppies. It is almost their birthright. These internal parasites vary from region to region but it is quite possible for one dog to become infected with more than one type at the same time. This is a common problem in dogs and demands awareness of symptoms on the part of the dog owner. The most important time to check for worms is at the time of purchase of the puppy or soon after. Symptoms vary with the type of infestation, the stage of the life cycle of the parasite and the degree of the infestation. Only a veterinarian can determine which type of parasite, if any, is present so that proper treatment can be given.

It would be a great disservice to parents and children not to mention that these five internal parasites can, under rare and unique circumstances, be transmitted to humans, but especially children. Several types of parasites enter the human body by the ingestion of contaminated material such as soil, water or even dog stools. Another form of entry is through skin contact (hookworms), usually by walking barefoot on contaminated material. It must be understood that routine medical examinations do not necessarily help a child's doctor detect parasitic infestation. What does help is the parent's alerting the child's doctor that the family dog is infested. Becoming aware of the symptoms of internal parasites in dogs helps parents know when to seek veterinary attention as well as pediatric attention. Treatment is simple and very effective for all.

If your dog tests positive for any of these parasites, it is advisable to have your children examined by a pediatrician, to be on the safe side. Proper sanitation of the dog's environment makes parasitic infestation difficult if not impossible.

These parasites are uncommon in children in the United States, although some cases are reported nationwide every year. Pinworms and flatworms are the parasites most commonly found in children and have no connection to pets whatsoever. Children are more likely to become ill from each other than from a dog.

Roundworm.   These are the most common of all internal parasites. Although they are quite unattractive in the adult stage, they are comparatively the least harmful of these parasites. Their presence is indicated by enlargement of the abdomen, loose stool or diarrhea, lethargy and stomach upset. These are transmittable to children if material containing larvae is ingested by the child. This has happened in areas with mild climates where the child is given to eating dirt that was contaminated with roundworm eggs. Roundworms can be very harmful once inside a child's blood system. It is for this reason that all puppies and young dogs living with small children should be checked for worms periodically and that parents be aware of the symptoms, while maintaining a clean environment for the dog as well as the children. It must be noted that the incidence of roundworm infestation in small children is uncommon.

Whipworm.   These parasites are often difficult to detect, even under a microscope, when the infestation is light. More than one stool examination is required. Symptoms are loss of weight, diarrhea, sometimes anemia. Treatment involves several applications of deworming medication plus periodic stool examinations. Good sanitation is the best preventive. Whipworm infection is worldwide in scope and is transmittable to humans by the ingestion of contaminated material. A pediatrician or family doctor should be consulted if your dog tests positive for this or any other internal parasite. Treatment is simple and effective for humans.

Hookworm.   The primary symptoms for hookworms are anemia due to chronic loss of blood and diarrhea caused by soreness in the stomach. It is a serious condition for a dog and must be corrected quickly. Puppies, older dogs and malnourished dogs will suffer collapse and even death if not treated. Watch for weight loss and an unnatural loss of housebreaking control. These symptoms plus a bloody stool should alert one to hookworm infestation. Veterinary treatment is necessary not only for the good of the dog but because the worms can be transmitted to humans through skin contact. It is important to understand that proper veterinary care in addition to good sanitation will eliminate this problem. If there is suspicion of human contact, discuss the matter with a pediatrician or the family doctor. Treatment is similar to the veterinary therapy, utilizing drugs to kill the parasites and some temporary diet control.

Tapeworm.   There are several species of tapeworm that can infect dogs. Intermediate hosts (such as fleas, lice, rodents, fish and snakes) are necessary during its life cycle. Eating uncooked meat can cause one type of tapeworm infestation. Symptoms are digestive upsets, poor appetite, dull coat and dry skin, weight loss and signs of stomach pain. Tapeworm is often detected by observing small segments of the worm in the animal's feces, in his sleeping quarters or clinging to the coat near the anus. A dog infested with tapeworms may occasionally be seen sitting down and dragging its hindquarters over the floor. This results partly from the irritation that worm segments cause when they pass through the intestines. However, this "scooting" behavior can also indicate other ailments. Treatment must both destroy the tapeworms already infecting the dog and control reinfection by eliminating or reducing contact with the intermediate hosts. Several treatments may be necessary to eliminate tapeworms. Seek veterinary care and have your children examined by a pediatrician or family doctor.

Heartworm.   The life cycle of this parasite is long and complex. In their first stage they are injected through the dog's skin by a host mosquito. They remain in the dog for several months, undergoing several changes in form and size. As small-size worms they enter a vein and work their way to the right side of the heart or the surrounding blood vessels and grow to full maturity. The female worm produces large quantities of newly hatched heartworms, called *microfilaria,* which circulate throughout the blood system. If such a dog is bitten by a mosquito, a quantity of the microscopic heartworms are carried off and, acting as an intermediate host, the mosquito passes them on to another dog or human that it bites. Thus the life cycle continues.

Adult heartworms can live in a dog's body for approximately five years, causing great physical damage and a shortened life span. The microfilaria can remain alive in the dog's bloodstream for more than three years while waiting for a mosquito to carry them to the next stage of development. Symptoms of mature heartworms in the dog are constant fatigue, gradual weight loss, weakness, coughing or labored breathing. It is necessary to seek veterinary care. Treatment is twofold. First, adult heartworms must be destroyed and then the microfilaria must be eliminated from the blood. Treatment requires a stay at the clinic and then medication at home. Heartworm is a very serious disease for dogs. Human contraction of the disease is rare but possible. Humans are more vulnerable in tropical and subtropical zones where large mosquito populations are a problem.

Heartworm disease prevention is available with the help of your veterinarian, and it is very effective. There is heartworm preventive medication that is administered to dogs every day during mosquito season. However, there can be no heartworm microfilaria present in the dog's body when the drug is given (orally) or it can cause serious medical problems. Therefore, it is customary for veterinarians to take a blood sample to be sure the dog is free of the parasite before prescribing the preventive medication. Mosquito control is the other aspect of prevention of this disease. The use of pesticides is advised and confining the dog indoors during peak mosquito hours. Some mosquito repellents are useful. Some communities close to the seashore or other bodies of water spray their areas for mosquitoes, but an individual can engage the services of a private outdoor exterminator. If your dog contracts heartworm, it is advisable to have the children checked by your family doctor or pediatrician.

External Parasites

Fleas, ticks, lice and mites are the primary villains that latch on to the outer body of the dog. The part of the country one lives in determines whether the problem is seasonal or year-round. In areas with warm or humid weather, such as Florida or California, fleas and ticks will be seen all the time. Your veterinarian is the best person to ask about this problem.

Once a dog becomes infested with an external parasite, his body must be treated with some form of pesticide. Sprays, dips, soaps and shampoos are all effective except in the case of mites. These microscopic parasites must be diagnosed and treated by a veterinarian. All areas that the dog inhabits must then be cleaned thoroughly with soap and water and attacked with a proper pesticide. A professional exterminator may be needed because it is absolutely essential to kill the insects in and around the house plus the eggs that may hatch several days after a cleanout.

All external parasites can and will attach themselves to humans if given the opportunity. For this reason it is important to be observant and treat the family pet and his environment at the first sign of infestation. Check all areas where the infested dog is allowed, including carpets, furniture, bedding, the children, their rooms and their toys (especially the stuffed ones). If there are any signs of fleas, ticks or lice, call in a professional exterminator.

Fleas.   There is nothing humorous about a dog infested with fleas. They are small, brown or black, wingless, rapid-moving insects that live and feed on the dog's body. Fleas bite into the dog's skin, take a blood meal, and scurry quickly to another spot for another bite. They are extremely irritating to the dog and do much more than itch. Sometimes they cause anemia and may spread disease as well as tapeworm. Sometimes a dog develops an allergy to the flea bite and will continue to scratch for months after the fleas are gone. Consult a veterinarian for various forms of relief of flea-bite allergy. If your dog constantly scratches various parts of his body and bites into his own coat, chances are quite high that he has fleas. He must be treated with any of the various forms of flea killers (sprays, dips, soaps, shampoos) according to the directions on the label. It is always best to ask a vet to recommend a specific pesticide that applies to your dog. Since eggs and larvae live in the dog's environment rather than on the dog, it is extremely important to spray the premises with an aerosol bomb every eight to ten days for a month to kill the newly hatched fleas. During this period dispose of the vacuum cleaner bag immediately after each use.

Lice.   Lice are small, black insects that live on the dog's body and take blood meals, as do fleas. The difference between the two is that fleas move from location to location on the body, while lice stay in one spot. If the dog scratches hard, these tiny creatures burrow in deeper. Unlike fleas, lice lay their eggs on the dog's coat by attaching them firmly to the follicles. The lice eggs are called nits and have light-colored, waxy bodies.

Treatment prescribed by a veterinarian may call for clipping the coat for removal of the nits; use of a series of insecticide treatments administered by the vet; a series of special shampoo baths; or the application of an insecticide spray or powder. Medication may be administered if the dog has been affected physically. During this period clean and disinfect all combs and brushes (including humans') and anything involving hair. Check everyone in the family for lice, including any other house pets.

Ticks.   Like fleas and lice, ticks feed on the blood of the host animal. There are several kinds of tick that attack dogs, and their life cycle is complicated. Only a short part of their lives is spent affixed to the skin of their hosts. It is the female that attaches itself to the host's skin and engorges itself with blood for the purpose of completing a mating and egg-laying process. An engorged female is gray and about the size of a small marble, with a much smaller male hovering close by. They are visible to the naked eye but one must part the dog's hair to see them. Check the head, neck, ears, feet (between the toes) and in the folds of skin on the body. While waiting for a host, they are to be found in tall grass and in crevices in streets, parks, vacant lots and around houses. It is possible to remove a tick oneself, providing the head is not allowed to remain in the wound. Rubbing alcohol dabbed on the tick with cotton usually will cause it to release its hold so that you can remove it without breaking off the mouth parts attached to the dog's skin. Use a tweezers to get all of it out. It is important to understand that the only way to dispose of a removed tick is to burn it in an ashtray or else it will survive to lay eggs and continue its life cycle. Do not flush the tick away.

Ticks can harm dogs and humans. They sometimes carry one of several serious diseases, including Rocky Mountain spotted fever. If you cannot cope with removing the tick yourself, have a veterinarian do it the very day of discovery. Once an engorged female is ready, it will drop off the dog's body and scurry away to a vertical object such as a wall or fence and commence to lay 1000 to 5000 eggs in a protected crack or crevice. Within three weeks many of these eggs enter their larval stage of life. If you discover ticks in your home or on your property, you are advised to talk to a professional exterminator.

Mites. Whenever your puppy or dog keeps pawing at her ears or if there is an apparent inflammation, you can assume it is the very common ear mite. These are small parasitic insects, barely visible to the naked eye, causing great discomfort and medical problems for dogs. They are minuscule white creatures that move. It is essential that they be identified and treated by a veterinarian. Two other types of mite cause sarcoptic mange and demodectic mange, which are serious skin conditions requiring veterinary treatment. Sarcoptic mange causes intense itching, hair loss and skin eruption. Demodectic mange does not cause itching but is evidenced by hair loss around the head and front legs and reddened, scaly skin. It is important to treat these unsightly and uncomfortable skin diseases not only for the sake of the dog. Sarcoptic mange is contagious to humans, but in a very limited form. It can only live three weeks on the human body but will reappear if the dog is not treated. Demodectic mange is a serious ailment for dogs. It is not contagious to humans.

First Aid

First Aid for dogs means emergency care until you can get veterinary help, and it can be the first line of defense in saving an animal's life. It is simply immediate, temporary treatment, meant to sustain life until professional care is available. It is by no means a cure and should be followed up with an immediate visit to a veterinarian.

Restraining an injured dog. *Make a muzzle.* A dog in pain may bite the hand that helps, so be prepared. Improvise a muzzle with gauze, string, a belt or a tie. Make a loop or half-knot and slip it over the dog's nose, halfway up. Pull it until it tightens. Bring the ends under the jaw, forming another half-knot. Secure the ends behind the dog's ears with a bowknot as you would tie a shoelace. Do not muzzle the dog too tightly. It may be necessary to tie the front paws (if they are not injured). You may now examime the animal for injuries without fear of being injured yourself.

Bleeding.   External bleeding is apparent. It comes from wounds, cuts, punctures, etc. Bleeding requires control of blood loss and prevention of infection. Superficial wounds show slight blood loss. Wash with soap and water and apply an antiseptic. Smear on a light film of Vaseline and cover with a gauze pad and tape. For persistent bleeding, it may be necessary to use a pressure bandage. Apply a gauze bandage and press it onto the wound with your hand. Keep applying pressure until the bleeding subsides. An alternate method is to tie cloth strips tightly around the gauze several times in order to create pressure over the bleeding area. Cover the bandage completely with adhesive tape. If no tape is available, tie the gauze or cloth strip by tearing it down the center and knotting the two ends.

Severe or deep cuts are serious. A severed artery shows light-colored blood rushing quickly. Dark-colored blood that flows slowly is from a vein. These types of lacerations or punctures extend beyond the skin into the tissue beneath. Place a gauze pad over the wound and apply pressure with your hand for several minutes, allowing the blood to collect on the dressing and to clot. If the blood soaks through, keep applying one pad on top of another. Maintain pressure on the wound. Wrap it completely with a bandage and cover the entire bandage with tape. See a veterinarian immediately.

Shock.   A condition known as shock may be caused by severe fright, injury or internal bleeding. It is a state of collapse caused by a failure of peripheral circulation. Look for apathy, prostration, weak pulse, hyperventilation, thirst, pale gums and inner eyelids, a temperature of 100° F or lower, cool extremities or panting. To prevent or counteract shock, bleeding must be arrested, pain relieved, and infection prevented. Reassure the animal, talking quietly as you might to a frightened youngster, and help preserve his or her body heat with a blanket (no electrical appliances). Keep the animal still and quiet and rush it to a veterinarian. Shock is a condition that will lead to death if not relieved quickly. If a dog has gone into shock, transport him immediately to a veterinarian. A dog in shock is likely to be unconscious, therefore you must keep the passageway in the mouth open. Clear the mouth of any fluids or obstructions and pull the tongue out to allow for clear breathing. Open the window of the car for fresh air. Keep the dog warm. Try to restore circulation to the cool extremities by inclining the body so that the head is lower than the rest of the body. Methodically massage the legs at the bottom and on the muscles. If breathing has stopped, apply artificial respiration and/or heart massage.

Broken bones.   Fractures can be determined by loss of the body's ability to bear its own weight, deformity, abnormal angulation, swelling in the affected area or by the protrusion of a bone. A simple fracture is one break. A comminuted fracture indicates two or more breaks. A compound fracture is a break that has punctured its surrounding tissue and may even protrude from the skin.

Muzzle the dog immediately. Restrain him as gently as possible. Immobilize the injured area with a splint. Use any firm object, such as a small plank of wood, a tree branch, heavy cardboard — even a metal tool — *so long as it extends far enough to brace the area above and below the break.* Use gauze or cloth strips to wrap the limb or other broken area in a layer of absorbent cotton or newspaper so that the splint will be padded evenly. Fix the splint with bandage, rope, twine or what-have-you. Do not tie it too tightly. *Do not attempt to set the bone.* Treat the animal for shock and rush him to the veterinarian.

Burns.   Burns are caused either by direct flame, electricity, friction, corrosive chemicals or scalding from hot liquids. The most common burns come from scalding water or other kitchen-related items such as soup, stew or coffee. Many a puppy has been attracted to the cord of an electrical cooking appliance and pulled it down on himself.

The most important remedy for first- or second-degree burns (where skin has *not* been destroyed) is to lower the temperature of the burned area with cold water or cold towels soaked in ice water. The sooner the area is cooled, the less tissue is damaged. Apply a thin film or antibiotic ointment, such as Bacitracin, and bandage with a thick covering of gauze pads and rolled gauze. *Do not use home remedies such as butter or lard.* Look for signs of shock, breathing difficulties, or coughing and see the veterinarian immediately.

For deep burns or burns of more than 50 percent of the body, apply

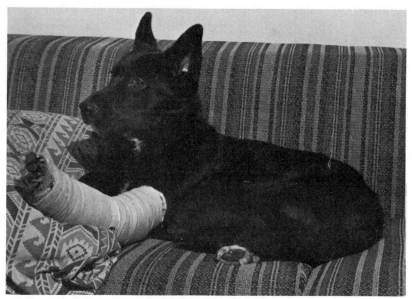

Never attempt to set a dog's broken bone yourself. Only a veterinarian can assure success.

a bandage or cloth soaked in cold water and seek professional emergency care.

Poison.   Poisoning is a large, complex subject. Find the telephone number of the nearest Poison Control Center in your area and keep it handy. This is important for the children as well as the dog. If you suspect that your dog (or child) has been poisoned, call the Poison Control Center and be prepared to tell them what you suspect the poisoning agent is. Empty containers and jars that held the offending substance should be at hand to tell them the brand name, lot number, date and possible list of ingredients. This information helps them instruct you properly. The label may also suggest antidotes and/or warn against certain treatments.

Poisons can enter the body by being swallowed or inhaled, by absorption through the skin, or by injection into the skin. When poison enters by mouth the symptoms are abdominal pain, possible vomiting and diarrhea. Breathing may be labored, accompanied by drool and a general lethargy. Inhaled poison creates hard breathing, the mouth-lining color's turning dark, possible sneezing and coughing. Poisons that are absorbed through the skin are indicated by sensitivity in the injured area, topical inflammation and possible peeling in the injured area. Injected poisons (bites and stings) are painful and swell at the injection point. Venom may produce slowing of the circulation and breathing. Muscles may tremble. Other symptoms of poisoning are severe odor on the body or from the dog's breath; burned areas on the coat, skin or mouth; radical change in behavior (including vomiting, diarrhea, convulsions); rapid breathing; or howling or whimpering from pain.

Emergency treatment.   When a dog swallows poison, the objective is to prevent it from being absorbed into the body. *However, only a veterinarian can save a dog's life if he has gone into convulsions or fallen unconscious.* If the dog has swallowed an acid (bleach, chlorine, battery fluid, etc.) or an alkali (ammonia, lye, drain cleaners, some cleaning products or petroleum distillates such as gasoline, kerosene, paint thinners and removers) or rodent poisons containing strychnine, try to find an antidote on the label of the product to administer. *Do not attempt to induce vomiting for these poisons.* First aid treatment calls for diluting the ingested poison by administering large quantities of liquid antacids (Maalox type), milk, milk of magnesia, baking soda mixed in tepid water, plain water or vegetable oil. If the poison is an acid, neutralize it with antacid (after administering the liquid dilution process above). If the poison is an alkali, neutralize it with equal amounts of vinegar and water or lemon juice and water (after administering the liquid dilution process). Several tablespoons given orally will suffice until you can get to a veterinarian.

Never induce vomiting for corrosive poisons, as they seriously burn and damage the esophagus. Do not induce vomiting for any ingested petroleum distillates, strychnine, acids or strong alkalis.

Do induce vomiting for ingested prescription drugs, patent remedies, insecticides, antifreeze (a deadly poison), all rodent poisons *not* containing strychnine, weak alkalis such as soap, laundry detergents, shampoos, dishwashing products and paint. Vomiting can be induced with ipecac syrup (obtained from a pharmacy) or by administering equal parts of hydrogen peroxide (3 percent solution) and water, using two tablespoons for each ten pounds of body weight. You can also try giving one tablespoon of salt mixed with one cup of tepid water. Use more for a large dog. After the dog has vomited, give him a quantity of milk to dilute the poison and several teaspoons of activated charcoal to further absorb and neutralize the remaining poison, and rush to the veterinarian, even if the symptoms have disappeared. Try to remember to take a sample of the vomitus to the vet for analysis.

Create a First Aid Kit

It is now possible to find pre-assembled first aid kits at various pet supply stores or advertised in pet magazines. However, it is best to assemble one at home to be sure it has everything you need for *your* dog. A suitable kit should contain the following items:

tincture of Merthiolate or Mercurochrome
Lambert Kay First Aid Antiseptic Skin Ointment
Bacitracin
antiseptic powder or spray
aromatic spirits of ammonia
mineral oil
Kaopectate (for diarrhea)
tongue depressors
sterile gauze bandage — 1 and 2 inches
ipecac syrup (to induce vomiting)
eye ointment
styptic powder (to stop bleeding)
Vaseline
scissors
tweezers
absorbent cotton balls
cotton applicators
large and small gauze pads
hydrogen peroxide (3 percent solution)
adhesive tape
rectal thermometer
liquid antacid (Maalox type)
charcoal tablets

GROOMING

An essential element for good health is hygiene and grooming. These go far in offering true preventive medicine. Grooming your dog is a wonderful activity for the kids as well as the four-legged family member. All the various aspects of keeping the dog clean and beautiful offer many opportunities for dogs and kids to get together in useful, constructive ways that solidify their relationships and allow the kids a sense of competency and accomplishment. Even the youngest child can help brother or sister or Mommy or Daddy with the dog's daily grooming needs and occasional ablutions. Older children are quite capable of taking on the entire responsibility for the dog's baths, daily brushing and minor coiffing.

Some breeds of dog require no trimming of their coats. However, most dogs need to have their coats clipped, which is to say the coat grows too long and must be trimmed with scissors or an electric clipper or both. This aspect of coat care requires training, experience and skill. It should not be attempted at home by those who know nothing about it. The dog will certainly come out a wreck. For that aspect of grooming it is best to take the dog to a professional grooming salon and have it done properly. However, combing, brushing, bathing, cleaning teeth, ears, eyes and trimming nails can be accomplished at home.

The Bath

The question of whether or not to bathe a dog perplexes many novice dog owners. The information given is mixed. The breeder may say the animal needs a bath once a month or before each dog show and the veterinarian may say avoid baths as much as you can. The truth is that too many baths can cause dry skin, dandruff, and maybe minor illness. However, dogs, like everyone else, get dirty and when they do they need a bath. When the dog walks in the room and everyone else leaves, it is time to throw him in the tub. It's hard to get close to a dirty, smelly dog, and such avoidance would defeat the idea of this book.

There is entirely too much fuss made over giving a dog a bath, anyway. Pet dogs do not need the constant, professional care given to show dogs. In warm weather, an adult dog does not even need a bathtub. He can simply be held in place in your backyard and washed down with a common garden hose. If the weather doesn't permit this, or if the dog lives in an apartment, use the bathtub. The sink is good for small dogs.

All dog grooming procedures require a firm but gentle manner. If your dog is obedience trained, give him a command that places him in a position that is convenient for you and the kids. Talk to the dog in a soothing tone of voice to get him as relaxed as possible. It is safe to as-

It should not be too difficult to get the kids to develop a workman-like attitude toward dog grooming by giving each person a specific job.

sume that your dog simply accepts grooming as inevitable at best and hates it at worst. The children mustn't be allowed to create pandemonium and get the dog stirred up. Although the atmosphere should be a pleasant one, fits of the giggles will only create hysteria in an already apprehensive dog. If the children cannot behave, then it is best to send them out to play and just get the job done. It should not be too difficult to get the kids to develop a workmanlike attitude toward dog grooming; give each person a specific job, no matter how slight. One can hold the shampoo while another lathers, etc. Make it a family affair with plenty of congratulations all around and perhaps a reward of cookies and ice cream or something special. The fun should be in working toward the accomplishment of a clean, handsome animal.

There are some simple procedures that should be performed before the dog becomes wet. Always brush the dog out before the bath. Do this right down to the skin. Use a natural bristle brush for dogs with short or medium coats. Pin brushes are good for long, flowing coats. Ask to see them at a pet supply shop and get one with pins that suit the length of your dog's coat. The object is to remove loose and dead hair and bits of loose skin particles along with dirt debris. Remove all mats and tangles from long coats (with the help of a bit of mineral oil or a commercial product formulated for this) before the bath. Without these procedures prior to bathing, the coat becomes a tangled mess and may be difficult to rinse and brush.

Fill the tub with approximately four inches of warm or tepid water, just enough to wet his paws. Pour a capful of dog shampoo in the water so that his pads are softening and being washed just by standing there. Place a wad of absorbent cotton in each ear to keep the water out and smear a bit of Vaseline in the corners of each eye to prevent the soap from irritating them. Some professional groomers prefer to stick their thumb in the dog's ear when wetting the dog, instead of absorbent cotton.

If you use the tub, use a rubber bathmat so the dog won't lose his balance. Secure him by placing a lead of some type around his neck and tie it to a secure place above his head (other than the hot-water tap). Leave a short slack in the lead so he cannot jump out of the tub. The dog can be held in place by an assistant holding the leash above the dog's head. Using a hand shower or simply scooping water up from the tub in a plastic container, wet the dog down from the neck to the tail, avoiding the head. Many dogs become frightened of baths and hate to have their heads washed. It is best to leave the head dry and do it last. Wet down the entire body, including the legs and underside of the torso.

Use a shampoo that is especially formulated for dogs. There is definitely a difference in the chemistry of the skin, called the pH factor. Knowledgeable dog people never use shampoo designed for humans, and that includes baby shampoo as well. Among the various dog shampoos available you may select a tearless one, a puppy shampoo, a medicated shampoo for sore skin, ones with coat conditioners, others with flea and tick insecticides added, and even some for dog coats of various colors and shades.

Apply the shampoo to the dog's coat much the way you would to your own hair. Using your hands work it into a good lather and shampoo all parts of the dog's body, including the tail, the belly, and the entire length of the legs. A rubber bristle shampoo brush helps the soap penetrate beneath the coat to the skin and stimulates the roots of the follicles. However, do not use such a brush on the dog's face. Now you can thoroughly rinse the soapy water with a hand shower or container of water. Rinse the dog's body completely. Do not leave soap on any part of the coat. Be as sensitive to the dog's acceptance of this as possible. You should rinse him gently and at a pace that does not upset him. Wet down and shampoo the top of the head and the front of the face after the rest of the body is soaped and rinsed. Use a washcloth for his face. The washcloth can also be used to clean inside the ears. There are commercial preparations for cleaning the dog's ears and others for cleaning his eyes. These are important aspects of grooming and hygiene. Simply follow the instructions on the package. It is not desirable to shampoo the dog twice unless he has long hair. Dogs with long fur should be given a creme rinse to make the coat easier to brush and less likely to tangle, but it is not necessary.

Remove him from the water to a warm room and squeeze the water from the coat with your hands. Next, towel dry the body with a blotting motion rather than a rubbing one. This too will make the coat more manageable. Remove the cotton from his ears. A short-coated dog can now dry outdoors if it's a summer day and you have a patio or deck. Brush him later. A long-coated dog should be dried with an electric, hand-held dryer and brushed at the same time. This speeds up the process and makes the coat light and airy. All dogs should be combed and brushed after a bath. There are many fine products that groom and condition the coat after the bath. Most of them are highly recommended. Simply follow the instructions on the label. When the kids are involved in bathing the dog, and they should be, this is the part that they love the most. The dog suddenly transforms from a scruffy playmate to a beautiful animal realizing his aesthetic potential.

Do not allow a slightly damp dog outdoors unless the weather is very warm and you don't care about his getting dirty all over again. Baths are fun when they're over with.

Trimming the Nails

Although it is nice to have good-looking nails, care of this part of the body has more importance than a matter of appearance. Unless a dog's nails are cut to a sensible length they begin to curl inward as they grow, and that leads to problems. The dog's gait will become awkward, along with his balance, and that could lead to problems of the spine, including the possibility of arthritis. Unclipped nails that have been permitted to grow inward can be painful to walk on. It is said that dogs living in the city wear them down by walking on the cement sidewalk. This is not always the case. Purchase a set of nail trimmers designed for dogs. A guillotine type is best for medium- to large-size dogs. A scissors type is more suited to small dogs. Trim the nails every month or two. Hold each paw firmly in one hand and clip off the tips of each nail. Dog nails are hard on the outside and soft on the inside. Do not trim off too much or you will cut into the quick and cause a slight bleeding. Have on hand a commercial product that stops bleeding. Styptic powder will do. Be firm but gentle and talk to the dog in a soothing tone of voice for all of these procedures. Trimming the dog's nails when he is a puppy gets him used to it and makes it easier later on. The same could be said of all grooming procedures.

Brushing and Combing

If you love taking photographs, have your camera ready the next time one of the kids combs and brushes the dog. If you pay close attention, you will see more loving and caring in that exchange between pet and child than in any other activity. The photo opportunity is a delightful one. Combing and brushing are responsibilities that almost every child can handle . . . to some degree. The wonderful thing about it is it can be done every day if you wish and can accommodate all the children as a satisfying chore. Believe it or not, this is one job the kids compete with each other to do. No matter how you work out the schedule, always allow it to be a kids' job.

All dogs, long- and short-coated, should be brushed daily to remove dead hair and dandruff. Long-haired dogs will develop mats, tangles and knots if they are not frequently brushed and combed. Short- and medium-haired dogs tend to be the shedders and daily brushing keeps shedding down to a manageable level. Brushing and combing not only cleans the coat and stimulates the skin, but also helps control dermatological ailments. Daily or even weekly grooming sessions allow the pet owner to catch significant body abnormalities such as lumps, lesions, cuts, scratches and even external parasites in their beginning stages. Nothing is more helpful for preventive medicine than frequent home examinations.

Brushes.   Long- and short-coated dogs all require a brush. The best type to get is a natural bristle brush, with the size of the bristles based on the length of the dog's coat. Consult a professional groomer or pet supply shop operator. Pin brushes are used for long-coated dogs of both large and small breeds. They are used when the coat is long and flowing in such breeds as cocker spaniels, borzois, Afghans and Shetland sheepdogs. A palm brush is an oval-shaped bristle brush held with a hand strap and used in the same manner as one curries a horse. They are best for dogs with medium to short coats. A hound glove resembles an oven mitt with either wire or fiber bristles on the palm side. It is used for general currying of the smooth-coated breeds, especially of the Hound Group.

Combs.   Stainless steel or some of the aluminum alloys make the best dog combs. For durability one should buy a quality comb. Match the length and spacing of the teeth to the characteristics of your dog's coat. The half-medium, half-fine comb is versatile and very useful. The medium teeth are for the main portion of the coat of an average dog. The fine teeth are for the more downy portions of the coat. They are made in sizes to accommodate any type or length of fur. There are other types of specialized combs that professional groomers and dog show people use, but they are very rarely needed by pet owners.

How to groom.   Most dogs must be brushed first and then combed. The brush stimulates the skin and the roots of the hair follicles while cleaning out dead hair and skin. It also strains the length of the fur for dirt and debris. A thorough brushing every day keeps the dog looking clean and healthy and avoids the necessity of too many baths. It's never a good idea to brush or comb a dry coat. Water run through the coat with your hands just before brushing is better than nothing at all. However, a bit of coat conditioner or dressing is better. There are many products available at pet supply shops. These will prevent the brush from creating static in the air, which results in snarls and tangles. Comb the dog out immediately following a brushing. This assures that all tangles and mats are smoothed away. Long, flowing comb strokes finish off the coat and make it quite beautiful looking.

When using the brush and comb, run the tools through the fur, getting the ends of the bristles or comb teeth as close to the skin as possible. Stroke the brush or the comb with the lay of the fur, never against it. Try to stroke the fur on all parts of the body, including the belly, the legs, tail, head and face. Use the fine portion of the comb for facial hair and downy places.

Dogs with short, shiny coats do not have to be combed. After brushing, a hound glove may be used instead. Many show people like to rub in a small quantity of coat conditioner with their hands and give the coat a glossy look by polishing the short fur with a silk handkerchief or a hank of velvet.

Grooming for health and hygiene is not too difficult and can very successfully involve the children. However, grooming can be much more than described here. If you are interested in meeting the grooming requirements of your breed for the show ring or simply because you want your dog to look his best, then there is much more involved. You may send the dog off every month to a professional groomer and have it accomplished to your satisfaction. Another way to do it is to attend dog shows and watch the exhibitors and handlers in the grooming area as they primp and fuss over the show dogs. Ask questions, make friends, and get involved. Next, purchase a book about your breed of dog that offers a complete chapter on grooming. There are entire books devoted to grooming procedures and many of them are quite important in their field. See the Suggested Reading List. Grooming can be simply a practical consideration or a total activity with your dog leading to other activities. No matter how far you go with it, however, it is important to bring the kids along with you. You will all be glad you did.

THE AGING DOG

Have you ever tried to explain the concept of time to a very young child? It is impossible. Jean Piaget, the great theorist of intellectual development in children, believed that a young child's idea of aging is static and without change. Very young children assume that "when growing stops, time apparently ceases to operate." Unfortunately, some adults see things much the same way and refuse to acknowledge the passage of time and its effects. Once the family dog reaches full maturity nothing further happens, as far as four-, five- and six-year-olds are concerned. It is difficult to explain the process of aging to a child because it involves the concept of the passage of time. However, because of the compression of the life cycle in dogs as compared to humans, the presence of a dog helps children begin to recognize the changes in living creatures as time passes. It is with total disbelief that a child views a photograph of a parent as a teenager. However, when an adult dog that is vigorous quite suddenly begins to slow down, turn gray, and manifest the behavior of old age, it is a reality that even a child must come to grips with. Even as elder statesman, the family dog continues to teach us all about being alive. The older dog is as valuable as the new puppy and should be cherished and honored for the years of unswerving love and loyalty. And like the frisky puppy, the aging dog needs to be seen in a special way, with special handling.

In dogs the aging process does creep up softly and is difficult to determine in the beginning stage. Some veterinarians and pet food manufacturers tell us it begins without much fanfare somewhere in the seventh year of life. Of course, it is different for each of the hundreds of breeds. You see, the size of the dog has a bearing on the life span. The average dog lives twelve or fifteen years, but the giant-size breeds, such as Great Danes and Irish wolfhounds, live much shorter lives. The very small breeds live longer, but so do some average-size dogs that have been blessed with a combination of sound genetics and good care. There is no way to predict the life span of an average dog. It is possible to stack the deck somewhat with good management and recognition of the needs of the maturing dog.

This does not mean going to an extreme. At seven years the dog's rate of metabolism slows down and the aging process begins. But it is important to understand that there are many great years ahead. I have witnessed dogs working for police departments handling the rigors of law enforcement (including the tough canine obstacle courses) at twelve years of age. No, spare your dog the cane and wheelchair until he asks for it. Gray hair and a slower gait does not mean your dog is ready for a gold watch, a pension and a trip to Hawaii. If you treat your pet like an old dog he will become "an old dog." No one can argue with the concept of an inevitable aging process. However, it can certainly be manipulated and put off for a while. Let decrepitude take a holiday. Here's how.

Avoid Stress

Nothing uses up a dog's life quicker than stress. It comes from two basic forces — extreme physical experience and anxiety caused by emotional activity. It is thought that emotional stress produces more disease than physical stress, which includes exposure to extreme heat and cold, pain, wounds, surgery and excessive exercise.

Emotional stress could be referred to as *distress*. It has been my experience that dogs become less adaptive as they get older. When they are forced to adapt to changes in the later part of their lives they become emotionally stressed, which in turn quickens the aging process or

even induces sickness. There is only so much resistance to stress that a dog's body can deliver before it begins to succumb.

When children go back to school after a long summer it can be hard on the aging dog to discover that the giggle factor has been removed. Of course we mustn't be too sentimental about it. Some dogs will be grateful for the peace and quiet. In either case, it would be very good for the older dog to be given some extra attention by the one who stays behind to get the Twinkies ready for the three o'clock rush. A little extra walk, a brush-up training session or even a conversation will go a long way in avoiding the stress of change. This is especially important if one or more of the kids go off to college and live away from home.

Boredom is the enemy. It is stressful for dogs of all ages, but especially so for older dogs. Do not consider your dog to be retired, despite his or her age. Retirement translates into having nothing to do and being turned into something useless. We all must feel useful and needed because the alternative is too awful. As with humans, work is good for dogs as long as they can be made to feel that they are having some effect on those with whom they live. If your dog can carry home the newspaper in her mouth, encourage her to do so and offer much praise for it. Some dogs believe they are guarding the house if they are

248

told to do so. Sometimes a dog feels useful by being asked for its companionship during household chores. Give your dog a job it is capable of doing, that it enjoys, and that members of the family appreciate.

Aging dogs must not be exposed to other dogs who are sick. They must not be moved from one home to another, especially to a strange, temporary home. Boarding an older dog at a kennel is extremely stressful. Do not allow a strange dog to challenge your mature dog's territory or position. This happens when the family decides to bring another pet into the house. Do not adopt a puppy or young adult if your older dog has always had the run of the house for herself. When it becomes obvious that a dog is very old and going to die, some parents attempt to protect the kids from the emotions of that experience by getting them a new puppy before the inevitable death of the old dog. This is wrong for both older dog and children. First, it robs the children of learning about their feelings and devalues the life of a loved one. Second, it is extremely hard on the old dog to cope with the vigor of a young dog, the loss of rank and territory and, finally, the inability to capture the attention of the adored children. If your aging lady or gentleman has had the house to herself or himself, do not take that privilege away. We must not punish anyone for getting older by thinking only of ourselves.

Give your dog a stress-free atmosphere with no drafts and a quiet place to sleep, someplace safe where he can get away from it all. It would not be outrageous to move the dog's bed into the master bedroom and away from the hectic roughhouse play of the children. All things in moderation is the key to a longer life.

Grooming the Aging Dog

The first signs of aging will be changes in the dog's coat. It begins to thin out a bit, perhaps turn gray, lose its gloss and ability to stay smooth. The skin begins to get dry and scaly and more dandruff is present. The haircoat is a dog's most aesthetic physical attribute and must not be allowed to fall victim to the aging process any more than necessary.

Grooming the dog every day is more important now than it used to be. Dead hair and skin must be removed and parasitic infestation avoided by daily brushing and combing. Be very gentle when unmatting and detangling the fur. Use a detangling product manufactured for this purpose. At this stage of life a proper dog brush is your pet's best friend. In addition to the natural bristle brush, purchase a soft-wire *slicker brush* for removing dirt and dead skin. A slicker brush is rectangular in shape with a slanted handle attached to its center. The metal teeth are bent inward and do a thorough job of preventing mats and tangles as well as removing dead material from the coat. But more important, the slicker brush stimulates the skin and helps the follicle roots secrete what natural oils are present, sending them up inside the hollow shaft of each hair. This not only makes the dog look better but actually helps fight off the various skin ailments that plague older dogs.

Bathing an older dog is just not worth the risk if it stresses him. If your dog has always enjoyed his bath, then for the sake of routine continue this course. The real risk of bathing older dogs is their susceptibility to respiratory infections caused by drafts and chills. When bathing the older dog, do it in a very warm room and keep him warm and draft-free for the rest of the day. Use a hand-held, electric dryer to get rid of the dampness in his coat as quickly as possible. You might look into products that refer to themselves as "dry baths." These are sprays and powders that are applied to the coat and then brushed out, taking with them dirt and debris.

Daily grooming also has the good effect of providing you with information about the dog's state of health. It is like a mini-examination. Look for skin rashes and irritations, patches of missing fur, parasites, cuts, bruises, lesions and lumps. All of these conditions should be looked at by a veterinarian. Keep the nails trimmed for the sake of balance and gait. Warts and lumps are common on the older dog's body, but if they seem to be growing or changing in shape and size, have the dog examined. Maintain ear and eye hygiene with a cotton ball dipped in warm water. At this point in the dog's life he or she is likely to lose some teeth and develop gum disease. Have this checked by the veterinarian.

Feeding the Older Dog

The principal caution involved in feeding older dogs is obesity. Older dogs need fewer calories but, ironically, are fed more by their owners out of love, sympathy or even pity. But the dog is done no favor when she is fed more calories than she can burn off at this time in her life. Ask a veterinarian about reducing the dog's caloric intake and avoid tidbits. (See "Older Dogs" in the "How to Feed Your Dog" section of this chapter.)

Exercise

Your aging companion must have some physical activity if life is to be worthwhile. We are not only concerned with the length of a dog's life but with the quality of that life. An arthritic dog tends to lie around more, but that only makes his condition worsen. Gentle, stimulating exercise helps a dog hold the line and slow down the progression of muscular and joint ailments.

If your dog cannot take the same long walks he did before, then give him shorter ones, but on a more frequent basis. It is good for his heart and lungs and keeps up muscle tone. There are also psychological benefits. Your and the children's constant attention keep the dog happy.

You might try brushing up on obedience commands or even teaching him a simple trick or two. (See the Suggested Reading List.) Keep the dog involved with the family by talking to him and getting him moving as much as possible. It does a lot of good to take him out with you on as many errands as possible. Do not go jogging with an older dog. Do not go for walks on very hot and humid days. Stay out of the rain. Stop and go home when the dog appears exhausted. Let him sleep after any play or exercises.

Frequent Medical Checkups

Preventive medicine is of the utmost importance to an older dog. Do not wait for sickness to strike. Seeing the veterinarian every six months is not excessive for a dog that is nine years or older. Maintain the dog's booster shots and other required vaccinations. As with humans, early detection increases the chances of surviving, and maybe even of curing sickness.

Rest

Try to find a happy balance between too much or too little rest. Just staying aware of rest as an important factor in your dog's life helps a great deal. Of course you do not want a dog that sleeps all the time. The reality is that an older dog requires more nap time than a younger one. Keep the kids away from the dog when he is catching forty or even eighty winks.

These are but a few of the measures that will surely prolong the life of your dog. No doubt others will occur to you as long as you remain

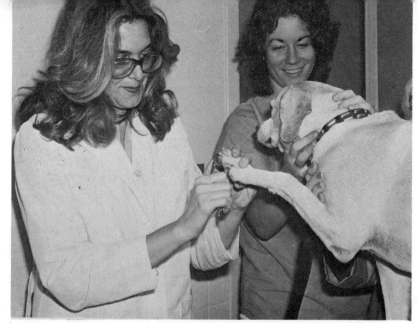

Older dogs require more frequent medical checkups. Allow a veterinarian to clip the nails of senior dogs.

sensitive to the dog's needs. Bear in mind that you are the only social security your dog will ever have.

Sometimes a dog seems to get cranky in old age. This is only partly true. Just like the rest of us, they have good days and bad days. Be patient and think of all the good times when the old dog is a bit more stubborn or cantankerous on any given day.

The Final Glidepath

When a dog dies it will be the first encounter with loss and ensuing grief for many children. Do not cheat your kids out of their emotions. Rather, help them express what they feel. Face the issue squarely and honestly and help them understand the *foreverness* of the loss. The loss of a pet stirs the imagination into trying to picture our own death. One can become quite upset or one can take an arrogant attitude. I, frankly, find it difficult to imagine a world without me in it. That is the view of most healthy children. Do not be afraid to discuss the death of a dog with the kids. They may cry, they may grieve, but they will not suffer. It will reinforce the value of life and give them a keen appreciation for what they have.

Tell the kids that the only true realities are time and other living beings. There is no control over time except to recognize it as a mea-

252

surement of life and thus enjoy what there is. As for other beings, the people and the creatures we come to know and love should be cherished and valued above everything else. Existence is a very dear and precious gift, to be enjoyed and savored like a burning log in winter or the tossing of a ball to your favorite dog. Tell the kids.

Suggested Reading List

READING FOR PLEASURE

Atkinson, Eleanor. *Greyfriar's Bobby.* New York: Grosset & Dunlop, 1940.

Baker, Stephen. *Games Dogs Play.* Cartoons by Roy McKie. New York: McGraw-Hill, 1982.

———. *How to Live with a Neurotic Dog.* Cartoons by Eric Gurney. New York: Pocket Books, 1976.

Baynes, Ernest Harold. *Animal Heroes of the Great War.* New York: Macmillan, 1925.

Benjamin, Carol Lea. *The Wicked Stepdog.* New York: Crowell, 1982.

Davis, Richard Harding. *The Bar Sinister.* New York: Scribners, 1930.

Downey, Fairfax, ed. *Great Dog Stories of All Time.* New York: Doubleday, 1962.

Kipling, Rudyard. *Collected Dog Stories.* New York: Doubleday, 1938.

Knight, Eric. *Lassie Come Home.* New York: Grosset & Dunlop, 1940.

Koehler, William R. *The Wonderful World of Disney Animals.* New York: Howell Book House, 1980.

London, Jack. *Call of the Wild.* New York: Grossett & Dunlop, 1915.

———. *Jerry of the Island.* New York: Grosset & Dunlop, 1917.

———. *White Fang.* London: Methuen, 1932.

Mery, Fernand. *The Life, History and Magic of the Dog.* New York: Grosset & Dunlop, 1970.

254

Ouida (Louisa de la Ramée). *A Dog of Flanders*. New York: Macmillan, 1929.

Peterson, Florence, ed. *The Big Book of Favorite Dog Stories*. New York: Platt & Munk, 1964.

Terhune, Albert Payson. *Lad of Sunnybank*. New York: Grosset & Dunlop, 1929.

————. *Loot*. New York: Grosset & Dunlop, 1940.

————. *My Friend the Dog*. New York: Harper & Brothers, 1926.

Truman, Margaret. *White House Pets*. New York: David McKay Company, Inc., 1969.

DOG BEHAVIOR

Pfaffenberger, Clarence. *The New Knowledge of Dog Behavior*. New York: Howell Book House, 1963.

Scott, John Paul, and Fuller, John L. *Dog Behavior: The Genetic Basis*. Chicago: University of Chicago Press, 1974.

Siegal, Mordecai. *The Happy Dog, Happy Owner Book*. New York: Howell Book House, 1984.

Tortora, Daniel, Ph.D. *Help! This Animal Is Driving Me Crazy*. New York: Playboy Press, 1977.

GENERAL, DOG CARE AND HEALTH

American Kennel Club. *The Complete Dog Book*. 15th ed., rev. New York: Howell Book House, 1975.

Barnes, Duncan, ed., and the staff of the American Kennel Club. *The AKC's World of the Pure-Bred Dog*. New York: Howell Book House, 1983.

Caras, Roger. *A Celebration of Dogs*. New York: Times Books, 1982.

————. *The Roger Caras Dog Book*. New York: Holt, Rinehart and Winston, 1980.

Carlson, Delbert G., D.V.M., and Giffin, James M., M.D. *Dog Owner's Home Veterinary Handbook*. New York: Howell Book House, 1980.

Hershhorn, Bernard S., D.V.M. *Active Years for Your Aging Dog*. New York: Hawthorn, 1978.

Howe, John. *Choosing the Right Dog*. Rev. ed. New York: Harper & Row, 1980.

Kalstone, Shirlee A. *Dogs: Breeds, Care, and Training.* New York: Dell, 1982.

Levinson, Boris M., Ph.D. *Pet-Oriented Child Psychotherapy.* Springfield: Charles C. Thomas, 1969.

———. *Pets and Human Development.* Springfield: Charles C. Thomas, 1972.

Margolis, Matthew, and Swan, Catherine. *The Dog in Your Life.* New York: Random House/Vintage, 1979.

Riddle, Maxwell. *Your Family Dog.* New York: Doubleday, 1981.

Siegal, Mordecai. *The Good Dog Book.* New York: Macmillan/Signet, 1978.

Tortora, Daniel F., Ph.D. *The Right Dog for You.* New York: Simon & Schuster, 1980.

GROOMING

Harmar, Hilary. *Dogs and How to Groom Them.* 2d rev. ed. New York: Arco, 1975.

Kalstone, Shirlee. *The Complete Poodle Clipping and Grooming Book.* New York: Howell Book House, 1981.

———. *Grooming All Toy Dogs.* New York: Howell Book House, 1976.

Stone, Ben, and Stone, Pearl. *The Stone Guide to Dog Grooming for All Breeds.* New York: Howell Book House, 1981.

DOG TRAINING

Benjamin, Carol Lea. *Dog Problems.* New York: Doubleday, 1981.

———. *Dog Training for Kids.* New York: Howell Book House, 1976.

Haggerty, Arthur J., and Benjamin, Carol Lea. *Dog Tricks.* New York: Howell Book House, 1982.

Monks of New Skete. *How to Be Your Dog's Best Friend.* Boston: Little, Brown, 1978.

Siegal, Mordecai, and Margolis, Matthew. *Good Dog, Bad Dog.* New York: Holt, Rinehart and Winston/Signet, 1973.

———. *Underdog.* New York: Stein & Day, 1974.

Index

Indifference to dog, 201–202
Infectious canine enteritis, 227
Infectious canine hepatitis, 223, 225–226
International Kennel Club of Chicago, 182
Ipecac syrup, 238
Irish setter, 34–35
Irish wolfhound, 48–49, 217, 247

Jealousy, 113–114
Jumping up, 192
Junior Showmanship competition, 16, 146, 181–182

Kaopectate, 239
Keeshond, 78–79
Kennel Club of Beverly Hills, 182
"Kennel cough," 227
Komondor puppies, 96

Labrador retriever, 29–30
Leadership, 7–9, 146, 148; of pack, 97–99, 120
Leash, 116, 136–137, 147–157
Leptospirosis, 223, 226
Lice, 232, 233
Life span, 49, 55, 57, 247
Litters, 24, 102; removing puppy from, 105
Loneliness, 94, 191
Loss of appetite, 223–224

Magazines, dog, 21, 26
Maintenance diet, 219
Male dogs, 24, 101–102, 203–204
Mange, 234
Marking territory, 99–100, 132
Mass-breeding, 18, 25, 26
Mastiffs, 53
Mating, 101–102, 202–203
Medical history, 21, 223
Medical problems, 194, 218, 223–225
Microfilaria, 231
Mineral oil, 239, 241
Minerals, 220
Mites, 20, 232, 234
Mixed-breed dogs, 91
Moisture content in dog food, 215, 216, 217
Mongrels. See Mutts
Mutts, 91–92
Muzzle, 234–235, 236

Nails, clipping, 198, 240, 243–244, 250
Naming dog, 109–112
National Academy of Science, 136, 214
National Association of Girls Clubs, 184
National Research Council, 219
Neonatal period, 103

Nervousness, 94
Neurotic dogs, 93–94
Neutering, 17, 24–25, 204. *See also* Castration
Newfoundland, 56–57
Night care of puppy, 188–189
Nilodor, 139–140
Nipping, 192
Noise-maker, 138–139, 143, 148
Non-sporting dogs, 25, 72–80
Norden Laboratories, 220
Nutrition requirements, 214–215, 217–220
"Nylabone," 192

Obedience training, 24, 93, 99, 105, 106, 116, 146–180, 194, 205
Obedience trials, 181
Obesity, 218, 220, 250
Odor, neutralizing, 139–140
"Okay" with "come" command, 178
Only child, and dog, 13
Ottawa Championship Show, 182
Otter hound, 50–51
Ovaban, 204
Ovariohysterectomy, 24, 204
Overfeeding, 218

Packs, 95–101, 104, 146, 147
Pairing, and "pair bond," 97
Paper training, 142–143
Parainfluenza, 223, 227
Parasites: external, 198, 232–234; internal, 20, 136, 198, 228–232
Parvovirus, 223, 227
Pedigree, 19–20, 25
Pembroke Welsh corgi, 88–89
Personalities, dog, 22, 23, 24; changes in, 226
"Pet quality" dogs, 20
Pet shops, 18–19
Phobias, 94
Play, 104, 135, 136, 137
Pointers, 26–27; Spanish, 31
Poison, 237–239; Poison Control Center, 237
Poltalloch terrier. See West Highland white terrier
Pomeranian, 22
Poodles, 23, 79–80
Practice, training, 152–153, 168, 180
Praise, 106, 132, 138–139, 147–148, 150, 178–179, 193
Prescription Diet, 220
Preventive medicine, 222–225
Progressive retinal atrophy, 18
Protection; dogs for, 16, 114–116; dog's need for, 116–118
Psychologists, dog, 93, 95